Spatial Microeconometrics

Spatial Microeconometrics introduces the reader to the basic concepts of spatial statistics, spatial econometrics and the spatial behavior of economic agents at the microeconomic level. Incorporating useful examples and presenting real data and datasets on real firms, the book takes the reader through the key topics in a systematic way.

The book outlines the specificities of data that represent a set of interacting individuals with respect to traditional econometrics that treat their locational choices as exogenous and their economic behavior as independent. In particular, the authors address the consequences of neglecting such important sources of information on statistical inference and how to improve the model predictive performances. The book presents the theory, clarifies the concepts and instructs the readers on how to perform their own analyses, describing in detail the codes which are necessary when using the statistical language R.

The book is written by leading figures in the field and is completely up to date with the very latest research. It will be invaluable for graduate students and researchers in economic geography, regional science, spatial econometrics, spatial statistics and urban economics.

Giuseppe Arbia is full professor of economic statistics at the Faculty of Economics, Catholic University of the Sacred Heart, Rome, and lecturer at the University of Italian Switzerland in Lugano. Since 2006 he has been president of the Spatial Econometrics Association and since 2008 he has chaired the Spatial Econometrics Advanced Institute. He is also a member of many international scientific societies.

Giuseppe Espa is full professor in economic statistics at the Department of Economics and Management of the University of Trento and the LUISS "Guido Carli" University of Rome.

Diego Giuliani is associate professor in economic statistics at the Department of Economics and Management of the University of Trento. He works primarily on the use and development of statistical methods to analyze firm-level microgeographic data.

Routledge Advanced Texts in Economics and Finance

27 Regional Economics, Second Edition
Roberta Capello

28 Game Theory and Exercises
Gisèle Umbhauer

29 Innovation and Technology
Business and Economics Approaches
Nikos Vernardakis

30 Behavioral Economics, Third Edition
Edward Cartwright

31 Applied Econometrics
A Practical Guide
Chung-ki Min

32 The Economics of Transition
Developing and Reforming Emerging Economies
Edited by Ichiro Iwasaki

33 Applied Spatial Statistics and Econometrics
Data Analysis in R
Edited by Katarzyna Kopczewska

34 Spatial Microeconometrics
Giuseppe Arbia, Giuseppe Espa and Diego Giuliani

For more information about this series, please visit: www.routledge.com/
Routledge-Advanced-Texts-in-Economics-and-Finance/book-series/SE0757

Spatial Microeconometrics

Giuseppe Arbia, Giuseppe Espa and
Diego Giuliani

LONDON AND NEW YORK

First published 2021
by Routledge
2 Park Square, Milton Park, Abingdon, Oxon OX14 4RN

and by Routledge
52 Vanderbilt Avenue, New York, NY 10017

Routledge is an imprint of the Taylor & Francis Group, an informa business

© 2021 Giuseppe Arbia, Giuseppe Espa and Diego Giuliani

The right of Giuseppe Arbia, Giuseppe Espa and Diego Giuliani to be
identified as authors of this work has been asserted by them in accordance
with sections 77 and 78 of the Copyright, Designs and Patents Act 1988.

All rights reserved. No part of this book may be reprinted or reproduced
or utilised in any form or by any electronic, mechanical, or other means,
now known or hereafter invented, including photocopying and recording,
or in any information storage or retrieval system, without permission in
writing from the publishers.

Trademark notice: Product or corporate names may be trademarks
or registered trademarks, and are used only for identification and
explanation without intent to infringe.

British Library Cataloguing-in-Publication Data
A catalogue record for this book is available from the British Library

Library of Congress Cataloging-in-Publication Data
A catalog record has been requested for this book

ISBN: 978-1-138-83374-6 (hbk)
ISBN: 978-1-138-83375-3 (pbk)
ISBN: 978-1-315-73527-6 (ebk)

Typeset in Galliard
by codeMantra

G.A. To Pietro, my first grandson
G.E. To the memory of my father, Salvatore
D.G. To Serena

Contents

Foreword	xiii
LUNG-FEI LEE	
Preface and acknowledgements	xix

PART I
Introduction   1

1 Foundations of spatial microeconometrics modeling   3
    1.1 A micro-level approach to spatial econometrics 3
    1.2 Advantages of spatial microeconometric analysis 5
    1.3 Sources of spatial micro-data 7
    1.4 Sources of uncertainty in spatial micro-data 8
    1.5 Conclusions and plan of the book 10

PART II
Modeling the spatial behavior of economic agents in a given set of locations   13

2 Preliminary definitions and concepts   15
    2.1 Neighborhood and the W matrix 15
    2.2 Moran's I and other spatial correlation measures 22
    2.3 The Moran scatterplot and local indicators of spatial correlation 26
    2.4 Conclusions 29

3 Basic cross-sectional spatial linear models   30
    3.1 Introduction 30
    3.2 Regression models with spatial autoregressive components 30
        3.2.1 Pure spatial autoregression 30
        3.2.2 The spatial error model 32

viii *Contents*

3.2.3 The spatial lag model 35
3.2.4 The spatial Durbin model 39
3.2.5 The general spatial autoregressive model with spatial autoregressive error structure 41

3.3 *Test of residual spatial autocorrelation with explicit alternative hypotheses 44*

3.4 *Marginal impacts 46*

3.5 *Effects of spatial imperfections of micro-data 48*
3.5.1 Introduction 48
3.5.2 Measurement error in spatial error models 49
3.5.3 Measurement error in spatial lag models 50

3.6 *Problems in regressions on a spatial distance 53*

4 Non-linear spatial models   57

4.1 *Non-linear spatial regressions 57*

4.2 *Standard non-linear models 58*
4.2.1 Logit and probit models 58
4.2.2 The tobit model 60

4.3 *Spatial probit and logit models 63*
4.3.1 Model specification 63
4.3.2 Estimation 65

4.4 *The spatial tobit model 72*
4.4.1 Model specification 72
4.4.2 Estimation 72

4.5 *Further non-linear spatial models 73*

4.6 *Marginal impacts in spatial non-linear models 74*

5 Space–time models   76

5.1 *Generalities 76*

5.2 *Fixed and random effects models 76*

5.3 *Random effects spatial models 77*

5.4 *Fixed effect spatial models 79*

5.5 *Estimation 80*
5.5.1 Introduction 80
5.5.2 Maximum likelihood 80
5.5.2.1 Likelihood procedures for random effect models 80
5.5.2.2 Likelihood procedures for fixed effect models 82
5.5.3 The generalized method of moments approach 83
5.5.3.1 Generalized method of moments procedures for random effects models 84
5.5.3.2 Generalized method of moments procedures for fixed effects models 85

5.6 *A glance at further approaches in spatial panel data modeling 85*

Contents   ix

PART III
Modeling the spatial locational choices of
economic agents   91

6 Preliminary definitions and concepts in point
   pattern analysis   93
   6.1 *Spatial point patterns of economic agents 93*
   6.2 *The hypothesis of complete spatial randomness 94*
   6.3 *Spatial point processes 95*
       6.3.1 Homogeneous Poisson point process 96
       6.3.2 Aggregated point processes 98
             6.3.2.1 Inhomogeneous Poisson point processes 98
             6.3.2.2 Cox processes 100
             6.3.2.3 Poisson cluster point processes 101
       6.3.3 Regular point processes 104
   6.4 *Classic exploratory tools and summary statistics for
        spatial point patterns 107*
       6.4.1 Quadrat-based methods 107
       6.4.2 Distance-based methods 110

7 Models of the spatial location of individuals   113
   7.1 *Ripley's K-function 113*
   7.2 *Estimation of Ripley's K-function 114*
   7.3 *Identification of spatial location patterns 116*
       7.3.1 The CSR test 116
       7.3.2 Parameter estimation of the Thomas
             cluster process 121
       7.3.3 Parameter estimation of the Matérn
             cluster process 124
       7.3.4 Parameter estimation of the log-Gaussian Cox
             process 126

8 Points in a heterogeneous space   127
   8.1 *Diggle and Chetwynd's D-function 127*
   8.2 *Baddeley, Møller and Waagepetersen's
        K_{inhom}-function 132*
       8.2.1 Estimation of K_{inhom}-function 133
       8.2.2 Inference for K_{inhom}-function 135
   8.3 *Measuring spatial concentration of industries:
        Duranton–Overman K-density and Marcon–Puech
        M-function 138*
       8.3.1 Duranton and Overman's K-density 139
       8.3.2 Marcon and Puech's M-function 140

x *Contents*

9 Space–time models   143

9.1 Diggle, Chetwynd, Häggkvist and Morris' space–time
K-function 143
    9.1.1 Estimation of space–time K-function 145
    9.1.2 Detecting space–time clustering of economic events 145
9.2 Gabriel and Diggle's STIK-function 148
    9.2.1 Estimation of *STIK*-function and inference 152

PART IV
Looking ahead: modeling both the spatial location
choices and the spatial behavior of economic agents   157

10 Firm demography and survival analysis   159

10.1 Introduction 159
10.2 A spatial microeconometric model for firm demography 161
    10.2.1 A spatial model for firm demography 161
        10.2.1.1 Introduction 161
        10.2.1.2 The birth model 162
        10.2.1.3 The growth model 163
        10.2.1.4 The survival model 163
    10.2.2 A case study 164
        10.2.2.1 Data description 164
        10.2.2.2 The birth model 166
        10.2.2.3 The growth model 169
        10.2.2.4 The survival model 170
    10.2.3 Conclusions 172
10.3 A spatial microeconometric model for firm survival 172
    10.3.1 Introduction 172
    10.3.2 Basic survival analysis techniques 173
    10.3.3 Case study: The survival of pharmaceutical
         and medical device manufacturing start-up
         firms in Italy 176
        10.3.3.1 Data description 176
        10.3.3.2 Definition of the spatial microeconometric
            covariates 177
        10.3.3.3 Definition of the control variables 180
        10.3.3.4 Empirical results 181
10.4 Conclusion 186

Appendices
Appendix 1: Some publicly available spatial datasets 187
Appendix 2: Creation of a W matrix and preliminary
               computations 188

Appendix 3: Spatial linear models 191
Appendix 4: Non-linear spatial models 192
Appendix 5: Space–time models 193
Appendix 6: Preliminary definitions and concepts in point
  pattern analysis 194
  Appendix 6.1: Point pattern datasets 194
  Appendix 6.2: Simulating point patterns 195
    Appendix 6.2.1: Homogeneous Poisson processes 195
    Appendix 6.2.2: Inhomogeneous Poisson processes 196
    Appendix 6.2.3: Cox processes 196
    Appendix 6.2.4: Poisson cluster processes 196
    Appendix 6.2.5: Regular processes 197
  Appendix 6.3: Quadrat-based analysis 197
  Appendix 6.4: Clark–Evans test 198
Appendix 7: Models of the spatial location of individuals 199
  Appendix 7.1: K-function-based CSR test 199
  Appendix 7.2: Point process parameters estimation by
      the method of minimum contrast 199
Appendix 8: Points in a heterogeneous space 200
  Appendix 8.1: D-function-based test of spatial
      interactions 200
  Appendix 8.2: K_{inhom}-function-based test of spatial
      interactions 202
  Appendix 8.3: Duranton–Overman K-density and
      Marcon–Puech M-function 203
Appendix 9: Space–time models 204
  Appendix 9.1: Space–time K-function 204
  Appendix 9.2: Gabriel and Diggle's $STIK$-function 205

Bibliography	207
Index	219

Foreword

Giuseppe Arbia, Giuseppe Espa and Diego Giuliani, invited me to read their monograph on *Spatial Microeconometrics* and to write a foreword for it. As a theoretical econometrician who has worked on both microeconometrics and spatial econometrics, I am glad to have the chance to write such a foreword to their book.

The three authors are statisticians, economists and educators. Their monograph on spatial microeconometrics has covered important spatial economic issues and models. The book is divided into two parts. The first half introduces and provides insights into popular simultaneous type equation models, such as the spatial autoregressive model (SAR), which capture contemporaneous interactions and spillover effects on economic outcomes of spatially located economic agents. The second half of the monograph concentrates on the location choices and spatial behavior of economic agents. The approach for the second half starts with spatial point processes. The merit of this monograph is that the authors provide for each spatial model an empirical application to illustrate the practical relevance of a spatial model specification and its implication of interactions via real data. While there are discussions on some regularity conditions for a model structure, the details are referred to the theoretical spatial econometric literature.

Chapter 1 provides the foundations of spatial econometric models with microeconomic justification, even though the popular SAR model has been introduced by statisticians, in the attempt to extend autoregression in time series to capture spatial correlation and/or spillover effects across spatial units. A time series has the time forwarding influence of past activities on current activity. However, for spatial interactions, in general, there is not a single forwarding direction of influence for spatial outcomes because the outcome of a spatial unit might have influences on all direct neighbors in all spatial directions. In order to capture neighboring spatial units' influences, typically, a spatial network matrix W_n would be constructed to capture possible, but relative influence of neighbors. Whether neighboring and networking units have significant influence on a spatial unit would then be summarized by an additional coefficient of the networking factor. Chapter 2 of the monograph introduces neighboring structures and the construction of the spatial network matrix W. With cross-sectional data on xiv *Foreword*

outcomes of spatial units, a preliminary interest is whether those outcomes are spatially correlated or not. A test statistic developed by Moran is the most useful statistic for testing purposes. Moran's test statistic lays the statistical foundation for spatial statistics and econometrics. Formal regression models with spatial interactions on outcomes as well as spatial correlation in disturbances are introduced. A regression equation with spatially correlated disturbances extends the regression model with serially correlated disturbances to the spatial situation. The Moran test of spatial correlation in the regression residuals is shown to be a Lagrange multiplier test. For estimation, the monograph has focused on the method of maximum likelihood (ML) and the generalized method of moments (GMM). For the SAR model, in the presence of exogenous variables, the orthogonality condition of exogenous variables and disturbances provides naturally the adoption of the two-stage least squares estimation method as the exogenous variables would be valid instrumental variables. In a regression framework, a classical social science model includes spatial interactions which describes how neighbors' exogenous characteristics influence the outcomes of a spatial unit. In spatial econometrics, an additional neighboring characteristic term is called a Durbin term. In a SAR model, one may include Durbin terms to capture directly exogenous effects due to interactions with neighbors. The subsequent sections of Chapter 3 point out the economic implications in terms of the marginal impact of a small change of an exogenous variable on the possible outcome. The marginal effects and multiplier effect are important, in particular, in SAR models as spillover effects due to neighbors are the key feature in such a model.

The regression and SAR models in Chapter 3 are linear models as they are linear in the dependent variables and their (main) coefficients. Linear models have the computational advantage in estimation, but, as in the classical microeconometric literature, individual decisions might involve discrete or limited outcomes. Discrete outcomes are usually modeled with probit or logit models. Limited outcomes are formulated with a censoring regression, which is known as a tobit model. In the classical microeconomics literature, individuals are assumed to make decisions only keeping in mind their self-interest, but do not take into account any possible externality in their decisions. On the contrary, spatial microeconometrics allows for individual decisions, taking into account the influence of possible decisions or actions of others in a game setting, even though their decisions might not take into account any externalities that their decision might generate. While in a SAR model, outcomes are the results of optimized decisions of each individual in a game setting, the SAR equation can be simply a linear equation. But for discrete choices and tobit models, there are limited points with probability involved so the resulting model could not be specified properly only with linear structures. Chapter 4 presents some of these non-linear models which take into account spill-over effects. There are two types of probit and tobit SAR models discussed in the monograph. One is a latent SAR underlying process but with observable binary or censored indicators. As the likelihood function for such a model is computationally complicated (as it involves multiple

Foreword xv

integrals), simplified estimation methods are discussed as they can be computationally tractable even if they might lose asymptotic efficiency for estimation. Other probit and tobit SAR models have a simultaneous structure in that the peer agents' chosen alternatives or limited outcomes have a direct influence on an agent's decision. The latent tobit SAR model can be computationally more attractive, but the estimation of the corresponding probit SAR would still be complicated. Furthermore, the corresponding discrete choice SAR model might have multiple Nash equilibrium, and tractable estimation methods remain to be considered. The asymptotic theory for estimators for such non-linear models has been developed in the theoretical spatial econometric literature. Asymptotic theories extend non-linear time series to spatial mixing and near-epoch dependence processes. These theories have not been presented in this monograph, but readers can refer to existing publications. Due to the non-linear structures of the spatial probit and tobit models, the monograph points out the importance of using marginal impacts for understanding economics implications of regressors in such models.

After the presentation of popular linear and non-linear spatial models for cross sectional data, Chapter 5 of the monograph considers panel data with space–time models. Cross-sectional models are static models. However, panel data models can incorporate dynamic adjustments and can identity effects of time-variant, but individual-invariant, explanatory variables. In a cross-sectional model, if an explanatory time variable stays constant for all units at each time, then its effect on outcomes cannot be identifiable because a cross-sectional invariant variable could not be separately identified from the intercept term in a model. With panel data models, since such an explanatory variable will have different values over time, its effect can then be identified. Another important feature of a panel data model is its ability to capture and identify effects of overall unobserved individual factors which do not change over time. In a cross-sectional model, those unobservables could only be captured as a part of the overall disturbance. Relevant unobservables in a cross-sectional model would not be allowed to correlate with included regressors in order to identify their specific effects. However, in a panel data model, time invariant unobservables can be treated as individual parameters for estimation, so their correlation with included regressors are allowed. That is the advantage of treating time-invariant, but unobserved individual variables with a fixed effect in a panel data model. If those time-invariant unobservables were not correlated with included regressors, they can be treated as a random component in the overall disturbance, which results in a random components model. As in the usual panel regression model, a Hausman test can validate whether individual effects are correlated with included regressors or not. Chapter 5 presents both fixed effects and random effects space-time models. In a spatial panel model, spatial and time lagged dependent variables can capture "diffusion" effects, while a cross sectional model cannot. In this chapter, the monograph discusses ML and GMM approaches. In a short panel time model, the GMM approach is of special interest as initial lagged endogenous variable would not be easily dealt with in the ML approach.

xvi *Foreword*

The second half of this monograph investigates spatial location patterns of economics agents (firms) and the growth and survival of firms taking into account spillover effects of existing firms. Chapter 6 considers the micro-geographical distribution of economic events and activities from the spatial statistics point of view. A spatial point process generates locations of objects on a plane and thus can be used to analyze spatial point patterns. A spatial point process is characterized by an intensity function, which describes an expected number of points per unit located within an infinitesimal region centered at the generic point x. If the intensity function is a constant through space, the point process is stationary. The hypothesis of complete spatial randomness (CSR) assumes that points have been generated under stationarity and independence. The homogeneous Poisson point process is the basic process which represents the CSR hypothesis. Other point processes generate aggregated or regular points patterns. Aggregation of points arises because of true contagion or apparent contagion. Apparent contagion relaxes stationarity. An inhomogeneous Poisson process can lead to apparent contagion while a Poisson cluster process leads to true contagion. The $\lambda(x)$ of the inhomogeneous Poisson process in a Cox process is stochastic, and $\lambda(x)$ and $\lambda(y)$ at different locations x and y can be correlated. Another form of violation of the CSR hypothesis is the spatial inhibition, which can be modeled with Matern's inhibition processes, the simple sequential inhibition process and the Strauss process. Traditional techniques provide formal tests for the CSR hypothesis. Chapter 7 introduces the K-function. Different spatial patterns in the CSR and the presence of "clustering" and "inhibition" can be captured by the K-function. In turn, one may introduce Monte Carlo procedures with the K-function to test for CSR. The K-function and its subsequent variants and extensions in the next chapters are useful mainly to perform static analysis of spatial distributions of economic agents' locations on a continuous space. Chapter 8 extends the modeling framework to a heterogeneous economics space by introducing inhomogeneous K-functions – such as the D-function and the K_{inhom}-function, which are distance-based measures of spatial concentration of industries and provide tools to assess the statistical significance of spatial interactions. Both the K-density and the M-function are proposed as adaptations of the K-function to industrial agglomeration. Chapter 9 extends the framework for location analysis to data with space and time. It concerns dynamic point patterns by introducing a spatio-temporal K-function, which separates the spatial and temporal dynamics. This function can be used to detect and measure space-time clustering. It can also be extended to be several possible diagnostic tools to detect independence between the spatial and temporal components of processes, as well as spatial-temporal clustering and spatial-temporal inhibition.

Chapter 10 considers more behaviors of firms in space and time. Firms are created at some random locations at some point in time, one models the way they operate, grow and attract or repulse other firms in their neighborhood. The authors formalize these processes of a firm with three model components, a birth model, a growth model and a death/survival model, which take into account the presence of spatial spillover effect, spatial externalities and spatial inhibition among economic agents. The firm formation process is modeled as an inhomogeneous Poisson process with an intensity function $\lambda(x)$ at location x driven by potential interaction effects of existing firms. The growth of a firm depends on its development at the beginning and competitive influences of other firms in the neighborhood. The death/survival component models a death/survival process taking into account competitive or cooperative influences of the other neighboring firms in the survival probability of a firm. Instead of discrete time for death/survival modeling, the final part of this chapter extends the survival data (or failure time) models to describe the death/survival component of the behavior of firms taking into account externalities in a continuous time setting. A case study with an Italian data provides an illustrative example for this chapter.

Lung-Fei Lee
Ohio State University

Preface and acknowledgements

This book is devoted to discussing a class of statistical and econometric methods designed to analyze individual micro-data which are observed as points in the economic space thus emphasizing the role of geographical relationships and other forms of network interaction between them.

Classical spatial econometrics is a field which traditionally studies the specificity of data observed within discrete portions of space, such as counties or regions. It owes its increasing popularity to the fact that applications can be found not only in regional and urban economics but also in a very wide variety of scientific fields like agricultural and health economics, resources and energy economics, land use, economic development, innovation diffusion, transportation, public finance, industrial organization, political sciences, psychology, demography, managerial economics, education, history, labor, criminology and real estate to name only a small subset of them.

Microeconometrics is a well-established field of research, which, however, generally neglects spatial and network relationships between economic agents.

Spatial microeconometrics represents the subfield which joins the efforts of these two fields. Although a spatial microeconometric approach had already been suggested in the late 1980s, at that time appropriate models had not been developed, adequate empirical data were not available and computing power was still inadequate to treat them anyway. Now that theoretical models have been fully developed and computing power has increased dramatically, there are no more obstacles and the field is rapidly growing under the impulse received by the widespread availability of detailed individual data linked to the Big Data advent and to the increased demand for empirical studies associated with them. Indeed, the availability of detailed databases coming from new data sources (e.g. crowdsourcing, cell phones, web scraping, internet of things, drones) makes it possible to eventually abandon the rather unrealistic representative agent paradigm that dominated the scene during the twentieth century and to start thinking in a totally different way by considering "the economy as a self-organizing system, rather than a glorified individual" to express it in Alan Kirman's words.

This book aims to draw the boundaries of this challenging new branch of studies.

xx *Preface and acknowledgements*

Going through the book, the reader will learn the specificities of treating data representing sets of interacting individuals with respect to the traditional microeconometric approach which treats their locational choices as exogenous and their economic behavior as independent. In particular, the reader will learn the consequences of neglecting such important sources of information on statistical inference and how to improve the model predictive performances exploiting them. The book introduces the theory, formally derives the properties of the models and clarifies the various concepts, discussing examples based on freely accessible real data that can be used to replicate the analyses for a better understanding of the various topics. It also instructs the readers on how to perform their own analyses, describing in detail the codes which are necessary when using the free statistical language R. This is an important and distinctive feature of the book in that, following the description of the procedures contained in the Appendix, all the models described in the text can be immediately put into action using the datasets which are of direct interest for the reader.

The book thus represents an essential reference for master's and PhD students as well as academic researchers who are engaged in the econometric analysis of empirical data in many branches of economics and in other neighboring fields like, such as environmental and epidemiological studies.

We believe that our work fills a gap in the literature with only marginal overlap with other existing textbooks on general spatial econometrics which are either explicitly focused on the analysis of regional data or do not consider the issues connected with the point pattern of individual agents and their locational choices.

The writing of this book has a long history that is perhaps worth telling briefly. Back in 1996 G.A. and G.E. wrote a book, entitled *Statistica economica territoriale* (Spatial Economic Statistics), published by the Italian publisher CEDAM (Arbia and Espa, 1996), that we like to think had a certain impact in the Italian academy and a certain role in diffusing those methodological practices among Italian researchers. The book was devoted to the econometric analysis of microdata, but it was limited to the study of the locational choices of individuals. At the time the two of us already had the idea of writing a second, more comprehensive, textbook which, in our minds, should also include the joint modeling of individuals' location decisions and their interactions. However, the time was not right for such a project. Even if the two of us perceived clearly the importance of such a comprehensive approach, the literature was still scarce and so incredibly scattered in many diverse disciplinary journals that it seemed impossible to bring it all within a single unified presentation accessible to all scholars. Furthermore, too many methodological problems were still waiting for satisfactory methodological answers. Indeed, most of the material we report in this book was still largely unwritten at the time and it materialized only after the turn of the new millennium. An important moment in the genesis of this book was the meeting with D.G., an enthusiastic student who at the time of the 1996 book was only 15-years-old. After he obtained his doctorate under the supervision of G.E. at the University of Trento, the three of us started a fruitful cooperation that still

Preface and acknowledgements xxi

goes on and that generated, in the last decade, a stream of papers on this subject. During this period the original plan of the book came back into discussion and we all agreed that the time was now right to engage the challenge of writing it.

What we had in mind was a book that could be used as a textbook for special topics in an econometrics course or in a course devoted specifically to spatial econometrics with an emphasis on individual spatial and network interaction. Despite the large class of models introduced from very different fields, we wanted to produce a book which was rather self-contained and whose understanding did not require any particular background beyond a working knowledge of elementary inferential statistics and econometrics at the level of an introductory academic course. The reader will judge if we achieved our aim.

The work has been demanding due to the vast literature examined and it was carried out jointly by the three of us in Rome (G.A.) and Trento (G.E. and D.G.) where we are currently located. Part of the work, however, was developed when G.A. was visiting the University of Illinois at Urbana-Champain, the universities of Sendai and Tsukuba in Japan, Stellenbosch University in South Africa, the Higher School of Economics in Moscow and the Centre for Entrepreneurship and Spatial Economics of Jönköping University in Sweden where he was invited to teach courses using some of the material reported here. We wish to take this chance to thank all these institutions for their interest in the subject and their warm hospitality.

An acceleration towards the production of the final draft, however, was provided by the lockdown measures imposed in Italy from March 9th to May 3rd 2020 to limit the diffusion of the SARS-CoV-2 during its pandemic. In those days, forced to stay at home for about two months with no teaching tasks to undertake and no distractions, we concentrated our efforts on the production of this book, trying to at least take some (small) advantage of the dramatic situation that was taking place around us. Even if this is perhaps not the best place for it, we feel it our duty to thank all the healthcare personnel for the incredible efforts they made in those days to contain the contagion even at the price, sometimes, of their own lives. Without them we would not be here today and their sacrifice can never be forgotten.

As it is common in these cases, the work has benefited by the comments and remarks received by a large number of people and we are happy to have here the chance to fulfil the pleasant duty to thank all of them in the occasion of submitting our draft to the publisher.

First of all, we wish to thank all the participants to the Spatial Econometrics Advanced Institute, a summer school held yearly in Rome since 2008 where G.A. and D.G. had a teaching role in recent years. The active presence of the students in class represented a great stimulus to collect the material in this book. In particular we wish to thank Giovanni Millo of Assicurazioni Generali (Trieste, Italy) who was first a student, and then for many years an instructor, at the summer school and who collaborated substantially to the drafting of Chapter 5.

Secondly, we would like to also thank Danila Filipponi, Simonetta Cozzi and Patrizia Cella of the Italian National Institute of Statistics in Rome for their

xxii *Preface and acknowledgements*

help and assistance in gathering the datasets used in some examples described in this book and Maria Michela Dickson and Flavio Santi of Trento University who carefully read previous drafts of the book and provided valuable comments and suggestions.

G.A.: I wish to dedicate this book to the newly born Pietro, my first grandson. I dedicated my first book to his mother Elisa back in 1989. Looking back to those years, it is sad to note how many of the people that were close to me at that time passed away, first of all my beloved parents, Francesco and Giulia. However, Pietro is now here and his arrival gives a positive sense to the time that has passed by. Therefore, this is my welcome to him, with whom I was so lucky to spend the last month in our country house in Tuscany alternating my last revisions of the book with the grandfather's important duty of assisting him in his first steps and his childish games. Even if he is the "special guest" here, in my dedication I cannot forget to give my thanks to my beloved wife Paola and to our three grown-up children: Elisa, Francesco and Enrica, although I have no more hope that they will ever read any of my books.

G.E.: I wish to dedicate this book to the memory of my father Salvatore who has always supported me in all my choices and inspired my love for statistics. I also would like to acknowledge the love and constant support of my sons Guido and Massimo.

D.G.: I wish to dedicate this book to my wife and partner, Serena, for her unwavering support and encouragement during the completion of this project.

To all of people mentioned above our thoughts are directed in this torrid and muggy day of an unusual mid-August when everybody else both in Rome and Trento seem to be on the beach despite the pandemic alert and we are here writing these that, hopefully, will be the last words of this book before it is published.

Rome, August 15th 2020
Ascension of Virgin Mary

Part I
Introduction

1 Foundations of spatial microeconometrics modeling

1.1 A micro-level approach to spatial econometrics

This book is devoted to the spatial econometric analysis of individual micro-data observed as points in the economic space (Dubé and Legros, 2014), sometimes referred to as "spatial microeconometrics" (Arbia et al., 2016). This branch is rapidly emerging onto the stage of spatial econometrics, building upon results from various branches of spatial statistics (Diggle, 2003) and on the earlier contributions of Arbia and Espa (1996), Duranton and Overman (2005), Marcon and Puech (2003; 2009; 2010) and Arbia et al. (2008; 2010; 2014a; 2014b; 2015b). In a relatively recent paper Pinkse and Slade (2010) heavily criticized the current developments of spatial econometrics, observing:

> The theory is in many ways in its infancy relative to the complexity of many applications (in sharp contrast to time-series econometrics, where the theory is well developed) ... due to the fact that it is almost invariably directed by what appears to be the most obvious extension of what is currently available rather than being inspired by actual empirical applications.

and:

> Many generic large sample results treat locations as both exogenous and fixed and assume that they are observations at particular locations of an underlying spatial process. ... Economists have studied the locational choices of individuals ... and of firms ... but generally treat the characteristics of locales as given. The purpose of much spatial work, however, is to uncover the interaction among (authorities of) geographic units, who choose, e.g., tax rates to attract firms or social services to attract households. ... An ideal model would marry the two; it would provide a model explaining both individuals' location decisions and the action of, say, local authorities. (Pinkse and Slade, 2010)

This new modelling strategy, which treats location as endogenous by taking into account simultaneously both individuals' locational choices and their economic

4   *Introduction*

decisions in their chosen location, represents the scope of the growing field of spatial microeconometrics.

As a matter of fact, a spatial microeconometric approach (unconceivable until only a few decades ago) is now more and more feasible due to the increasing availability of very large geo-referenced databases in all fields of economic analysis. For instance, the US Census Bureau's Longitudinal Business Database provides annual observations for every private-sector establishment with a payroll and includes approximately 4 million establishments and 70 million employees each year. Sourced from US tax records and Census Bureau surveys, the micro-records document the universe of establishments and firms characterized by their latitude–longitude spatial coordinates (Glaeser and Kerr, 2009). Examples of this kind can be increasingly found in all branches of economics including education, health economics, agricultural economics, labor economics, industrial economics, house prices, technological diffusion and many others. We will discuss them in the next section.

The availability of these detailed geographical databases now makes it possible to model individuals' economic behavior in space to gain information about economic trends at a regional or macro-level. A spatial microeconometric approach had already been suggested some 30 years ago by Durlauf (1989), at a time when data allowing this kind of approach were not yet available, appropriate models had not been developed and computing power was limited. Durlauf criticized the mainstream macroeconomy, pointing out that "macroeconomic modeling currently relies upon the representative agent paradigm to describe the evolution of time series. There is a folk wisdom that heterogeneity of agents renders these models unsatisfactory approximations of the macroeconomy". He then proceeded to describe a "lattice economy" where a "collection of agents are distributed across space and time" and "macroeconomy consists of many simple agents simultaneously interacting". Durlauf (1989; 1999) suggested a parallel between physics and economic analysis. In particular he concentrated on the links existing between formal individual choice models and the formalism of statistical mechanics, which suggested that there are many useful tools that applied economists could borrow from physics. Just as in statistical mechanics models explain how a collection of atoms can exhibit the correlated behavior necessary to produce a magnet, in economics one may devise models aimed at explaining spatially interdependent behaviors. The basic idea in statistical mechanics, that the behavior of one atom is influenced by the behavior of other atoms located nearby, is indeed very similar to the hypothesis that forms the basis of all spatial econometric studies that individual or collective decisions depend upon the decisions taken in other neighboring regions or by neighboring economic agents.

According to Kirman (1992) the traditional approach considers "the aggregate behavior of the economy as though it were the behavior of a single representative agent". However there is strong evidence that "heterogeneity and dispersion of agents' characteristics may lead to regularity in aggregate behavior" and that "once we allow for interdependence ... consistency between microeconomic characteristics and macroeconomic characteristics may be lost" and, finally, "strong local random interacting agents who are *a priori* identical may produce macroeconomic irregularities". Kirman concludes his work by stating that we must change our attitude and start thinking "of the economy as a self-organizing system, rather than a glorified individual".

Perhaps the most radical criticism in this respect is, however, presented by Danny Quah (1993), who states:

> Modern macroeconomics concerns itself, almost by definition with substitution of consumption and production across time. The macroeconomist wishes to understand the dynamic of inflation and asset prices, output and employment, growth and business cycles. Whether in doing so, one uses ideas of search and nonconvexities, intertemporal substitution and real business cycles, sticky prices and wages, or dynamic externalities, one implicitly assumes that it is the variation in economic activity across time that is the most useful to analyse. But why must that variation be the most important?

In doing so the macroeconomist "almost exclusively focuses on aggregate (rather than disaggregate) shocks as the source of economic fluctuations" ignoring "rich cross-sectional evidence on economic behaviour" and losing "the ability to say anything about the rich heterogeneous observations on economic activity across space, industries, firms and agents". These criticisms should be distinguished from those implying the

> failure of aggregation to a representative agent (e.g. Forni and Lippi, 1997; Kirman, 1992). There, the researcher points out the inability to represent aggregate behaviour because of individual heterogeneity. Here I assert instead that it is individual heterogeneity that is more interesting even from the perspective of wishing to understand macroeconomic behaviour.

However in introducing such concepts into the discussion and ignoring the empirical tools, "researchers have used empirical ideas that are altogether uninformative. Those econometricians who model dynamic adjustment have done so not because adjustment occurs only in time and not in space, but because time series methods are already readily available for the former and not the latter" (Quah, 1993). The quoted sentences can be considered in some sense the manifesto of spatial microeconometrics.

1.2 Advantages of spatial microeconometric analysis

The biggest advantage of a spatial microeconometric approach over orthodox spatial econometrics is the possibility of treating location and distances as endogenous thus allowing the modeling of both economic variables and locational choices within the same methodological framework (Pinkse and Slade, 2010). Spatial microeconometrics present many distinctive features with respect to orthodox spatial econometrics based on regional data and with respect to standard

6 *Introduction*

microeconometrics. Concerning the general field of microeconometrics, Cameron and Trivedi report six distinctive features: (i) discreteness and nonlinearity, (ii) greater realism, (iii) greater information content, (iv) microeconomic foundations, (v) disaggregation and heterogeneity and (vi) dynamics (Cameron and Trivedi, 2005). The lack of theories to support regional econometric modelling (Pinkse and Slade, 2010; Corrado and Fingleton, 2012) is one of the deeper criticisms against spatial econometrics restrictively conceived, which can, at most, lead to the identification of technical relationships with little or no possibility of drawing causal inferences. On the contrary, a spatial microeconometric approach provides the possibility of identifying more realistic models because hypotheses about economic behavior are usually elicited from theories related to the individual choices of economic agents. The inconsistency between microeconomic theories and macro-relationships has long been discussed in the economic literature (Pesaran et al., 1987; Klein, 1946). As a matter of fact, a relationship estimated at an individual level, such as a production function, may be regarded as a behavioral relationship that, for the single firm, embodies a particular interpretation of the causal mechanism linking inputs to outputs. However, the same relationship at an aggregate level does not depend on profit maximization but purely on technological factors (Klein, 1946). The relatively cavalier fashion with which most empirical studies shift from one unit to the other has seldom been criticized in the literature (Green, 1964; Hannan, 1970; Haitovsky, 1973). Traditionally economists have been faced with this problem in the analysis of family budgets: if we estimate a linear consumption function on aggregate data the impact of income on consumption has nothing in common with the individual marginal propensity to consume (Modigliani and Brunberg, 1955; Stocker, 1982).

The aggregation problem is a particularly relevant feature of the spatial econometrics of regional data that can be tackled by estimating models at a micro-geographical level. In fact, geographically aggregated data within discrete portions of space are based on arbitrary definitions of the spatial observational units, and, in this way, they introduce a statistical bias arising from the discretional characterization of space. This issue is very well known in the statistical literature, where it is referred to as the "modifiable areal unit problem" or MAUP (Arbia, 1989). The modifiable areal unit problem is more severe than the traditional modifiable unit problem (Yule and Kendall, 1950), because regional data are usually very irregular aggregations of individual characterized by large differences in terms of the size and the shape of the various spatial units. The MAUP manifests itself in two ways: (i) the scale problem, dealing with the indeterminacy of any statistical measure to changes in the level of aggregation of data, and (ii) the aggregation problem, having to do with the indeterminacy of any statistical measures due to changes in the aggregation criterion at a given spatial scale. The effects of aggregation on standard econometric models are well known, dating back to the early contributions of Prais and Aitchinson (1954), Theil (1954), Zellner (1962), Cramer (1964), Haitovsky (1973). More contributions were made by Barker and Pesaran (1989), Okabe and Tagashira

Foundations of spatial microeconometrics 7

(1996), Tagashira and Okabe (2002) and Griffith et al. (2003). The main results found in the literature are that the estimators of regression's parameters have a larger variance when using aggregated rather than individual data, leading to false inferential conclusions and to the acceptance of models that should be discarded. Orcutt et al. (1968), through a microsimulation study, pointed out that "detailed study of the individual regression indicates a tendency to reject the null hypothesis more frequently than the usual sampling theory suggests. ... Perhaps this is why economic theories are almost never rejected on the basis of empirical evidences." Similar conclusions were reached by Arbia (1989), who considered a spatial random economy constituted by many interacting agents. He noticed that "even a small amount of autocorrelation between the individuals can produce the ecological fallacy effect".[1] The loss in efficiency due to aggregation depends on the grouping criterion and it is minimized when individuals are grouped so as to maximize the within-group variability. The effects of MAUP on different statistical measures, pioneered by Gehlke and Biehl (1934), Yule and Kendall (1950), Robinson (1950) and Openshaw and Taylor (1979), have been studied at length by Arbia (1989) who derived the formal relationship between the Pearson's correlation coefficient at the individual level and the same coefficient at the aggregate level when data are spatially correlated. Arbia and Petrarca (2011) presented a general framework for analyzing the effects of MAUP on spatial econometric models showing that the efficiency loss, connatural to any aggregation process, is mitigated by the presence of a positive spatial correlation parameter and conversely exacerbated by the presence of a negative spatial correlation. This result is intuitive: positive spatial correlation implies aggregation between similar values thus preserving variability, while negative spatial correlation implies aggregation between very different values thus implying a more dramatic increase of variability.

1.3 Sources of spatial micro-data

The large availability of geo-coded data in many fields has increased enormously the potential applications of spatial microeconometrics, opening new possibilities for modeling the individual economic behavior in fields like education, industrial economics, hedonic house prices, health economics, agricultural economics, labor economics, business, crime, social networks and technological diffusion to name only a few.

Indeed the advent of Big Data (Arbia, forthcoming) has brought a revolution in terms of the data availability at an individual level so that the sources of spatial micro-data are now no longer limited to archives, administrative records or panels, as they were in the recent past. In fact, they more and more include alternative data sources such as satellite and aerial photographs, information obtained through drones, crowdsourcing, cell phones, web scraping, the internet of things (IOT) and many others. In particular, common examples of increasingly popular alternative spatial data sources are represented by crowdsourcing (data voluntarily collected by individuals), web scraping (data extracted from

8   *Introduction*

websites and reshaped in a structured dataset) and the internet of things. These typologies of data with the addition of a spatial reference are commonly known as "volunteered geographic information" (VGI) (Goodchild, 2007). Crowd-sourced data are common in many situations. An example is represented by data collected through smart phones in order to measure phenomena that are other-wise difficult to quantify precisely and quickly, such as food prices in developing countries (see e.g. Arbia et al., 2020) and epidemiological data (Crequit et al., 2018). The practice of extracting data from the web and using them in statisti-cal analyses is also becoming more and more popular, such as collecting online prices in the real estate market (Beręsewicz, 2015; Boeing and Waddell, 2017; Arbia and Nardelli, 2020) or in consumer goods. A very good example in this re-spect is constituted by the Billion Prices Project (Cavallo and Rigobon, 2016) an academic initiative that collects prices from hundreds of online retailers around the world on a daily basis to conduct economic research.

The internet of things consists of a system of interrelated computing devices which are provided with the ability to automatically transfer data over a network. An example is constituted by electronic devices to monitor the quality of the air in metropolitan areas (see e.g. <https://www.wiseair.it>).

There are two pieces of information that are needed in order to conduct a micro-level spatial econometric analysis. The first is derived from the traditional observation of attributes, while the second is the exact geographical location of the observed individuals and can take the form of UTM/GPS coordinates. Many spatial econometric methods are based on the possibility of accessing the exact individual locations and calculating inter-point distances between them. In many situations such information is obtained automatically in the process of data acquisition. For instance, in the case of crowdsourcing from cell phones data are related to the coverage area of a cellular system which is divided into non-overlapping *cells*. In areas where the cells are very dense the individual's position can be assessed with a high degree of precision. Moreover, when col-lected from the internet of things, data are transmitted automatically containing both the attribute information and the GPS coordinates. Conversely, when the coordinates cannot be observed directly, the process of geo-coding often implies converting addresses into geographical coordinates, such as in the case of web scraping house-price data from real estate companies. In this case the task can be automatically accomplished through the use of such programs as Google Maps Geocoding API. Travel distances or times for a matrix of origins and destina-tions based on recommended routes from a start to an end point can be similarly obtained through Google Maps Distance Matrix API.

1.4 Sources of uncertainty in spatial micro-data

Having described briefly the major advantages of a micro-approach to spatial econometrics, let us now present the typical problems emerging when we use micro-data that are, in contrast, irrelevant in the use of regional aggregated data in statistical analyses. When using regional data in spatial econometrics almost invariably (i) the spatial units (regions) constitute the whole population, (ii) there are no missing data and (iii) the location of the observations is known exactly. Conversely, when we use individual geo-coded data, we encounter various forms of data imperfection that can mask the real phenomena up to the point of distorting dramatically the inferential conclusions: data are often based on a sample, some data may be missing and they may very frequently contain both attribute and locational errors.

Dealing with spatial micro-data, there is still a certain degree of ambiguity in the literature on the concept of uncertainty and missing data. In order to clarify this issue, let us distinguish the case of missing data from the case of missing location. In practice we can encounter four different cases that must be distinguished because the consequences (and the solutions) are intuitively different in each situation. These will be discussed in turn in the present section

The first case is missing spatial data and spatial location, when both the location and some measurements are unknown. We know of the presence of some individuals in a certain area but not exactly where they are, and, furthermore, we do not have information about some or all their characteristics. Some individuals are simply not observed in the study area. A second situation within this context is missing spatial data, when the location of individuals is known exactly, but we are unable to observe the characteristics of some or all of the individuals. This happens, for instance, when we know of the presence of a firm and its exact GPS location, but some or all information is missing at a certain moment of time (e.g., the number of employees or the production realized by the firm in that location). This case represents the traditional case of missing data as it has been treated at length in the statistical literature (Little, 1988; Little and Rubin, 2002; Rubin, 1976; Roderick and Rubin, 2007) where solutions have been suggested to replace the observations that are missing following different interpolating strategies (e.g., the expectation-maximization (EM) algorithm by Dempster et al. (1977) and multiple imputation methods (Rubin, 1987)). These approaches, however, do not adequately treat the nature of spatial data and do not suggest solutions to the problem of locating the information that is artificially recovered in the space.

A further cause of uncertainty is unintentional positional error: that is, when observations on individuals are available, but their location is missing or not known with certainty. For instance, we have a list of firms in a census tract and we also have observations on some of their statistical characteristics, but we do not know their exact address within the area. In this case it is common to assign the individual to the centroid of each area, but this procedure generates a positional error (see Cozzi and Filipponi, 2012, for the archive of firms managed by the Italian National Statistical Institute). In this situation, not only are the traditional statistical procedures proposed in the literature to minimize the fallacies produced by missing data useless, but even their consequences on statistical modeling are still largely unknown (see Bennett et al., 1984; Griffith et al., 1989). Finally, we can encounter the case of intentional positional error (Arbia et al., 2015a) where both location and measurement of the single individuals are

10   *Introduction*

known, but the individuals' positions might be geo-masked before making them publicly available to preserve respondents' confidentiality. In Section 3.4.2 we will discuss some of the effects of these data imperfections on spatial econometric modeling. Further sources of errors derive from measurement errors (Greene, 2018) and from the misalignment which might occur when data are collected at different levels of resolution (Mugglin et al., 2000; Banerjee and Gelfand, 2002; Madsen et al., 2008).

Last but not least, a problem that it is often overlooked when analyzing spatial micro-data is the fact that they often refer to individuals that are not observed in the whole population but only in a sample.

When data are observed for the whole population we refer to them as a "mapped point pattern" whereas in the second case we refer to a "sample point pattern". In this respect, a common characteristic of many new unconventional data collection sources is represented by the collection of sample data which lack any precise statistical sample design. In crowdsourcing, for instance, participation is generally voluntary, meaning that the population is self-selecting. A similar problem emerges when extracting data that were published on web platforms and social media without taking into account the process that lead to their publication. This situation is described in statistics as "convenience sampling" in the presence of which, as it is well known, no sound probabilistic inference is possible (Hansen et al., 1953), as, in general, all the optimal properties of the estimators are lost. More precisely, while in a formal sample design the choice of observations is suggested by a precise mechanism which allows the calculation of the probabilities of inclusion of each unit (and, hence, sound probabilistic inferences), with convenience collection no probability of inclusion can be calculated thus giving rise to over- and under-representativeness of the sample units.

1.5 Conclusions and plan of the book

In this first chapter we have introduced the main ideas on which spatial microeconometrics are grounded, and we discussed the advantages and the drawbacks connected with such an approach. The rest of the book is organized into three parts. Part II deals with methods and models for the spatial behavior of a single economic agent observed in a set of locations which are assumed to be exogenously given. This involves introducing some preliminary concepts in Chapter 2, discussing cross-section linear and non-linear models in Chapters 3 and 4, and dynamic space–time models in Chapter 5. In Part III, we will concentrate our attention on the position of the individual economic agent and discuss methods to model its spatial locational choices. After a preliminary chapter (Chapter 6) we will consider approaches to modeling the spatial location of the individual agent in a homogeneous (Chapter 7) and heterogeneous (Chapter 8) space. These approaches are extended to include the temporal dimension in Chapter 9.

Part IV unites the methods discussed in Parts II and III, considering modeling strategies where both the spatial location and the spatial behavior of the economic agents are considered endogenous with a strong emphasis on the spatial aspects of firm demography and survival analysis. This discussion is reported in Chapter 10 which also concludes the book with a discussion of the many open questions and research challenges connected with the current and future development of this new discipline.

Note

1 The "ecological fallacy" is the extending of conclusions and relationships observed at an aggregated level to the level of individuals.

Part II

Modeling the spatial behavior of economic agents in a given set of locations

2 Preliminary definitions and concepts

2.1 Neighborhood and the W matrix

The classical linear regression model assumes normal, exogenous and spherical disturbances (Greene, 2018). However, when we observe a phenomenon in, say, n regions, non-sphericalness of residuals may arise due to the presence of spatial autocorrelation and spatial heterogeneity among the stochastic terms, in which case the optimal properties of the ordinary least squares (OLS) are lost. Before introducing various alternatives to the basic model, let us, however, introduce some preliminary concepts. In fact, we can intuitively define spatial correlation as a feature of data describing the fact that observations that are close together are more correlated than observations that are far apart (the "first law of geography" (Tobler, 1970)). However, a formal definition requires a clarification of the concept of "closeness". At the heart of spatial econometrics methods is the definition of the so-called "weights matrix" (or "connectivity matrix"). The simplest of all definitions is the following:

$$
{}_nW_n = \begin{bmatrix} w_{11} & \cdots & & w_{n1} \\ \cdots & w_{ij} & & \\ & & & \\ w_{1n} & & w_{nn} \end{bmatrix} \tag{2.1}
$$

in which each generic element is defined as

$$
w_{ij} = \begin{cases} 1 & \text{if } j \in N(i) \\ 0 & \text{otherwise} \end{cases} \tag{2.2}
$$

$N(i)$ being the set of neighbors of location j. By definition we have that $w_{ii} = 0$.

Many different alternative definitions of the W matrix are possible.

A first definition is based on an inverse function of the distance: $w_{ij} = d_{ij}^{-\alpha}; \quad \alpha > 0$ where often $\alpha = 2$ due to the analogy with Newton's law of universal gravitation. This first definition, however, presents the disadvantage of producing very dense W matrices an issue that can create computational problems with very large datasets.

16 Spatial behavior of economic agents

A second definition considers a threshold distance (say d^*) introduced to increase the sparseness of the W matrix thus reducing the computational problems emerging when dealing with large datasets (see Figure 2.1b). We can then have simple binary matrices where $w_{ij} = \begin{cases} 1 \text{ if } d_{ij} < d^* \\ 0 \text{ otherwise} \end{cases}$ or, alternatively, a combination with the inverse distance definition where $w_{ij} = \begin{cases} d_{ij}^{-\alpha} \text{ if } d_{ij} < d^* \\ 0 \text{ otherwise} \end{cases}$. Finally, we can adopt a k nearest neighbors definition where $w_{ij} = \begin{cases} 1 \text{ if } i \in N^k(i) \\ 0 \text{ otherwise} \end{cases}$ where $N^k(i)$ is the set of the k nearest neighbors to point i (see Figure 2.1a).

Quite often the W matrices are standardized to sum unity in each row an operation called "row standardization". In this case we have:

$$w_{ij}^* = \frac{w_{ij}}{\sum_{j=1}^{n} w_{ij}}; \; w_{ij}^* \in W^* \tag{2.3}$$

This standardization may be very useful in some instances. For example, by using the standardized weights we can define the matrix product

$$L(y) = W^* y \tag{2.4}$$

in which each single element is equal to:

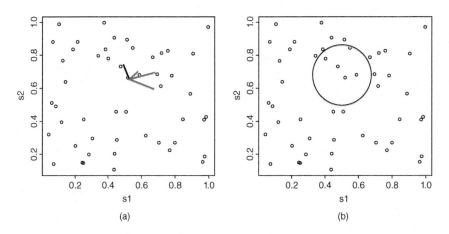

Figure 2.1 K-nearest neighbors contiguity criterion ($k = 4$): (a) only the first k nearest neighbors are considered; maximum threshold criterion; (b) all points within a radius d^* are considered neighbors to the point located in the center.

$$L(y_i) = \sum_{i=1}^{n} w_{ij}^* y_j = \sum_{i=1}^{n} \frac{w_{ij} y_j}{\sum_{i=1}^{n} w_{ij}} = \frac{\sum_{j \in N(i)} y_j}{\# N(i)} \qquad (2.5)$$

with $\#N(i)$ representing the cardinality of the set $N(i)$. The term in Equation 2.5 represents the average of variable y observed in all the individuals that are neighbors to individual i (according to the criterion chosen in defining W). It therefore assumes the meaning of the "spatially lagged value" of y_i and for this reason is often indicated with the symbol $L(y)$ by analogy with the lag operator in time-series analysis. This definition assumes no directional bias in that all neighbors affect individual i in the same way (for alternatives, see Arbia, 1990; Arbia et al., 2013).

An important aspect of W matrices is represented by their "density", defined as the percentage of non-zero entries a value that ranges between 0 and $\frac{n-1}{n}$ when all off-diagonal entries are non-zero. The complement to 1 of the density is called the "sparsity" of a matrix. Dense W matrices should be avoided as they may involve severe computational problems in terms of computing time, storage and accuracy especially when the sample size is very large (see Arbia et. al., 2019b).

Example 2.1

Some simple examples of W matrices for sets of points are reported here. Consider, initially, a map of ten individual points (Figure 2.2). From this dataset we can build up four different W matrices employing the different neighborhood criteria illustrated above.

i   The first W matrix can be built up as a simple binary threshold distance by fixing a conventional threshold at a distance of, say, 0.45 (R Command: {spdep}-dnearneigh) (Table 2.1). The matrix can then be row-standardized obtaining Table 2.2.

ii   The second alternative is to build up a W matrix using the nearest neighbor criterion (R Command: {spdep}-knearneigh). We obtain Table 2.3, which is standardized by definition.

iii   As a third alternative we consider the squared inverse distance criterion. We first obtain the pair-wise distance matrix (Table 2.4) and then the W matrix is obtained calculating in each entry the squared inverse distance (keeping 0 in the main diagonal) (Table 2.5), which can be row-standardized, obtaining Table 2.6.

iv   Finally we build up a combination of cases ii and iii using the squared inverse distance below a threshold (<0.45). The unstandardized version is in Table 2.7, which, once row-standardized, becomes Table 2.8.

18 *Spatial behavior of economic agents*

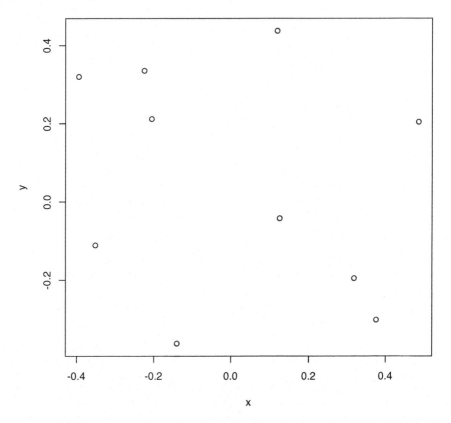

Figure 2.2 Map of ten points in a unit square.

Table 2.1 Binary threshold distance W matrix (threshold = 0.45) built on the basis of the points reported in Figure 2.2 (unstandardized)

										Row sum
0	0	0	1	0	0	0	1	0	0	2
0	0	1	1	0	1	0	0	0	0	3
0	1	0	1	0	0	1	0	0	0	3
1	1	1	0	0	0	1	0	1	0	5
0	0	0	0	0	1	0	0	1	1	3
0	1	0	0	1	0	0	0	1	0	3
0	0	1	1	0	0	0	0	0	0	2
1	0	0	0	0	0	0	0	1	1	3
0	0	0	1	1	1	0	1	0	1	5
0	0	0	0	1	0	0	1	1	0	3

Preliminary definitions and concepts 19

Table 2.2 Binary threshold distance W matrix (threshold = 0.45) built on the basis of the points reported in Figure 2.2 (row standardized)

										Row sum
0.00	0.00	0.00	0.50	0.00	0.00	0.00	0.50	0.00	0.00	1.00
0.00	0.00	0.33	0.33	0.00	0.33	0.00	0.00	0.00	0.00	1.00
0.00	0.33	0.00	0.33	0.00	0.00	0.33	0.00	0.00	0.00	1.00
0.20	0.20	0.20	0.00	0.00	0.00	0.20	0.00	0.20	0.00	1.00
0.00	0.00	0.00	0.00	0.00	0.33	0.00	0.00	0.33	0.33	1.00
0.00	0.33	0.00	0.00	0.33	0.00	0.00	0.00	0.33	0.00	1.00
0.00	0.00	0.50	0.50	0.00	0.00	0.00	0.00	0.00	0.00	1.00
0.33	0.00	0.00	0.00	0.00	0.00	0.00	0.00	0.33	0.33	1.00
0.00	0.00	0.00	0.20	0.20	0.20	0.00	0.20	0.00	0.20	1.00
0.00	0.00	0.00	0.00	0.33	0.00	0.00	0.33	0.33	0.00	1.00

Table 2.3 Nearest neighbor distance W matrix built on the basis of the points reported in Figure 2.2

0	0	0	0	0	0	0	1	0	0
0	0	0	0	0	1	0	0	0	0
0	0	0	0	0	0	1	0	0	0
0	0	1	0	0	0	0	0	0	0
0	0	0	0	0	0	0	0	1	0
0	0	0	0	1	0	0	0	0	0
0	0	1	0	0	0	0	0	0	0
1	0	0	0	0	0	0	0	0	0
0	0	0	0	1	0	0	0	0	0
0	0	0	0	1	0	0	0	0	0

Table 2.4 Pair-wise distance matrix of the points reported in Figure 2.2

0.000	0.844	0.486	0.416	0.702	0.840	0.519	0.329	0.578	0.728
0.844	0.000	0.434	0.436	0.722	0.433	0.518	0.895	0.691	0.887
0.486	0.434	0.000	0.245	0.757	0.662	0.122	0.673	0.662	0.877
0.416	0.436	0.245	0.000	0.515	0.479	0.360	0.482	0.418	0.633
0.702	0.722	0.757	0.515	0.000	0.359	0.875	0.464	0.125	0.170
0.840	0.433	0.662	0.479	0.359	0.000	0.781	0.723	0.396	0.527
0.519	0.518	0.122	0.360	0.875	0.781	0.000	0.751	0.775	0.989
0.329	0.895	0.673	0.482	0.464	0.723	0.751	0.000	0.354	0.433
0.578	0.691	0.662	0.418	0.125	0.396	0.775	0.354	0.000	0.217
0.728	0.887	0.877	0.633	0.170	0.527	0.989	0.433	1.000	0.000

20 *Spatial behavior of economic agents*

Table 2.5 Squared inverse distance W matrix built on the basis of the points reported in Figure 2.2 (unstandardized)

0.000	1.405	4.233	5.791	2.027	1.416	3.718	9.259	2.995	1.889
1.405	0.000	5.320	5.250	1.918	5.327	3.731	1.250	2.091	1.271
4.233	5.320	0.000	16.723	1.743	2.283	67.630	2.205	2.280	1.299
5.791	5.250	16.723	0.000	3.774	4.351	7.721	4.304	5.731	2.494
2.027	1.918	1.743	3.774	0.000	7.738	1.307	4.651	64.476	34.587
1.416	5.327	2.283	4.351	7.738	0.000	1.638	1.913	6.371	3.597
3.718	3.731	67.630	7.721	1.307	1.638	0.000	1.771	1.663	1.023
9.259	1.250	2.205	4.304	4.651	1.913	1.771	0.000	7.971	5.342
2.995	2.091	2.280	5.731	64.476	6.371	1.663	7.971	0.000	21.289
1.889	1.271	1.299	2.494	34.587	3.597	1.023	5.342	21.289	0.000

Table 2.6 Squared inverse distance W matrix built on the basis of the points reported in Figure 2.2 (row standardized)

										Row sum
0.000	0.043	0.129	0.177	0.062	0.043	0.114	0.283	0.091	0.058	1.000
0.051	0.000	0.193	0.190	0.070	0.193	0.135	0.045	0.076	0.046	1.000
0.041	0.051	0.000	0.161	0.017	0.022	0.652	0.021	0.022	0.013	1.000
0.103	0.094	0.298	0.000	0.067	0.077	0.138	0.077	0.102	0.044	1.000
0.017	0.016	0.014	0.031	0.000	0.063	0.011	0.038	0.528	0.283	1.000
0.041	0.154	0.066	0.126	0.223	0.000	0.047	0.055	0.184	0.104	1.000
0.041	0.041	0.750	0.086	0.014	0.018	0.000	0.020	0.018	0.011	1.000
0.239	0.032	0.057	0.111	0.120	0.049	0.046	0.000	0.206	0.138	1.000
0.026	0.018	0.020	0.050	0.561	0.055	0.014	0.069	0.000	0.185	1.000
0.026	0.017	0.018	0.034	0.475	0.049	0.014	0.073	0.292	0.000	1.000

Table 2.7 Squared inverse distance with a threshold (0.45) W matrix built on the basis of the points reported in Figure 2.2 (unstandardized)

0.000	0.000	0.000	5.791	0.000	0.000	0.000	9.259	0.000	0.000
0.000	0.000	5.320	5.250	0.000	5.327	0.000	0.000	0.000	0.000
0.000	5.320	0.000	16.723	0.000	0.000	67.630	0.000	0.000	0.000
5.791	5.250	16.723	0.000	0.000	0.000	7.721	0.000	5.731	0.000
0.000	0.000	0.000	0.000	0.000	7.738	0.000	0.000	64.476	34.587
0.000	5.327	0.000	0.000	7.738	0.000	0.000	0.000	6.371	0.000
0.000	0.000	67.630	7.721	0.000	0.000	0.000	0.000	0.000	0.000
9.259	0.000	0.000	0.000	0.000	0.000	0.000	0.000	7.971	5.342
0.000	0.000	0.000	5.731	64.476	6.371	0.000	7.971	0.000	21.289
0.000	0.000	0.000	0.000	0.029	0.000	0.000	0.187	0.000	0.000

Preliminary definitions and concepts 21

Table 2.8 Squared inverse distance with a threshold (0.45) W matrix built on the basis of the points reported in Figure 2.2 (row standardized)

										Row sum
0.000	0.000	0.000	0.385	0.000	0.000	0.000	0.615	0.000	0.000	1.000
0.000	0.000	0.335	0.330	0.000	0.335	0.000	0.000	0.000	0.000	1.000
0.000	0.059	0.000	0.186	0.000	0.000	0.754	0.000	0.000	0.000	1.000
0.141	0.127	0.406	0.000	0.000	0.000	0.187	0.000	0.139	0.000	1.000
0.000	0.000	0.000	0.000	0.000	0.072	0.000	0.000	0.604	0.324	1.000
0.000	0.274	0.000	0.000	0.398	0.000	0.000	0.000	0.328	0.000	1.000
0.000	0.000	0.898	0.102	0.000	0.000	0.000	0.000	0.000	0.000	1.000
0.410	0.000	0.000	0.000	0.000	0.000	0.000	0.000	0.353	0.237	1.000
0.000	0.000	0.000	0.054	0.609	0.060	0.000	0.075	0.000	0.201	1.000
0.000	0.000	0.000	0.000	0.134	0.000	0.000	0.866	0.000	0.000	1.000

The various definitions present relative advantages and drawbacks. In particular, the distance threshold criterion (case i) may produce isolated locations with no neighbors if the threshold is too small which makes it impossible to derive the spatially lagged variable. On the other hand, it may lead to very dense matrices with each location related to many others (possibly all of them) if we are forced to use a large threshold to include at least one neighbor for each location. We mentioned already the problems raised by dense W matrices. The nearest neighbor definition (case ii) produces a matrix which is not symmetrical, which can be a problem in some instances, but it should be equally remarked that none of the other definitions lead to a symmetrical matrix once they are standardized.

Similarly to case i, the squared inverse distance criterion (case iii) leads by definition to fully dense matrices, so that a reasonable compromise could be represented by the squared inverse distance with a threshold (case iv).

Example 2.2

Now suppose that in the ten locations reported in the point pattern of Example 2.1, we observe the following values of a hypothetical variable Y:

Location	1	2	3	4	5	6	7	8	9	10
Y	102	113	103	116	94	115	100	91	91	103

Using the four different W matrices described above we can calculate the spatially lagged variable using the expression reported in Equation 2.5 (R Command: {spdep}-lag.listw). We obtain Table 2.9.

22 Spatial behavior of economic agents

Table 2.9 Spatially lagged variable computed using four different neighborhood criteria

Y	Spatial lag, L(Y)			
	Threshold distance	Nearest neighbor	Squared inverse distance	Squared inverse distance with threshold
102	103	91	101	101
113	110	115	105	111
103	108	100	103	103
116	102	103	102	102
94	102	91	98	97
115	98	94	101	98
100	110	103	104	105
91	98	102	101	99
91	104	94	98	98
103	91	94	95	91

2.2 Moran's I and other spatial correlation measures

The most widely used measure for spatial autocorrelation is based on a general measure of spatial correlation introduced by Moran (1950) and proposed by Cliff and Ord (1972) as a test statistic for the null of uncorrelation among ordinary least squares regression residuals. As is known, in the presence of significant residual autocorrelation, the OLS estimators, although still unbiased and consistent, lose their efficiency and in general will produce larger standard errors. As a consequence, the test of hypothesis will be biased (Greene, 2018). Notice that Moran's I was introduced in the literature before the analogous measure for time-series regression residuals: the celebrated Durbin–Watson statistic (Durbin and Watson, 1951) even if, as already noted, its extension to deal with regression residuals was published only later (Cliff and Ord, 1972). The Durbin–Watson statistic can be defined as a special case of Moran's I by simply defining an appropriate W matrix (see e.g. Arbia, 2006). In its essence Moran's I takes the form of a correlation between the regression disturbances, call them ε, and their spatially lagged values, that is:

$$Corr(\varepsilon, L\varepsilon) = \frac{Cov(\varepsilon, L\varepsilon)}{\sqrt{Var(\varepsilon)Var(L\varepsilon)}} \qquad (2.6)$$

From Equation 2.6, by using the definition of spatial lag given in Equation 2.4 and assuming (by analogy to what happens with stationary time series) that:

$$Var(\varepsilon) = Var(L\varepsilon) \qquad (2.7)$$

we have

$$Corr(\varepsilon, L\varepsilon) = \frac{Cov(\varepsilon, L\varepsilon)}{Var(\varepsilon)} = \frac{\varepsilon^T W \varepsilon}{\varepsilon^T \varepsilon} \qquad (2.8)$$

However, it can be shown that, due to the nature of the spatial lag definition, Equation 2.7 does not hold for spatial data, where we have instead $Var(\varepsilon) \geq Var(L\varepsilon)$ (see Arbia, 1989). One of the effects of this inequality is that the measure introduced in Equation 2.8 is not limited by 1 in absolute value, but possesses narrower limits given by $|I| \leq \sqrt{\dfrac{Var(L\varepsilon)}{Var(\varepsilon)}}$. However, partly for historical reasons, and more substantially for the equivalence that can be demonstrated with a Lagrange multiplier test (see Section 3.7), this definition is currently prevailing in the literature and is the most widely implemented in software routines (alternatives are discussed in Whittle, 1954; Cliff and Ord, 1981 and more recently in Li et al., 2007). In its original definition Moran's I considers the biased estimator of the variance in the denominator of Equation 2.8 and a normalizing factor for the numerator equal to the sum of the weights. As a consequence the empirical counterpart of Equation 2.8 can be expressed as:

$$I = \frac{n e^T W e}{e^T e [\sum_i \sum_j w_{ij}]} \tag{2.9}$$

with the symbol e indicating the empirical residuals of a regression. When the weight matrix is row-standardized then $\sum_i \sum_j w_{ij} = n$ and the previous expression simplifies as:

$$I = \frac{e^T W e}{e^T e} \tag{2.10}$$

Cliff and Ord (1972) derived the sampling distribution of Moran's I under two different hypotheses: (i) randomization and (ii) normality of residuals. In the first case the sampling distribution is obtained by considering all possible permutations of the observed data on the spatial system and calculating Moran's I in each of them. They also proved that the asymptotical distribution is normal irrespective of the hypothesis chosen with an expected value that also does not depend on the hypothesis and that is expressed by:

$$E(I) = \frac{n \; tr(M_x W)}{S_0 (n - k)} \tag{2.11}$$

with $S_0 = \sum_i \sum_j w_{ij}$, $M_x = I - P_x$ and $P_x = X(X^T X)^{-1} X^T$. In contrast, its variance depends on the hypothesis selected. In particular, if we assume normality of the residuals, it can be expressed as:

$$Var(I) = \left(\frac{n}{S_0}\right)^2 \frac{tr(M_x W M_x W^T) + tr(M_x W)^2 + [tr(M_x W)]^2}{(n-k)(n-k+2)} - E(I)^2 \tag{2.12}$$

24 Spatial behavior of economic agents

Notice that Moran's I suffers from the limitation of not being based on an explicit alternative hypothesis. However, due to the already mentioned equivalence of the test to a LM test (proved by Burridge, 1980), this is not a major drawback. The discussion of an alternative for the null of no residual correlation cannot be made before we present some plausible explicit formulations which will not be presented until Section 3.7.

Example 2.3

Let us consider here the dataset Boston, downloadable from the R library spdep, which refers to house prices observed in 506 location in the city of Boston, Massachusetts. The data were collected by Harrison and Rubinfield (1978) and integrated by Gilley and Pace (1996) and are very popular in spatial econometrics (see Figure 2.3). For each location the dataset reports the UTM (Universal Transverse Mercator system) coordinates, the house price and a set of covariates. Our model explains the price of the house as a function of the nitric oxide

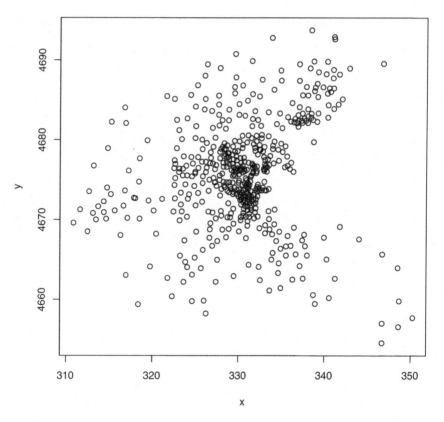

Figure 2.3 Map of 506 locations in Boston, Massachusetts. Source: R library spdep.

Preliminary definitions and concepts 25

Table 2.10 Output of the regression of the house price as a function of NOX of 506 locations in the city of Boston. Estimation method: OLS

Parameter		Standard error	t-test	p-value
Intercept	41.346	1.811	22.83	< 2e – 16
NOX	–33.916	3.196	3.196	< 2e – 16

R^2 = 0.1826; adjusted R^2 = 0.181; F-statistic = 112.6 (p-value < 2e – 16); AIC = 3584.455; BIC = 3597.135

Table 2.11 Moran's I of the residuals of the regression reported in Table 2.10

	Observed value	Expected value	Variance	z-test	p-value
Moran's I	0.195	–0.0033	0.00017	15.09	< 2e – 16

concentration (parts per 10 million). The result of the estimation of the model with the OLS are reported in Table 2.10 together with the main test statistics (R Command: {stat}-lm).

For the calculation of Moran's I on the residuals, we consider the definition of the weight matrix based on a distance threshold with a threshold which is derived as the minimum distance to ensure that each point has at least one neighbor. The distances are calculated based on the UTM coordinates. The matrix obtained with this criterion has a density of 14.27% (percentage of non-zero weights) and an average number of neighbors equal to 72.22. On this basis we calculated Moran's I on the regression residuals (R Command: {spdep}-lm.morantest). Results are reported in Table 2.11. Moran's I reveals the presence of a very strong and significant positive spatial autocorrelation among the regression residuals, which undermines the use of the OLS criterion for parameter's estimator and the interpretation of the related hypothesis testing procedures.

An alternative measure of spatial correlation with respect to Moran's I is represented by Geary's index (Geary, 1954) which is based on a completely different rationale. Instead of building the index as a correlation between actual and spatially lagged values, as in Moran's I, Geary's index is based on the squared difference between two neighboring values. The formal expression is the following:

$$C = \frac{(n-1)\sum_i \sum_j w_{ij}(X_i - X_j)^2}{2\sum_i \sum_j w_{ij} \sum_i (X_i - \bar{X})^2} \qquad (2.13)$$

Similar values between neighboring observations (positive spatial correlation) will give rise to a low index, whereas when the difference between neighboring values is large (implying positive spatial correlation) it will produce a low value

26 *Spatial behavior of economic agents*

of the index. The index is obviously always positive. In particular, Geary (1954) showed that the index ranges between 0 and 2, with 1 corresponding to the absence of spatial correlation, values > 1 indicate negative spatial correlation and finally values of the index < 1 indicate positive spatial correlation. The expected value and the variance of the index under the null of no spatial correlation where derived by Geary (1954) who also proved normality thus allowing the standard hypothesis testing procedures. Similarly to Moran's I, however, no explicit alternative hypothesis is specified.

2.3 The Moran scatterplot and local indicators of spatial correlation

Both Moran's I and Geary's index are global measures in that they allow us to test for a spatial pattern over the study area as a whole. However, individual behaviors are typically heterogeneous in space. Therefore, it could happen that the presence of significant spatial correlation in smaller sub-sections of the study areas is not observed in a single global index due to the presence of other sub-sections displaying negative or no spatial correlation. A way of measuring this effect is to define local measures that look at the spatial correlation of the phenomenon within smaller partitions. This approach is referred to as the analysis of "local indicators of spatial association" (LISA) (Anselin, 1995). The LISA are exploratory tools that can be employed on data before starting the formal modelling through regression analysis to identify patterns of spatial correlation among the variables of interest.

While many different local indicators can be defined (see Anselin, 1995), here we will present only two of them, namely the local version of Moran's I and the Getis–Ord statistic.

Local Moran's I represents a decomposition of global Moran's I (Anselin, 1995) and can be expressed as:

$$I_i = \frac{\sum_j w_{ij}(X_i - \bar{X})(X_j - \bar{X})}{n^{-1}\sum_j (X_j - \bar{X})^2} \tag{2.14}$$

where w_{ij} are the elements of a weight matrix defined in Section 2.1, X_i ($i = 1, 2, ..., n$) are the observed values of the variable X in location i and $\bar{X}$ is the sample mean of X. As is clear, Equation 2.14 represents the single addend of Equation 2.9 and basically constitutes the contribution of each individual unit to the global measure. Positive values of local Moran's I indicate a clustering of high values in the neighborhood of high values or, alternatively, a clustering of low values in the neighborhood of low values. These are generally indicated as HH (for high–high, called "hot spots") or LL (for low–low, called "cold spots"). Conversely, negative values of the local index indicate the presence

Preliminary definitions and concepts 27

of spatial outliers where there is a significant concentration of low values in the neighborhood of high values or, alternatively an extra concentration of high values in the neighborhood of low values. These points are indicated respectively as HL or LH points. The significance of each local indicator can be then calculated either assuming asymptotic normality (by using the formal expressions derived for the expected value and the variance) or, alternatively, using Monte Carlo simulated sampling distributions.

Example 2.4

A sample output of the R procedure for local Moran's I (procedure localmoran) is reported in Table 2.12. The outcome of the procedure is a vector of values which represent the single contribution to global Moran's I (elements I_i in Equation 2.14) with the associated significance level. Table 2.12 includes only a sample of rows from the output of local Moran's I related to the variable house price in the R dataset Boston already illustrated in Example 2.3 (R Command: {spdep}-localmoran). Significant local spatial correlations are highlighted in bold.

Table 2.12 Local Moran's I of house prices in Boston

Location	I_i	$E(I_i)$	$Var(I_i)$	z-score	Significance
1	$-8.913755e-02$	-0.001980198	0.037846512	-0.448013484	0.67
...	...	...	...	...	...
15	0.170	-0.002	0.025	1.090	0.137
16	-0.027	-0.002	0.022	0.621	0.267
17	-0.027	-0.002	0.025	-0.156	0.562
18	0.234	-0.002	0.026	1.450	0.073
19	0.098	-0.002	0.024	0.642	0.260
20	0.190	-0.002	0.023	1.265	0.102
21	0.367	-0.002	0.024	2.369	**0.009**
22	0.133	-0.002	0.026	0.831	0.203
23	0.312	-0.002	0.026	1.961	**0.025**
24	0.590	-0.002	0.026	2.218	**0.013**
25	0.287	-0.002	0.027	1.747	**0.040**
26	0.295		0.025	1.883	**0.030**
...	...	...	...	...	...

A second measure of local spatial correlation is based on the local concentration of values in the neighborhood of each individual. This second local index was introduced by Ord and Getis (1992) and it assumes the following expression:

$$G_i = \frac{\sum_j w_{ij} X_i}{\sum_j X_j} \tag{2.15}$$

where w_{ij} are the elements of the usual weight matrix. The index G_i is thus the share of the total amount of the variable X which is concentrated in the neighborhood of the i-th individual. In the same paper (Ord and Getis, 1992) the authors derived the expected value and variance of G_i so that formal testing procedures are available. A further paper (Getis and Ord, 1995) introduced a modified version of the statistics where the values are standardized to facilitate the interpretation. The modified index is expressed as:

$$G_i^* = \frac{\sum_{j=1}^{n} w_{ij} X_j - \bar{X} \sum_{j=1}^{n} w_{ij}}{S\sqrt{\frac{\sum_{j=1}^{n} w_{ij}^2 - \left(\sum_{j=1}^{n} w_{ij}\right)}{n-1}}} \qquad (2.16)$$

where S is the standard deviation of the variable X.

The modified G^* is a Gaussian z-score so that hypothesis testing can be run straightforwardly. Positive values of the statistics indicate clustering of high values (coded as HH), while negative values indicate clustering of low values (coded as LL).

A further tool is represented by the Moran scatterplot, a graphical exploratory tool introduced by Anselin (1995) that can help in identifying local

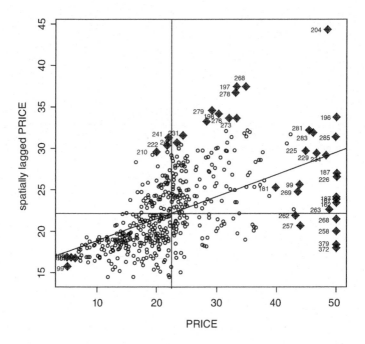

Figure 2.4 Moran scatterplot of house prices in Boston.

patterns of spatial correlation. It is obtained as a simple scatterplot which places the value of the variable (say X) on the horizontal axes and the corresponding spatially lagged value on the vertical axes (say WX).

Example 2.5

As an example of a Moran scatterplot, Figure 2.4 considers again the house prices in 506 locations reported in the dataset Boston already used in Examples 2.3 and 2.4. The global value of Moran's I is positive and highly significantly ($I = 20.1892$, p-value $< 2.2e - 16$) as it evident by the increasing regression line drawn on the graph. However, in addition to this global information, the graph also shows the presence of a large number of outliers (points observed in quadrants 2 and 4) which relate to prices that are much higher (or much lower) than the average of the neighboring locations (R Command: {spdep}-moran.plot).

2.4 Conclusions

This chapter aimed to introduce the fundamental concepts of spatial analysis which will constitute the backbone of the rest of this part of the book and, in some sense of the whole book. We have introduced, in particular, the notion of the W matrix which is the fundamental tool in the spatial regression models which we will discuss in Chapters 3 and 4. The notion of spatial autocorrelation among regression residuals has also been approached by introducing various measures and hypothesis test statistics. Finally, we have also introduced some exploratory tools much used in the literature before facing the problem of specifying a plausible behavioral regression model which contemplates the presence of spatially interacting individual agents.

3 Basic cross-sectional spatial linear models

3.1 Introduction

This chapter discusses different specifications of linear spatial econometrics. In particular, Section 3.2 is devoted to a detailed presentation of the basic models belonging to the SARAR (1,1) (spatial autoregressive with additional autoregressive error structure) class. Section 3.3 introduces the associated tests for residual spatial correlation. Section 3.4 approaches the problem of quantifying the marginal effects in a spatial econometric linear model. In Section 1.4 we discussed the possible presence of spatial imperfection that may occur when dealing with micro-data. This topic is taken up again in Section 3.5 discussing how these imperfections may affect spatial econometric regression analysis with a particular emphasis on locational error and missing spatial data. Finally, Section 3.6 is devoted to the particular case, that occurs frequently in spatial microeconometrics, when a distance is used as a predictor in a regression model and how data imperfections related to missing data or locational error may seriously undermine the estimation and hypothesis testing procedures.

3.2 Regression models with spatial autoregressive components

3.2.1 Pure spatial autoregression

The simplest of the models containing a spatial autoregressive component is the autopredictive model where the independent variable is regressed on its spatial lag without including any further predictors.

This specification is known in the literature as the "purely spatial autoregressive model" (SAR) which can be expressed by the following equation:

$$y = \rho W y + \varepsilon \qquad\qquad |\rho| < 1 \qquad\qquad (3.1)$$

where y is a vector and W a weight matrix (see Section 2.1) which is assumed to be non-stochastic and exogenously given. In addition, the residuals are assumed to be normally and independently distributed as $\varepsilon \approx i.i.d.N(0, \sigma_\varepsilon^2{}_n I_n)$ and ρ and

σ_ε^2 are parameters to be estimated. Kelejian and Prucha (1998) proved that, when the W matrix is row-standardized, the model requires the constraint that $|\rho| < 1$.

From Equation 3.1 we have that:

$$(I - \rho W) y = \varepsilon \tag{3.2}$$

Hence:

$$y = (I - \rho W)^{-1} \varepsilon \tag{3.3}$$

From Equations 3.1 and 3.3 we derive:

$$E(y) = 0 \tag{3.4}$$

and

$$Var(y) = \Omega = \sigma_\varepsilon^2 (I - \rho W)^{-1} (I - \rho W)^{-T} \tag{3.5}$$

whence the log-likelihood associated with the model can be straightforwardly derived as:

$$l(\rho, \sigma_\varepsilon^2) =$$
$$= const - \frac{n}{2} \ln(\sigma_\varepsilon^2) - \frac{1}{2} \ln \left| (I - \rho W)^{-1}(I - \rho W)^{-T} \right| - \frac{1}{2\sigma_\varepsilon^2} y^T$$
$$\left[(I - \rho W)^{-1}(I - \rho W)^{-T} \right]^{-1} y \tag{3.6}$$

This last expression cannot be maximized analytically due to its high degree of non-linearity in the parameters and can only be maximized numerically.

Example 3.1

As an example of the pure autoregressive model, let us consider the dataset of the 794 local units in the province of Macerata (Italy) in four industrial sectors, namely food, textiles, wood, and software and IT consulting active between 2011 and 2014. The dataset is provided by the Italian National Statistical Institute (ISTAT) and collected in the archive ASIA. The dataset contains the following variables: unit code, province code, communal code, province name, communal name, GPS x–y coordinates in 2014, sector of activity code, number of employees in 2011 and in 2014 and volume of business in 2011 and 2014. The map of the 794 industries is given in Figure 3.1.

For the definition of the W matrix we employ a threshold distance-based definition which leads to a density of 7.09% and an average number of neighbors of 53.7. We concentrated on the study of the autoregression in the variable "business volume per employee". We obtain the estimation results in Table 3.1 (R Command: {spatialreg}-spautolm). The table reports the usual t-test for the

32 *Spatial behavior of economic agents*

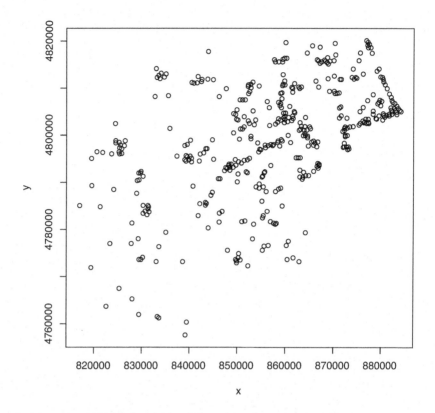

Figure 3.1 Map of 794 industries in Macerata province. Source: Italian National Statistical Institute.

Table 3.1 Output of the auto-regression for the variable business volume per employee of 794 industries in Macerata province

Parameter		Standard error	t-test	p-value
Intercept	848273	29831	28.436	< 2.2e – 16

ρ = –0.299; LR test value: 3.7598 (p-value = 0.0525); log-likelihood = –13226.49; AIC = 26459

intercept term and a likelihood ratio test for the spatial parameter ρ. The results show a significant negative spatial autocorrelation thus indicating a tendency for small firms to locate near to large firms.

3.2.2 *The spatial error model*

A second linear regression model considers the presence of regressors and the possibility of spatially correlated residuals. It is specified as follows:

$$y = X\beta + u \tag{3.7}$$

$$u = \rho W u + \varepsilon \qquad\qquad |\rho| < 1 \qquad\qquad (3.8)$$

where X is a matrix of regressors and W a weight matrix. Both X and W are assumed to be non-stochastic and exogenously given. In addition, the residuals are assumed to be conditionally normally distributed as: $\varepsilon | X \approx i.i.d. N(0, \sigma_\varepsilon^2 {}_n I_n)$ and β, ρ and σ_ε^2 are parameters to be estimated. The second equation considers a purely spatial regression model for the error terms. Again if the W matrix is row-standardized, the model require the constraint that $|\rho| < 1$.

This model is known as the "spatial error model" (SEM) (Anselin, 1988; Arbia, 2014a). If $\varepsilon | X \approx i.i.d. N(0, \sigma_\varepsilon^2 {}_n I_n)$, the model implies an error term which is both heteroscedastic and autocorrelated. In this case, if the value of the parameter ρ was known, a generalized least squares (GLS) procedure could be applied, which is not the case in practical situations. Furthermore the error is also correlated with the spatially lagged variable Wy, so, in principle, an instrumental variable procedure should be adopted as an alternative to OLS in order to accommodate endogeneity. In the literature two estimation methods were suggested: maximum likelihood (ML) and feasible GLS (FGLS).

From Equation 3.4 it is straighforward to derive:

$$u = y - X\beta \qquad\qquad (3.9)$$

The term u is normally distributed with a variance–covariance matrix Ω, so we can easily obtain the likelihood function as:

$$L(\rho, \sigma_\varepsilon^2, \beta) = const \, \sigma_\varepsilon^2 |\Omega|^{-\frac{1}{2}} \exp\left\{ -\frac{1}{2\sigma_\varepsilon^2} u^T \Omega^{-1} u \right\} \qquad\qquad (3.10)$$

But u is a purely autoregressive model, so the explicit expression for Ω is given by Equation 3.5. Substituting and taking the log, we have:

$$l(\rho, \sigma_\varepsilon^2, \beta) =$$

$$= const - \frac{n}{2}\ln(\sigma_\varepsilon^2) - \frac{1}{2}\ln\left|(I - \rho W)^{-1}(I - \rho W)^{-T}\right|$$
$$- \frac{1}{2}(y - Z\beta)^T \left[(I - \rho W)^{-1}(I - \rho W)^{-T}\right]^{-1}(y - Z\beta) \qquad (3.11)$$

This expression corresponds to deriving the likelihood function of the transformed regression model $y^* = X^*\beta + \varepsilon$, where $y^*(\rho) = y - \rho Wy$ and $X^*(\rho) = X - \rho WX$.

Lee (2004) proved that the ML estimators are consistent and asymptotically normal. The log likelihood equation (3.11) cannot be maximized analytically due to the high degree of non-linearity so that we have to resort to numerical maximization, a procedure that can be demanding for large datasets. The problem in the maximization is linked to the determinant $\ln|I - \rho W|$ because this has to be calculated for each of the values of ρ in a grid search. This was already a problem in the 1970s with only hundreds of data due to the limited computer

34   *Spatial behavior of economic agents*

capabilities at the time. This lead Ord to suggest the following decomposition ("Ord's decomposition" (Ord, 1975)):

$$\ln|I - \rho W| = \ln\left[\prod_{i=1}^{n}(1 - \rho\varphi_i)\right] \tag{3.12}$$

where ϕ_i represents the i-th eigenvector of the weight matrix W. This decomposition simplifies enormously the computation, but, if n is very large, it does not eliminate completely the accuracy problems because the spectral decomposition is also approximated in very large matrices as remarked by Kelejian and Prucha (1998). To overcome the computational problems Kelejian and Prucha (1998) suggested an alternative estimation strategy called feasible generalized least squares (FGLS).

Indeed, if the parameter ρ was known, then we could use the GLS estimators which will coincide with the OLS estimators on the transformed variables. So FGLS are obtained by deriving an estimator for ρ and then estimate the transformed model $y^* = X^*\beta + \varepsilon$, where $y^*(\rho) = y - \rho Wy$ and $X^*(\rho) = X - \rho WX$.

The FGLS estimators can be obtained as follows. First of all we derive a consistent estimate of β, say $\tilde{\beta}$. Secondly, we use $\tilde{\beta}$ in order to obtain an estimate of the residuals u, in Equation 3.9, say $\hat{u}$. Thirdly we use $\hat{u}$ to estimate ρ in Equation 3.8, using a generalized method of moments (GMM) procedure (see Hall, 2005). Let us call this estimate $\hat{\rho}$. Fourthly we use $\hat{\rho}$ to transform Equation 3.7 as follows.

$$(I - \hat{\rho}W)y = (I - \hat{\rho}W)Z\beta + \varepsilon \tag{3.13}$$

Finally, since the residuals of Equation 3.13 are normally and independently distributed, we estimate β by OLS as in a simple GLS procedure. (The interested reader is referred to Arbia, 2014a, for further details on the method.)

Example 3.2

As an example of an SEM, let us consider again the ASIA dataset of the 794 industries in Macerata used in Example 3.1. We start by estimating a non-spatial reduced production function in 2011 where the value added (proxied by the volume of business) is expressed as a linear function of the number of employees. The OLS estimation results are reported in Table 3.2. The F-test is highly

Table 3.2 Output of the SEM regression of the volume of business expressed as a linear function of the number of employees in 794 industries in Macerata province estimated with OLS

Parameter		Standard error	t-test	p-value
Intercept	−380887	77384	−4.922	1.05e − 06
Employees	170410	1427	119.392	< 2e − 16

F-test = 1.425e + 04 (p-value < 2.2e − 16); AIC = 24199.53; BIC = 24213.42

Basic cross-sectional spatial linear models 35

Table 3.3 Output of the SEM regression of the volume of business expressed as a linear function of the number of employees in 794 industries in Macerata province estimated with ML

Parameter		Standard error	t-test	p-value
Intercept	−381370	10880	−35.052	< 2.2e − 16
Employees	170435	1423	119.770	< 2.2e − 16

ρ = −0.197; LR-test = 5.2874 (p-value = 0.02148); Wald statistics = 2.182 (p-value = 0.13963); AIC = 24196; BIC = 24214

Table 3.4 Output of the SEM regression of the volume of business expressed as a linear function of the number of employees in 794 industries in Macerata province estimated with FGLS

Parameter		Standard error	t-test	p-value
Intercept	−380573.4	152681.4	−2.4926	0.01268
Employees	170409.8	1425.5	119.5479	< 2e − 16
ρ	0.49687	9507.7	5.226e − 05	0.999

significant and leads to the acceptance of the model. Furthermore both parameters are significant at the usual confidence level. The beta parameter shows the expected added value of an additional employee.

Let us now estimate the SEM using the maximum likelihood technique using again a threshold distance-based weight matrix as in Example 3.1 (R Command: {spdep}-errorsarlm). The results are reported in Table 3.3. The tests now show that the regression coefficient related to the number of employees is still significant and both coefficients are very close to those estimated with OLS, but the standard errors are very different. The parameter ρ is positive and highly significant if evaluated through the likelihood ratio test.

To finish with, let us estimate the same spatial error model using the FGLS estimators discussed in Section 3.4.3 (R Command: {spatialreg}-GMerrorsar). The results are reported in Table 3.4. The FGLS estimates substantially confirm the point estimation provided by OLS and ML estimation. However, standard errors are generally larger and the ρ coefficient is now not significant.

3.2.3 The spatial lag model

A third alternative is constituted by the "spatial lag model" (SLM) which can be expressed as:

$$y = \lambda Wy + X\beta + u. \quad |\lambda| < 1 \tag{3.14}$$

with $u|X \approx i.i.d.N(0, \sigma_u^2 {}_n I_n)$ (Anselin, 1988; Arbia, 2006).

In this case a problem of endogeneity emerges in that the spatially lagged value of y is correlated with the stochastic disturbance (see Arbia, 2014a). As a

36 *Spatial behavior of economic agents*

consequence, due to the presence of endogeneity, a GLS procedure cannot be employed and in the literature two alternatives estimators have been suggested: ML and the two-stage least squares (2SLS) (Greene, 2018).

To introduce the ML estimators, first of all notice that, re-writing Equation 3.14 as $(I - \lambda W)y = Z\beta + u$ we have:

$$y = (I - \lambda W)^{-1} Z\beta + (I - \lambda W)^{-1} u \tag{3.15}$$

So that:

$$E(y) = E\left[(I - \lambda W)^{-1} Z\beta + (I - \lambda W)^{-1} u \right] = (I - \lambda W)^{-1} Z\beta \tag{3.16}$$

and

$$E\left(yy^T\right) = \sigma_\varepsilon^2 (I - \lambda W)^{-1} (I - \lambda W)^{-T} = \sigma_\varepsilon^2 \Omega \tag{3.17}$$

Hence the likelihood of y can be expressed as:

$$L(\sigma^2, \lambda, \beta; y) =$$
$$const \left| \sigma_\varepsilon^2 \Omega \right|^{-\frac{1}{2}} \exp\left\{ -\frac{1}{2\sigma_\varepsilon^2} \left[y - (I - \lambda W)^{-1} Z\beta \right]^T \Omega^{-1} \left[y - (I - \lambda W)^{-1} Z\beta \right] \right\} \tag{3.18}$$

and, therefore, the log likelihood as:

$$l(\sigma^2, \lambda, \beta; y) =$$
$$const - \frac{1}{2} \ln \left| \sigma_\varepsilon^2 \Omega \right| - \frac{1}{2\sigma_\varepsilon^2} \left[y - (I - \lambda W)^{-1} Z\beta \right]^T \Omega^{-1} \left[y - (I - \lambda W)^{-1} Z\beta \right] \tag{3.19}$$

Using the expression reported in Equation 3.5, the determinant of the matrix $\sigma_\varepsilon^2 \Omega$ can be written as:

$$\left| \sigma_\varepsilon^2 \Omega \right| = \left| \sigma_\varepsilon^2 (I - \lambda W)^{-1} (I - \lambda W)^{-T} \right| = \sigma_\varepsilon^{2n} \left| (I - \lambda W)^{-1} (I - \lambda W)^{-T} \right| =$$
$$\left| \sigma_\varepsilon^2 \Omega \right| = \sigma_\varepsilon^{2n} \left| (I - \lambda W) \right|^{-2} \tag{3.20}$$

Using this expression in Equation 3.19 we obtain:

$$l(\sigma^2, \lambda, \beta; y) =$$
$$const - \frac{1}{2} \ln \left(\sigma_\varepsilon^{2n} \left| I - \lambda W \right|^{-2} \right) - \frac{1}{2\sigma_\varepsilon^2} \left[y - (I - \lambda W)^{-1} Z\beta \right]^T \tag{3.21}$$
$$\left[(I - \lambda W)^{-1} (I - \lambda W)^{-T} \right]^{-1} \left[y - (I - \lambda W)^{-1} Z\beta \right] =$$

which after some tedious, but straighforward, algebra (Arbia, 2014) leads to:

$$l(\sigma^2, \lambda, \beta; y) =$$
$$const - \frac{n}{2} \ln \sigma_\varepsilon^2 + \ln \left| I - \lambda W \right| - \frac{1}{2\sigma_\varepsilon^2} \left[(I - \lambda W)y - Z\beta \right]^T \left[(I - \lambda W)y - Z\beta \right] \tag{3.22}$$

which can be maximized numerically.

To overcome the endogeneity problem, as an alternative, we can also use a 2SLS. One problem with this strategy is the identification of proper instruments which are relevant and exogenous: that is, correlated with Wy (relevance) and uncorrelated with the error term (exogeneity). In this respect, in order to eliminate the endogeneity of Wy, Kelejian and Prucha (1999) suggested the optimal instruments matrix given by the n-by-$3k$ matrix $_nH_{3k} = \left[X, WX, W^2 X \right]$.

Let us now write Equation 3.14 as:

$$y = M\theta + u \qquad (3.23)$$

with M the matrix of regressors which includes the lagged value of y given by: $_nM_{k+1} = [Wy, X]$ and the vector of unknown parameters given by $_n\theta_1 = [\lambda, \beta_k]$.

In the first of the two-stage procedure, the independent variables M are regressed against the instruments H through the instrumental regression:

$$M = H\gamma + \eta \qquad (3.24)$$

with η an error term. The parameters in Equation 3.24 can be estimated by OLS, thus giving:

$$\hat{\gamma} = (H^T H)^{-1} H^T M \qquad (3.25)$$

through which we derive the estimated value of M, say $\hat{M}$, which is given by:

$$\hat{M} = H\hat{\gamma} = H(H^T H)^{-1} H^T M \qquad (3.26)$$

In the second stage of the two-stage procedure, we estimate the relationship between y and the instrumented regressors using OLS, that is:

$$y = \hat{M}\theta + u \qquad (3.27)$$

This finally leads to the two-stage estimators of the vector θ given by:

$$\hat{\theta}_{2SLS} = \left(\hat{M}^T \hat{M} \right)^{-1} \hat{M}^T y \qquad (3.28)$$

Example 3.3: House price determinants in Boston

Let us consider an example of the spatial lag model based on the dataset Boston already presented in Example 2.3.

Let us start by calculating a simple regression model estimated by OLS. We wish to test if the price of the house can be expressed as a function of the variables RM (number of rooms), NOX (nitric oxides concentration in parts per 10 million), RAD (Index of Accessibility to Radial Highways) and DIS (distance from five Boston employment centers). The results of a simple OLS estimation are reported in Table 3.5 together with the test statistics. The F-test is highly significant and leads to the acceptance of the model. Furthermore, all variables

38 Spatial behavior of economic agents

are also significant at the usual confidence level and of the expected sign. We employed three W matrices based on (i) a distance-based weight matrix considering as neighbors two points if their distance was less than 3.99 units, (ii) 4 nearest neighbors and (iii) inverse distance with a threshold of 3.99 units.

Table 3.6 summarizes the calculation of Moran's I for the hypothesis of spatial correlation of the residuals according to the various W matrix specifications. The test shows that there is evidence of a positive and highly significant spatial correlation in the regression residuals irrespective of the W matrix definition adopted. This result shows the robustness of the conclusions and motivates further analysis to try and remove the residual spatial correlation and improve the efficiency of the estimates. In our case, we can hypothesize that house prices change smoothly through space displaying positive spatial correlation. Hence an SLM seems an appropriate specification, expressing the price of a house as a function of the price observed for the neighboring houses.

First of all, let us estimate the model using the ML technique and the threshold distance W matrix definition (R Command: {spdep}-lagsarlm). We obtain the results in Table 3.7. The z-tests show that, again, as in the OLS case, all variables are highly significant, with a sign which is in accordance with the OLS estimation and with the theoretical expectations. In addition, both the likelihood ratio test and the Wald test statistics show that the parameter λ of the spatial lag of the price is highly significant. Similar results are obtained by employing different weight matrix definitions.

Table 3.5 Output of the SLM regression of house prices expressed as a linear function of other variables in Boston estimated with OLS

Parameter	Estimated value	Standard error	t-test	p-value
Intercept	−12.018	4.093	−2.936	0.003
RM	8.030	0.406	19.784	< 2e − 16
NOX	−20.677	4.111	−5.029	6.87e − 07
DIS	−0.793	0.203	−3.509	0.0005
RAD	−0.183	0.039	−4.655	4.15e − 06

F-test = 161.8 (p-value = 2.2e − 16); AIC = 3272.801; BIC = 3298.16

Table 3.6 Moran's I of residual spatial correlation

W matrix definition	Observed value	Expected value	Variance	z-test	p-value
Distance threshold	0.074	−0.005	0.0001	6.239	2.199e − 10
K = 4 nearest neighbors	0.571	−0.008	0.0008	20.055	2.2e − 16
Inverse distance with threshold	0.181	−0.006	0.0002	12.967	2.2e − 16

Basic cross-sectional spatial linear models **39**

Table 3.7 Output of the SLM regression of house prices expressed as a linear function of other variables in Boston estimated with ML

Parameter	Estimated value	Standard error	z-test	p-value
Intercept	−20.325	4.272	−4.757	1.93e − 06
RM	7.315	0.398	18.335	< 2.2e − 16
NOX	−14.671	4.141	−3.542	0.0004
DIS	−0.733	0.193	−3.788	0.0001
RAD	−0.153	00.038	4.009	6.099e − 05

$\lambda = 0.417$; LR-test = 35.08 (p-value = 3.16e − 09); Wald statistics = 37.75 (p-value = 8.0426e −10); AIC = 3239.7; BIC =3269.306

Table 3.8 Output of the SLM regression of house prices expressed as a linear function of other variables in Boston estimated with 2SLS

Parameter	Estimated value	Standard error	t-test	p-value
λ	0.481	0.080	5.970	2.37e − 09
Intercept	−21.599	4.252	−5.079	3.783e − 07
RM	7.205	0.414	17.396	< 2.2e − 16
NOX	−13.749	4.122	−3.335	0.0008
DIS	−0.736	0.194	−3.786	0.0001
RAD	−0.148	0.038	−3.863	0.0001

Let us also estimate, for the sake of comparison, the same SLM with the same distance threshold W matrix employing the 2SLS technique leading to Table 3.8 (R Command: {spdep}-stsls). The 2SLS procedure leads to results that are comparable with the ML estimation in terms of the sign, the magnitude and the significance of each variable. The significance of the parameter λ is also confirmed and with a value that is very similar to the one estimated by ML. Notice, also, that the ML method requires the hypothesis of normality, while the 2SLS does not require any distributional hypothesis.

3.2.4 The spatial Durbin model

A special case of the spatial error model is the "spatial Durbin model" (SDM) by analogy with the time series model introduced by Durbin. In its expression we find in the list of predictors the lagged values of both the dependent and some or all the independent variables. It can be written as:

$$y = \lambda Wy + \gamma WX + X\beta + u. \quad |\lambda| < 1 \qquad (3.29)$$

This model is very much used in spatial econometrics applications. Since the variables X are assumed to be non-stochastic, so are their spatially lagged values and, as a consequence, no additional problems emerge from the estimation point of view with respect to the SLM presented in the previous section. However, the model can be theoretically motivated in different ways.

For a first motivation, consider again the SEM model presented in Section 3.2.2.

40 *Spatial behavior of economic agents*

$$y = X\beta + u \tag{3.7}$$

$$u = \rho W u + \varepsilon \qquad\qquad |\rho| < 1 \tag{3.8}$$

The second equation can be written as $\varepsilon = (I - \rho W)$, so that pre-multiplying the first equation by the term $(I - \rho W)$, we have:

$$(I - \rho W) y = (I - \rho W) X\beta + (I - \rho W)\ u \tag{3.30}$$

Which can be re-written as:

$$y = \rho W y + X\beta - \rho W X\beta + \varepsilon \tag{3.31}$$

which, with the additional constraint $\gamma = -\rho\beta$, is again the SDM presented in Equation 3.29. This form is defined as the constrained structural form of the SDM (LeSage and Pace, 2009).

Thus, the more complex SDM model can be reduced to the simpler SEM model, if some constraints on the coefficients of SDM are satisfied. (For more details about this issue, which is known as the spatial common factor problem, see Anselin, 1988.)

A second motivation is founded on the notion of omitted variables (Greene, 2018). Omitted variable biases may easily arise in spatial modeling because unobservable factors such as location amenities, highway accessibility, or neighborhood prestige (for example) may exert an influence on the dependent variable. In empirical cases, it is extremely unlikely that explanatory variables are able to capture these types of latent influences, so that the presence of omitted variables can be considered as the rule rather than the exception in spatial models. In this respect LeSage and Pace (2009) suggest that the use of an SDM may mitigate the bias connected with this problem because some of the unexplained effects due to omitted variables can be captured by the term WX.

A third motivation is the likely presence of unobserved heterogeneity in a spatial model. For this reason, we can specify a spatial model that contains an individual effect modeled as a separate intercept for each individual spatial unit. LeSage and Pace (2009) show that an SDM specification can help in mitigating the effects due to unobserved heterogeneity.

Beyond the empirical evidences, there are some theoretical motivations that support the use of the SDM specification (see e.g. Elhorst, 2010; 2014). First of all, the SDM produces unbiased estimates even if the true data generating process is an SLM or an SEM whereas if the SDM is the true data generating process, alternative specifications will suffer for omitted variable bias (see e.g. LeSage and Pace 2009; Elhorst 2014).

Example 3.4: House price determinants in Boston (continued)

In Example 3.3 we estimated an SLM seeking to explain the spatial variability of house prices among 506 census tracts in Boston. Let us repeat the exercise with the SDM by adding a spatial lag for the four independent variables.

Basic cross-sectional spatial linear models 41

Table 3.9 Output of the SDM regression of house prices expressed as a linear function of other variables in Boston estimated with ML

Parameter	Estimated value	Standard error	t-test	p-value
Intercept	−51.999	12.490	−4.163	3.139e − 05
RM	7.024	0.423	15.595	< 2.2e − 16
NOX	−18.620	4.536	−4.104	4.05e − 5
DIS	−1.122	0.725	−1.546	0.122
RAD	−0.202	0.049	−4.044	5.257e − 05
Lag.RM	4.295	1.904	2.2009	0.027
Lag.NOX	20.489	10.748	1.906	0.037
Lag-DIS	0.903	0.757	1.193	0.233
Lag.RAD	−0.021	0.108	−0.194	0.846

λ = 0.267; LR-test = 3.733 (p-value = 0.05); AIC = 3238.478; BIC =3284.97

The results of model estimation using the ML estimation technique are displayed in Table 3.9 (R Command: {spdep}-lagsarlm). The results are comparable to those of the models estimated in Example 3.3 in terms of the significance and the sign of the variables, although the introduction of the new variables lead the variable DIS to become non-significant. In addition, the lagged variable of variable RM and NOX are also significant and contribute to the explicative power of the model. The parameter λ is also positive and significantly different from zero.

3.2.5 *The general spatial autoregressive model with spatial autoregressive error structure*

The SEM and SLM can be subsumed into a single model which contemplates both specifications. This is commonly referred to in the literature as the SARAR model (Kelejian and Prucha, 1998), although it was also called the "general spatial model" by Anselin (1988) and the "spatial autocorrelated" (SAC) model by LeSage and Pace (2009).

The SARAR model can be written as follows:

$$y = X\beta + \lambda Wy + u. \quad |\lambda| < 1 \tag{3.32}$$

$$u = \rho Wu + \varepsilon. \quad |\rho| < 1 \tag{3.33}$$

with $\varepsilon | X \approx i.i.d. N(0, \sigma_{\varepsilon}^2 {}_n I_n)$.

For many years in the literature it was believed that such a complete model was not identifiable. However, Kelejian and Prucha (1998) proved that this only happens when $\beta = 0$ a case that we are not usually interested in spatial econometrics (see Arbia, 2014a, for a formal proof).

The model described in Equations 3.32 and 3.33 presents two major estimation problems. First of all, for SLM components it suffers from a problem of endogeneity associated with the presence of the variable *Wy*. Secondly, for the spatial correlation in the residuals, we cannot employ a GLS strategy unless the

42 *Spatial behavior of economic agents*

parameter ρ is known. A first obvious solution to estimate the two equations is to resort to an ML solution.

From Equation 3.32 we have:

$$E(y) = (I - \lambda W)^{-1} X\beta \tag{3.34}$$

and

$$E(yy^T) = \sigma_\varepsilon^2 (I - \lambda W)^{-1} (I - \rho W)^{-1} (I - \lambda W) (I - \rho W) = \sigma_\varepsilon^2 \Omega \tag{3.35}$$

hence, maintaining the hypothesis of normality on the disturbances, we have:

$$y \approx N \left[(I - \lambda W)^{-1} X\beta; \sigma_\varepsilon^2 \Omega \right] \tag{3.36}$$

From this result, the likelihood function is easily derived:

$$L(\sigma_\varepsilon^2, \rho, \lambda, \beta; y) =$$
$$c(\sigma_\varepsilon^2)^{-n/2} |I - \lambda W||I - \rho W| exp \left\{ -\frac{1}{2\sigma_\varepsilon^2} \left[y - (I - \rho W)^{-1} X\beta \right]^T \Omega \left[y - (I - \rho W)^{-1} X\beta \right] \right\} \tag{3.37}$$

so that the associated log likelihood is thus expressed as:

$$l(\sigma_\varepsilon^2, \rho, \lambda, \beta; y) =$$
$$= c - \frac{n}{2} \ln(\sigma_\varepsilon^2) + \ln|I - \lambda W| + \ln|I - \rho W|$$
$$- \frac{1}{2\sigma_\varepsilon^2} \left[y - (I - \rho W)^{-1} X\beta \right]^T \Omega \left[y - (I - \rho W)^{-1} X\beta \right]$$

which, using Equation 3.35, explicit expression for Ω and after some algebra becomes:

$$l(\sigma_\varepsilon^2, \rho, \lambda, \beta; y) = c - \frac{n}{2} \ln(\sigma_\varepsilon^2) + \ln|I - \lambda W| + \ln|I - \rho W|$$
$$- \frac{1}{2\sigma_\varepsilon^2} \left[(I - \rho W) (y - X\beta - \lambda Wy) \right]^T \left[(I - \rho W) (y - X\beta - \lambda Wy) \right] \tag{3.38}$$

Equation 3.38 can be maximized numerically to derive the ML estimators of the parameters, but the maximization procedures can become computationally demanding with large datasets. Furthermore, there is no formal proof of the large sample properties of the estimators. However, we can consider an alternative estimator that combines together the FGLS approach considered for an SEM with the 2SLS employed for an SLM. This will lead to a spatial version of 2SLS called the "generalized spatial two-stage least squares" (GS2SLS) procedure introduced by Kelejian and Prucha (1998) which accounts for both the problem of endogeneity of Wy and the problem of spatial correlation among the stochastic disturbances. The method is essentially an extension of the 2SLS methodology

Basic cross-sectional spatial linear models 43

already illustrated for the SLM, but combined with the GMM estimator presented for the SEM.

To implement the procedure we first of all obtain a consistent estimate for the parameters β and λ using the 2SLS procedure to account for the problem of endogeneity. Let us indicate these initial estimates with the symbols $\tilde{\beta}$ and $\tilde{\lambda}$. These initial estimates are then used to obtain an estimate of u in Equation 3.33, say $\hat{u}$ which in turn can be used to estimate ρ in Equation 3.34 with the generalized method of moments procedure and we call it $\hat{\rho}$. We now can transform our model as follows:

$$\left(I - \hat{\rho}W\right)y = \left(I - \hat{\rho}W\right)X\beta + \varepsilon \tag{3.39}$$

The final estimation of the parameters of the transformed model are obtained using 2SLS using as instruments the following three transformed variables $\left(I - \hat{\rho}W\right)X$; $W\left(I - \hat{\rho}W\right)X$ and $W^2\left(I - \hat{\rho}W\right)X$. Kelejian and Prucha (1998) showed that, under the model's assumptions, the GS2SLS estimators thus derived are consistent with an explicit expression for the asymptotic variances that can be used in the hypothesis testing procedures.

However, the GS2SLS estimators are not asymptotically fully efficient. Lee (2003) suggested an asymptotically fully efficient alternative estimator known in the literature as best feasible GS2SLS (BFGS2SLS) which achieves the theoretical lower bound for the variance in large samples. The computation of the instruments in the 2SLS part of the procedure, however, can be numerically challenging in very large samples. For this reason Lee (2003) himself derives a numerical algorithm computationally simpler which does not differ substantially from the GS2SLS in terms of efficiency.

Example 3.5: House price determinants in Boston (continued)

Let us consider once again the use of the Boston data and try to improve the explicative power of the regression model by considering a full SARAR model. If we employ the ML estimation technique and the usual weight matrix based on a distance threshold we obtain the estimates in Table 3.10 (R Command: {spdep}-sacsarlm). The parameter ρ related to the residual spatial autocorrelation,

Table 3.10 Output of the SARAR regression of house prices expressed as a linear function of other variables in Boston estimated with ML

Parameter	Estimated value	Standard error	t-test	p-value
Intercept	−19.835	5.523	−4.385	1.15e − 05
RM	7.312	0.405	18.016	< 2.2e − 16
NOX	−15.037	4.281	−3.512	0.0004
DIS	−0.739	0.197	−3.739	0.0001
RAD	−0.154	0.039	−3.970	7.174e − 05

λ =0.037 (p-value = 0.835); ρ = 0.407 (p-value = 3.664e − 06); AIC = 3241.7; BIC = 3275.5

44　*Spatial behavior of economic agents*

Table 3.11 Output of the SARAR regression of the volume of house prices expressed as a linear function of other variables in Boston estimated with GS2SLS

Parameter	Estimated value	Standard error	t-test	p-value
Intercept	−22.199	4.151	−5.347	8.942e − 08
RM	7.223	0.413	17.471	< 2.2e − 16
NOX	−13.138	4.063	−3.233	0.001
DIS	−0.715	0.186	−3.847	0.0001
RAD	−0.147	0.037	−3.935	9.668e − 05

λ =0.08 (p-value = 0.835); ρ = 0.483 (p-value = 8.942e − 08)

is positive and significantly different from zero, while the parameter λ is also positive, but not significantly different from zero. This would lead to the rejection of the SARAR model in favor of the SEM model where only the ρ parameter is significant. If we estimate the same model using the GS2SLS procedure we obtain Table 3.11 (R Command: {spatialreg}-gstsls). These results basically confirm the findings obtained with ML estimation in terms of the sign, the magnitude and the significance of the coefficients.

3.3　Test of residual spatial autocorrelation with explicit alternative hypotheses

In Chapter 2 we introduced a testing procedure for the hypothesis of spatial uncorrelation among OLS residuals based on Moran's I (Moran, 1950). In the previous sections of the present chapter we introduced some alternative formulations to the classical linear regression model based on various ways of taking into account the spatial dependence: the spatial error, the spatial lag, the spatial Durbin and the SARAR models. All of these models, in principle, can be considered as alternatives to the case of uncorrelation in a testing the null of spatial uncorrelation thus overcoming a pitfall of Moran's I which, in contrast, does not have any explicit alternative hypothesis.

In particular the literature has concentrated on alternative hypotheses that take the form of either a spatial lag or a spatial error using a maximum likelihood approach to build up a Lagrange multiplier test (Greene, 2018). If the alternative hypothesis is specified as a SEM the log likelihood function assumes the expression derived in Equation 3.23. As a consequence, in this case, Equation 3.11 the Lagrange multiplier test can be expressed as:

$$LM_{SEM} = \frac{n^2}{tr\left(W^T W + WW\right)} \left[\frac{\hat{\varepsilon}^T W \hat{\varepsilon}}{\hat{\varepsilon}^T \hat{\varepsilon}}\right]^2 \tag{3.40}$$

which is simply the square of Moran's I, as demonstrated by Burridge (1980). So, using Moran's I or the LM test reported in Equation 3.40 is inferentially equivalent.

Basic cross-sectional spatial linear models   45

In contrast, if the alternative hypothesis is specified in the form of an SLM, the log likelihood is specified in Equation 3.22 and the Lagrange multiplier becomes:

$$LM_{LAG} = \frac{n^2}{Q} \left[\frac{\hat{\varepsilon}^T Wy}{\hat{\varepsilon}^T \hat{\varepsilon}} \right]^2 \tag{3.41}$$

with $Q = \left(WX\hat{\beta} \right)^T (I - M_x) \frac{WX\hat{\beta}}{\hat{\sigma}_\varepsilon^2} + T$, $M_x = X \left(X^T X \right) X^T$, $T = tr \left(W^T W + WW \right)$ and $\hat{\beta}$ and $\hat{\sigma}_\varepsilon^2$ the maximum likelihood estimators of the corresponding parameters. Being derived as Lagrange multiplier tests, both LM_{SEM} and LM_{LAG} are asymptotically distributed, under the null, as a χ^2 with 1 degree of freedom. However, the two test statistics are not independent on one another. As a consequence, we could only test the alternative hypothesis that the alternative model is a SEM assuming that there is not a spatial lag component or vice versa. To tackle this drawback, Anselin et al. (1996) proposed a robust version of both tests which can be expressed as follows:

$$RLM_{SEM} = \frac{1}{T(1-TQ)} \left[\frac{n\hat{\varepsilon}^T W\hat{\varepsilon}}{\hat{\varepsilon}^T \hat{\varepsilon}} - TQ^{-1} \frac{n\hat{\varepsilon}^T Wy}{\hat{\varepsilon}^T \hat{\varepsilon}} \right]^2 \tag{3.42}$$

for the alternative hypothesis of an SEM with the symbols already introduced and, respectively, using an SLM as an alternative:

$$RLM_{LAG} = \frac{1}{Q-T} \left[\frac{n\hat{\varepsilon}^T W\hat{\varepsilon}}{\hat{\varepsilon}^T \hat{\varepsilon}} - \frac{n\hat{\varepsilon}^T Wy}{\hat{\varepsilon}^T \hat{\varepsilon}} \right]^2 \tag{3.43}$$

Example 3.6: House price determinants in Boston (continued)

Let us consider the test of hypothesis on the residuals of the OLS regression estimated in Example 3.3 by using the explicitly alternative hypothesis of an SEM and an SLM. If we use the SEM as an alternative we obtain the same inferential conclusions of Moran's I, as demonstrated by Burridge (1980). All other tests are reported in Table 3.12 (R Command: {spdep}-lm.LMtests). The table shows that both the SLM and the SEM are significant alternatives to the hypothesis of no

Table 3.12 Robust residual correlation tests for the SLM of house price determinants in Boston

Test statistic	Test value	p-value
LM_{ERR}	30.474	3.383e – 08
LM_{LAG}	53.098	3.173e – 13
RLM_{ERR}	1.483	0.223
RLM_{LAG}	24.106	9.118e – 07

46 *Spatial behavior of economic agents*

spatial correlation in the residuals of the OLS regression. However, the robust version of the Lagrange multiplier tests leads us to choose a spatial lag model as an alternative.

3.4 Marginal impacts

In a standard linear regression model the regression parameters can be straightforwardly interpreted as the partial derivative of the dependent variable y with respect to the independent variables, that is the variation induced on variable y by a unitary increase in the single independent variable X_i. Due to the independence assumed between the observed units this variation is constant for all observations and there is no spillover: a change in variable X in one location has only an effect on variable y in the same location and not on the other locations. However, this interpretation is not correct in a spatial regression where the change in variable X in one location also has an effect on variable y in the neighboring locations.

Consider, for instance, the model presented in Example 3.3 which aimed to explain the price of a house as a function of four variables: NOX concentration, number of rooms, accessibility of radial highways and average distance from five Boston employment centers. The model estimates in Example 3.3 forecasts that, for instance, the lower the level of NOX the higher the house value. However, in an SLM, an increase in the price of a house would also produce a decrease of the price of houses located in the neighboring locations due to the transmission mechanism connatural with the SLM.

The problem of correctly interpreting the marginal effects in a spatial regression model has been treated in the literature by Kelejian et al. (2006), LeSage and Pace (2009) and Arbia et al. (2019) amongst others. The formal solution to the problem consists in evaluating all the marginal effects as the matrix of the partial derivatives in each specific model. If we consider the spatial error model the partial derivative of y with respect to X in Equation 3.7 is still represented by the vector β and no spillover effect is present. In contrast, in the SLM we have a different result. First of all, notice that Equation 3.12 can also be written in reduced form as:

$$y = (I - \lambda W)^{-1} X\beta + (I - \lambda W)^{-1} u \tag{3.44}$$

so that the vector of the expected values is equal to:

$$E(y) = (I - \lambda W)^{-1} X\beta \tag{3.45}$$

and the matrix of the partial derivatives can be expressed as:

$$S = \frac{\partial}{\partial X} E(y) = (I - \lambda W)^{-1} \beta \tag{3.46}$$

where each entry is defined as $s_{ij} = \dfrac{\partial E(y_i)}{\partial X_j}$ and represents the impact of a unitary change of the variable X observed in location j on the variable y observed in location i. This impact is different from β and it is emphasized by a positive value of λ and reduced by a negative value of λ.

In order to facilitate the interpretation of a potentially very large n-by-n matrix, LeSage and Pace (2009) suggested three summary measures, namely:

i The "average direct impact" (ADI) which expresses the impact produced on average by a change in X_i on y_i for each observation. This can be simply expressed as the average of the diagonal elements of the matrix S, that is:

$$ADI = n^{-1} tr(S) \tag{3.47}$$

ii The "average total impact" (ATI) which expresses the impact produced on average by each unit. This can be expressed as the average of all the elements of matrix S, that is:

$$ATI = n^{-1} i^T S i \tag{3.48}$$

with i the unitary vector.

iii The "average indirect impact" (AII) obtained as the difference between the two preceding measures or the average of the off-diagonal elements of S:

$$AII = ATI - ADI \tag{3.49}$$

LeSage and Pace (2009) also suggested consideration of two vector measures. The first is represented by the "average total impact to" an observation (ATIT), which is the average impact produced on one single observation by all other observations, that is the row average of the S matrix:

$$ATIT = n^{-1} S i \tag{3.50}$$

The second is the "average total impact from" an observation (ATIF) which represents the average impact produced by one single observation on all other observations, that is the columns average of the S matrix:

$$ATIT = n^{-1} i^T S \tag{3.51}$$

Measures of relative impact for a general SARAR model can be similarly obtained by taking the derivatives of the appropriate reduced form expressions.

For each of the preceding measures it is possible to run significance tests based either on Monte Carlo or asymptotic distributions (Arbia et al., 2019).

Example 3.7: House price determinants in Boston (continued)

If we take again the example of house prices considered in Example 3.3, we obtain the following results in Table 3.13 (R Command: {spatialreg}-impacts). In the OLS framework the interpretation is straightforward. For instance, if with some air-quality policy we are able to achieve a reduction of 1 part per million

48 *Spatial behavior of economic agents*

Table 3.13 Summary measures of marginal impacts for the SLM of house price determinants in Boston

	OLS	SLM	ADI	AII	ATI
λ		0.417			
Intercept	-12.018	-20.325			
RM	8.030	7.315	7.383	5.155	12.539
NOX	-20.677	-14.671	-14.807	-10.339	-25.147
DIS	-0.793	-0.733	-0.739	-0.516	-1.255
RAD	-0.183	-0.153	-0.154	-0.107	-0.262

of NOX we will observe an increase in house values of \$20,677 attributable to the improved environmental quality. Similar interpretations are possible for the other variables. However, within the spatial lag framework it would be wrong to interpret the regression slope in the same way. Indeed, the "direct" effect of decreasing NOX by 1 ppm is not an increase of price of \$20,677, but rather a larger increase of \$25,147 (ATI) because of the additional \$10,339 due to the indirect effect (AII). Indeed, improving the air quality in one location will increase house prices in that location, but also in the neighboring locations which in turn (due to the spatial lag mechanism), will produce a further increase in house prices. Thus, the impact is greater if we consider an SLM in place of the traditional a-spatial model due to the positive spatial correlation estimated with the parameter λ. Similar considerations can be made for the other variables. For instance, improving the house accessibility by 1 unit (thus reducing variable DIS) would increase the house value by \$262 and not only by \$154 due to the presence of the positively correlated spatial lag variable. A negative spatial lag correlation would conversely reduce the total impact with respect to the direct impact.

3.5 Effects of spatial imperfections of micro-data

3.5.1 Introduction

We have seen in Chapter 2 that the use of the pairwise inter-point distances to build up W matrices is a common practice when dealing with the individual point data that constitute the basis of spatial microeconometric models. However, this choice can introduce measurement errors in a regression context when data are affected by the different inaccuracies that we have discussed in Section 1.4. In this section, in particular, we will discuss the cases when data are incomplete (missing or sample data points) or individuals' location is not known with certainty. If we measure inaccurately the inter-point distances, we will introduce a measurement error in the W matrix and, in this way, in all the spatially lagged variables that are considered in the model, both dependent and independent. As is known (Greene, 2018), in the presence of a measurement error in the independent variables, the parameters' estimators are less efficient and inconsistent with an additional persistent bias towards zero (attenuation effect). This effect is well known in general

Basic cross-sectional spatial linear models 49

econometrics (Greene, 2018) and in time-series analysis (Grether and Maddala, 1973; Dagenais, 1994), but it has only recently received attention in a spatial context (Le Gallo and Fingleton, 2012). In this section we will present some useful results in this area to clarify how uncertainty about the spatial data may affect the accuracy of the result of spatial regressions. We will discuss in turn the effects of measurement and locational error on SEMs and SLMs.

3.5.2 Measurement error in spatial error models

We start by considering the effects of measurement errors induced by incomplete data and uncertain location on the spatial error model. In this case, it is easy to show that data uncertainty does not produce any bias, but only an underestimation of the error variance. In fact, in this case the error component of the model (see Equation 2.11) can be written as $Wu = \bar{W}u + v$ with $\bar{W}$ the error-contaminated weight matrix and v the measurement error. In the case of incomplete data (e.g. due to missing observations), the $\bar{W}$ matrix is a non-stochastic term which depends only on the spatial pattern of the missing data and, as a consequence:

$$E(v) = E\left(Wu - \bar{W}u\right) = \left(W - \bar{W}\right)E(u) = 0 \tag{3.52}$$

but

$$Var\left(v\right) = Var\left(Wu - \bar{W}u\right) = \left(W - \bar{W}\right)^2 Var\left(u\right) \tag{3.53}$$

In contrast, in the case of locational error, $\bar{W}$ becomes a random variable which depends on the error mechanism, so that we have again no effect on the expected value of v, in that:

$$E(v) = E\left(Wu - \bar{W}u\right) = E\left(W - \bar{W}\right)E(u) = 0 \tag{3.54}$$

since the contamination process can be assumed independent of u. However, for the same reason we can express the variance of v as:

$$Var(v) = Var\left(Wu - \bar{W}u\right) = Var\left[\left(W - \bar{W}\right)u\right] = Var\left(\bar{W}u\right) = Var\left[\bar{W}\left(I - \rho W\right)^{-1}e\right] =$$
$$= \left(I - \rho W\right)^{-2} Var\left(\bar{W}e\right) \tag{3.55}$$

because, from Equation 2.11, $u = \left(I - \rho W\right)^{-1}e$, so that, eventually, we have that the variance of the measurement error is equal to:

$$Var(v) = \left(I - \rho W\right)^{-2}\left[Var\left(\bar{W}\right)E(e)^2 + Var(e)E(\bar{W})^2 + Var\left(\bar{W}\right)Var(e)\right] =$$
$$= \left(I - \rho W\right)^{-2} Var\left(e\right)\left[E(\bar{W})^2 + Var(\bar{W})\right] = \left(I - \rho W\right)^{-2} Var\left(e\right)\left[E(\bar{W})\right]^2 \tag{3.56}$$

where the inflation factor on the error variance is now expressed by the term $\left(I - \rho W\right)^{-2}\left[E(\bar{W})\right]^2$.

3.5.3 Measurement error in spatial lag models

The effects of data uncertainty on a spatial lag model are more severe than in the case of a spatial error model but also more interesting. Let us start by considering the case where data are either a random sample from a larger population or are missing completely at random (*Roderick and Rubin, 2007*). Let us also consider, for the sake of illustrating the essential concepts, the case of a purely spatial autoregressive model (Equation 3.1) which, expressed in algebraic terms, can be written as:

$$y_i = \lambda \sum_{j=1}^{n} w_{ij} y_j + \varepsilon_i \tag{3.57}$$

with w_{ij} as the generic element of true n-by-n weight matrix. Let us now define $\overline{w}_{ij}$ as the generic element of the observed $(n - m)$-by-$(n - m)$ weight matrix, where m observations are missing. The spatially lagged variable in Equation 3.1 will be then affected by a measurement error that can be expressed by:

$$u_i = \sum_{j=1}^{n} w_{ij} y_j - \sum_{j=1}^{n-m} \overline{w}_{ij} y_j \tag{3.58}$$

From this definition we have:

$$E(u_i) = \sum_{j=1}^{n} w_{ij} E(y_j) - \sum_{j=1}^{n-m} \overline{w}_{ij} E(y_j) = 0 \tag{3.59}$$

because in a purely spatial model $E(y_j) = 0$ (see Section 3.2.1), and:

$$Var[u_i] =$$
$$Var(y) \left[\sum_{j=n-m+1}^{n} d_{ij}^{-2} + 2 \sum_{j=1}^{n} \sum_{l=1}^{n} w_{ij} w_{il} Corr\left(y_j y_l\right) - 2 \sum_{j=n-m+1}^{n} \sum_{j=1}^{n-m} w_{ij} \overline{w}_{il} Corr\left(y_j y_l\right) \right] \tag{3.60}$$

where d_{ij} is the distance between each location i and the missing location j (see Arbia, 2016, for a proof). Commenting on Equation 3.60 we can reach the following conclusions.

First of all, the presence of missing data produces a heteroscedastic measurement error because $Var[u_i]$, in general, will be non-constant. This in turn introduces heteroscedasticity of the error component.

Secondly, the attenuation effect on the estimator of λ will be more severe if the distance between each point and the missing points is small, in which case the term $\sum_{j=n-m+1}^{n} d_{ij}^{-2}$ will be large. This happens when the missing data are clustered in space.

Thirdly, the attenuation effect on the estimator of λ will be emphasized in the presence of a positive spatial correlation between all n observations of the dependent variable (the term $\sum_{j=1}^{n}\sum_{l=1}^{n}w_{ij}w_{il}Corr\left(y_j y_l\right)$ in Equation 3.60). Indeed, if the observations display no spatial correlation, then Equation 3.60 simplifies into $Var\left[u_i\right]=Var(y)\sum_{j=n-m+1}^{n}d_{ij}^{-2}$ and the attenuation effect depends only on the position of the missing points and it is minimized when they are scattered in the space (so that the distances d_{ij} on average are large).

Fourthly, the attenuation effect on the estimator of λ will be reduced by a positive spatial correlation between the observed and the missing points. In this case, intuitively, at least part of the information which are lost with the missing data, can be recovered using the information contained in the observed points which are similar due to the positive spatial correlation. In fact, the term $\sum_{j=n-m+1}^{n}\sum_{j=1}^{n-m}w_{ij}\overline{w}_{il}Corr\left(y_j y_l\right)$ in Equation 3.60 expresses the fact that if location i is close to both the observed location j and the missing location l, and, furthermore, j and l are positively correlated, we can exploit their correlation to recover part of the lost information thus mitigating the attenuation effect.

Finally, the worst situation is when the missing points are clustered in space and the missing observations are negatively correlated with the non-missing observations. In fact, in this case, the information which is lost cannot be recovered by exploiting the similarity with the observations that are available in the neighborhood of the missing data.

Let us now move to discuss the effects of measurement errors due to "locational uncertainty". In this respect an interesting case that can be treated analytically emerges when data are intentionally geo-masked to protect the individuals' confidentiality as often happens: for example, in many health econometrics studies (see Section 1.4). In particular, we can investigate the effects of a procedure known as the "random direction, random distance method" (Collins, 2011; USAID, 2013) or "uniform geo-masking" (Arbia et al., 2015a) used by the Department of Homeland Security (DHS) in the US to preserve confidentiality. This mechanism transforms the coordinates, displacing them along a random angle (say δ) and a random distance (say θ) both obeying a uniform probability law $\theta \overset{iid}{\approx} U(0,\theta^*)$ and $\delta \overset{iid}{\approx} U(0,360°)$ respectively, with θ^* the maximum distance error and with θ and δ mutually independent and independent of the variable y. Since in spatial microeconometrics, we invariably refer to spatial coordinates observed on a two dimensional continuous surface, it is useful to slightly modify our notation and to indicate with the symbol $y_{<ij>}$ the variable y observed at the point of coordinates $<i,j>$ and with $d_{<ij>,<lm>}$ the distance between point $<i,j>$ and point $<l,m>$.

With this new notation the purely spatial autoregressive model introduced in Section 3.2.1 can be re-written as:

$$y_{<ij><lm>}=\lambda\sum_{<lm>}w_{<ij><lm>}y_{<ij><lm>}+\varepsilon_{<ij>} \tag{3.61}$$

52 Spatial behavior of economic agents

with $\varepsilon_{(ij)} \approx i.i.d. N\left(0, \sigma_\varepsilon^2\right) \forall i, j$ and $w_{<ij><lm>} = d_{<ij><lm>}^{-2}$. Consequently, the measurement error on the spatially lagged variable can be expressed as:

$$u_{<ij><lm>} = \sum_{<lm>} w_{<ij><lm>} y_{<lm>} - \sum_{<lm>} \overline{w}_{<ij><lm>} y_{<lm>} \tag{3.62}$$

with $\overline{w}_{<ij><lm>} = \overline{d}_{<ij><lm>}^{-2}$ representing (with the usual notation) the weight matrix based on error-contaminated distances. Let us, first of all, examine the effect of a measurement error on the distance. If we define such an error as $\nu_{<ij><l,m>} = \overline{d}_{<ij>,<l,m>}^{2} - d_{<ij>,<l,m>}^{2}$, we have (see Arbia, 2016, for the proofs):

$$E(\nu_{<i, j><l,m>}) = \frac{2}{3} \theta^{*2} \tag{3.63}$$

and

$$Var(\nu_{<ij><l,m>}) = Var(\overline{d}_{<ij>,<l,m>}^{2}) = \frac{113}{600} \theta^{*4} \tag{3.64}$$

Equation 3.63 shows that the observed pairwise distances after geo-masking are expected to be greater than the true distances and, as expected from the intuition, both the expected value and the variance of the error are increasing functions of the maximum displacement radius θ^*. Furthermore, the measurement error on the spatially lagged variable will be such that:

$$E(u_{<ij>}) = 0 \tag{3.65}$$

and

$$Var(u_{<ij>}) = Var(y) \sum_{<lm>} \left[\mu_{\overline{w}}^2 + \sigma_{\overline{w}}^2 \right] \tag{3.66}$$

with the explicit expressions for $\mu_{\overline{w}}^2$ and $\sigma_{\overline{w}}^2$ given by:

$$\mu_{\overline{w}}^2 = \frac{1}{d_{<ij><lm>}^2} - \frac{1}{d_{<ij><lm>}^2 + \frac{2}{3}\theta^{*2}} - \frac{\frac{113}{600}\theta^{*4}}{2\left(d_{<ij><lm>}^2 + \frac{2}{3}\theta^{*2}\right)^2} \tag{3.67}$$

(Arbia, 2016) and by:

$$\sigma_{\overline{w}}^2 = \frac{\frac{113}{600}\theta^{*4}}{\left(d_{<ij><lm>}^2 + \frac{2}{3}\theta^{*2}\right)^4} \tag{3.68}$$

respectively (see Arbia, 2016, for the proofs).

Equation 3.67 shows the effects of an intentional locational error.

First of all, the intentional location error introduces a downward bias on the elements of the W matrix (since all elements in Equation 3.66 are positive)

Secondly, for locations that are distant (when $d \to \infty$), the bias of the elements of the W matrix becomes negligible since in this case $E(w_{<ij>,<l,m>} - \overline{w}_{<ij>,<l,m>}) \to 0$

Thirdly, for locations that are nearby, when $d \to 0$, the bias converges to the finite value $E(w_{<ij>,<l,m>} - \overline{w}_{<ij>,<l,m>}) \to \dfrac{339}{1600}$ which depends on the structure of the weight matrix before and after geo-masking, that is, ultimately, on the geo-masking procedure employed.

Furthermore, using the results of Equations 3.67 and 3.68 in Equation 3.66, we obtain:

$$Var(u_{<ij>}) =$$

$$Var(y) \sum_{<lm>} \left[\left(\frac{1}{d^2_{<ij><lm>}} - \frac{1}{d^2_{<ij><lm>} + \frac{2}{3}\theta^{*2}} - \frac{\frac{113}{600}\theta^{*4}}{2\left(d^2_{<ij><lm>} + \frac{2}{3}\theta^{*2}\right)^2} \right)^2 + \frac{\frac{113}{600}\theta^{*4}}{\left(d^2_{<ij><lm>} + \frac{2}{3}\theta^{*2}\right)^4} \right]$$

$$(3.69)$$

This expression leads us to several interesting conclusions.

First of all, with location error heteroscedasticity is introduced into the model due to the fact that $Var[u_i]$ in Equation 3.66, in general, will be non-constant.

Secondly, the attenuation effect is, obviously, null when $\theta^* = 0$ and it is also reduced to zero if points are scattered. In fact, when $d \to \infty$, $Var(u_{<ij>}) \to 0$. It is, conversely, emphasized if points are clustered in space in that it becomes larger when $d \to 0$.

Finally, the attenuation effect is a complex function of the maximum displacement distance θ^* and of the pairwise distances between the observed points.

3.6 Problems in regressions on a spatial distance

In many spatial microeconometric studies, the distance between each observed individual economic agent and a conspicuous point is often used as a predictor in a regression model. For instance, in health economics it is common practice to postulate a relationship between a health outcome for each individual (such as the effect of a health policy) and the individual's distance from a clinic or a hospital. Similar examples may be found in labor economics, education, hedonic price studies and industrial economics to name but a few. In principle, there is no obstacle to using the OLS procedure to estimate the parameters of a regression with a distance used as an independent variable. However, as we have shown in Section 3.5, the presence of missing data or locational errors produces the effect that pairwise distances are biased upwards and produce a measurement error on

54 *Spatial behavior of economic agents*

spatial autoregressive models. A similar effect can be observed when a distance is used as a regressor (see Arbia et al., 2015a). In this section we will report some useful theoretical results with the aim of illustrating the dangers that are hidden in this procedure.

Let us consider the simple linear model with only the square of the distance as a regressor:

$$y_{<i,j>} = \alpha + \beta d^2_{<ij>} + \varepsilon_{<i,j>} \tag{3.70}$$

which, although admittedly not very realistic, helps in illustrating the main points. In Equation 3.70, without loss of generality, we can assume that the conspicuous point is located in the origin of a squared area, so that the distance between $<i,j>$ and the conspicuous point can be simply expressed as $d^2_{ij} = (i^2 + j^2)$. Consider further the case of a uniform geo-masking (illustrated in Section 3.5) where the coordinates are displaced along a random angle and a random distance. The observed distance after geo-masking, can now be expressed as $\bar{d}^2_{ij} = (i + \theta Cos\delta)^2 + (j + \theta Sin\delta)^2$ using polar coordinates. By defining the measurement error as $u_{ij} = (\bar{d}^2_{ij} - d^2_{ij})$, (similarly to the case discussed in Section 3.5) Arbia et al. (2015a) proved that the geo-masking produces an upward bias and a non-constant variance, respectively given by:

$$E(u_{ij}) = \frac{\theta^*}{3} \neq 0 \tag{3.71}$$

and

$$Var(u_{ij}) = \frac{17}{180}\theta^{*4} + \frac{2}{3}\theta^{*2}d^2_{ij} \tag{3.72}$$

So, consistently with the results reported in Section 3.5, the variance of the measurement error increases with the maximum displacement distance θ^* and as we move away from the conspicuous point (the term d_{ij}). We can use this result to provide an explicit expression to the estimation variance and for the attenuation effect induced by measurement error. We have, respectively:

$$Var(\widehat{\beta}) = \frac{\beta^2 \left(\frac{17}{180}\theta^{*4} + \frac{2}{3}\theta^{*2}d^2_{ij} \right) + \sigma^2_v}{n\sigma^2_{d^2}} \tag{3.73}$$

and

$$p\lim(\widehat{\beta}) = \beta \left(\frac{\sigma^2_{d^2}}{\sigma^2_u + \sigma^2_{d^2}} \right) = \beta \left(\frac{\sigma^2_{d^2}}{\frac{17}{180}\theta^{*4} + \frac{2}{3}\theta^{*2}d^2_{ij} + \sigma^2_{d^2}} \right) \tag{3.74}$$

(see again Arbia et. al., 2015a) which leads to the intuitive results that the greater the maximum displacement distance in a geo-masking procedure, the lower the precision and the larger the attenuation effects. This result is useful for practical purposes because the data producers, before geo-masking the data, can calculate the appropriate expression when choosing the maximum location error (θ^*) so as to limit the negative consequences on any subsequent econometric analysis. Furthermore, using Equation 3.74, the data producer could disclose to the end users and to the practitioners the level of attenuation that is expected given the chosen level of the geo-masking procedure.

The results reported here for linear models were extended to the case when a distance is used as a regressor in a discrete choice model (Arbia et al., 2019b).

Example 3.7

In order to illustrate the effects described in this chapter, let us consider a set of simulated data where 100 individuals are observed in a unit square study area as shown in Figure 3.2. Taking these points as given, we have that in Equations 3.73 and 3.74 d_{ij}^2 = 0.520151 (considering for operational reasons the mean of all squared distances from the origin) and $\sigma_{d^2}^2$ = 0.1592879.

With reference to these artificial data Figure 3.3 reports the behavior of the attenuation effect for Gaussian (lower curve) and uniform (upper curve) geo-masking for the values of the maximum displacement distance θ^* ranging between 0 and 1.44 (1.44 being the theoretical maximum possible distance in a unitary square). Two features emerge from the inspection of the graph. First,

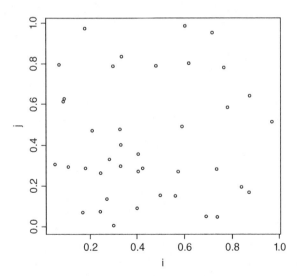

Figure 3.2 100 simulated individuals observed in a unit square study area.

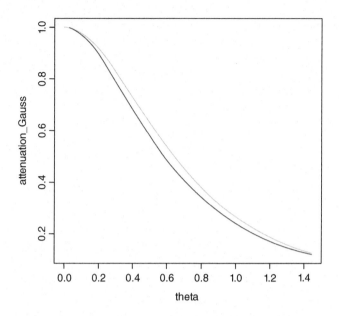

Figure 3.3 Attenuation effect for Gaussian (lower curve) and uniform (upper curve) geo-masking as a function of the maximum displacement.

the attenuation increases dramatically already at small levels of θ^*. Secondly, the Gaussian geo-masking, other things being constant, produces more severe consequences on the estimation of β than the uniform geo-masking. This type of graph could be used by data producers to calibrate the optimal value of θ^* and to communicate to the practitioners the resulting level of attenuation they should expect from a regression analysis.

4 Non-linear spatial models

4.1 Non-linear spatial regressions

In Chapter 3 we considered the case of linear spatial regressions. In this chapter we will extend the analysis to non-linear models. Non-linear models can emerge for different reasons. One important instance is when the dependent variable can assume only a limited number of discrete outcomes. There are many examples of cases where this modeling framework is useful in spatial microeconometrics. For instance, we might be interested in explaining patient's choices in health economics or school choices in educational economics. But many other examples can be found: for instance, when studying the presence or absence of a certain technology in a set of firms in industrial economics, consumer choice regarding different shopping centers, in electoral behavior, in criminal behavior and in a large number of other situations. We refer to these cases as to "discrete choice modeling" (see Greene, 2018). A second important class of non-linear models emerges when the dependent variable is limited by censoring or truncation (Greene, 2018). Surprisingly, despite the interest of non-linear models from an applied perspective, in the spatial econometrics literature they have received comparatively less attention than the models presented in Chapter 3, partly because of the higher analytical complexity involved and the associated higher computational effort required even in moderately large samples. In the case of non-linear models the framework presented in Chapter 3 cannot be employed, and it needs to be adjusted to respect the statistical nature of the datasets employed. The various specifications of spatial non-linear models follow the general strategy used in the literature to deal with non-spatial non-linear models with a particular emphasis on the "logit", "probit" and "tobit" specifications adapted to account for the presence of spatial dependence in the dependent variable. In what follows we will present some of the most popular spatial versions of these models. The interested reader is referred to the works of Beron and Vijverberg (2004), Fleming (2004), Smirnov (2010) and LeSage and Pace (2009) for more thorough reviews.

58   *Spatial behavior of economic agents*

4.2 Standard non-linear models

4.2.1 Logit and probit models

We will start by introducing standard discrete choice specifications based on the idea of a utility function associated with a latent continuous variable y^* which can be studied through a linear regression model:

$$y^* = X\beta + \varepsilon \qquad \varepsilon \cong i.i.d. \tag{4.1}$$

where the error terms are independent, with a distribution that can be differently specified. We imagine that if the utility variable y^* exceeds a certain threshold, say a, then the associated binary variable y is equal to 1 and 0 otherwise. Formally we can express this condition as $y = I(y^* > 0)$ with $I(.)$ the indicator function such that $I(a > 0) = \begin{cases} 1 & \text{if } a > 0 \\ 0 & \text{otherwise} \end{cases}$. When the utility y^* is greater than 0, then the economic event materializes (such as the decision to go to a certain hospital or to enroll in a certain school). Equation 4.1 represents a basic linear regression model but expressed in terms of an unobservable utility variable, y^*. The phenomenon of interest can only be observed through the variable y. If we are interested in the probability that the event is realized we can calculate:

$$P(y_i = 1|X) = P(y_i^* > 0|X) = P(X_i\beta > \varepsilon|X) = P(\varepsilon < X_i\beta|X) = F(X_i\beta)$$
$$= \int_{-\infty}^{\mu_i} f(\mu)\, d\mu \tag{4.2}$$

and, similarly for $P(y_i = 0|X)$. With the symbol $F(x)$ in Equation 4.2 we indicate the cumulative probability distribution function, with $f(x)$ the associated density function such that $f(x) = \dfrac{\partial}{\partial x} F(x)$ and with $\mu = X\beta$ the systematic component of the model which in this literature is called the "index function" (Greene, 2018). If we specify different distribution functions in Equation 4.2 we obtain different discrete choice models (for a review, see Greene, 2018). The most popular are the probit and logit specifications. In particular, if in Equation 4.2 we define $F(.)$ as the standardized normal probability distribution function, say $F(.) = \Phi$, we obtain the probit model. If conversely we define $F(.)$ as a standardized logistic distribution, say $F(.) = \Lambda$, we produce the logit model. The standardized logistic distribution has, by definition, zero expected value and a variance equal to $\pi^2/3$. However, since the value of the dichotomous variable y depends only on the sign of y^* and not its absolute value, it is not affected by the amount of the variance so that it is not a limitation to standardize it to 1.

A popular estimation method for both the probit and the logit is the maximum likelihood approach. Indeed, the likelihood function can be easily built up as the probability of drawing a random sample, of size say n, from a sequence of independent Bernoulli variables. This is equal to:

$$L(\beta) = P(Y_1 = y_1, \ldots, Y_n = y_n | X) = P(Y_1 = y_1 | X) \ldots P(Y_n = y_n | X) \tag{4.3}$$

where Y_i represents a random variable and y_i its sample realization. In the standard setting due to the hypothesis of Equation 4.1, we have:

$$L(\beta) = \prod_{y_i=1} F(X_i\beta) \prod_{y_i=0} \left[1 - F(X_i\beta)\right] \tag{4.4}$$

where $\displaystyle\prod_{y_i=1}$ represents the product for all values of y such that $y_i = 1$ and similarly

for $\displaystyle\prod_{y_i=0}$. Since y_i is dichotomous, we can express Equation 4.4 as:

$$L(\beta|X) = \prod_{i=1}^{n} F(X_i\beta)^{y_i} \prod_{y_i=0} \left[1 - F(X_i\beta)\right]^{y_i-1} \tag{4.5}$$

The log likelihood follows straightforwardly as:

$$l(\beta) = \ln\left[L(\beta)\right] = \sum_{i=1}^{n} y_i \left\{\ln F(X_i\beta) + (1 - y_i)\ln\left[1 - F(X_i\beta)\right]\right\} \tag{4.6}$$

which can only be maximized numerically due to its non-linearity. From Equation 4.6 it follows the score function:

$$\frac{\partial}{\partial\beta} l(\beta) = \sum_{i=1}^{n} \left[\frac{y_i f_i}{F_i} + (1 - y_i)\frac{-f_i}{1 - F_i}\right] x_i = 0 \tag{4.7}$$

First of all, let us assume that the probability distribution function has a logistic specification which defined the logit model, and, furthermore, let us set in Equation 4.7 $F_i = \Lambda_i = \Lambda(X_i\beta)$. Equation 4.7 becomes (Greene, 2018):

$$\frac{\partial}{\partial\beta} l(\beta) = \sum_{i=1}^{n} (y_i - \Lambda_i) X_i = 0 \tag{4.8}$$

From Equation 4.8 we also obtain the elements of the Hessian matrix as:

$$\frac{\partial^2}{\partial\beta^2} l(\beta) = \sum_{i=1}^{n} \Lambda_i (1 - \Lambda_i) X_i X_i^T \tag{4.9}$$

which forms the basis for the calculation of Fisher information matrix to be used in confidence interval estimation and hypothesis testing.

As an alternative, we can assume that the errors in Equation 4.1 are normally distributed, leading to a probit model. In this case the score function is equal to:

$$\frac{\partial}{\partial\beta} l(\beta) = \sum_{y_i=0} \frac{-\varphi_i}{1 - \Phi_i} X_i + \sum_{y_i=1} \frac{\varphi_i}{\Phi_i} X_i = 0 \tag{4.10}$$

60 *Spatial behavior of economic agents*

with $\phi_i = \phi(X_i\beta)$, the standard normal density function such that $\varphi = \dfrac{\partial \Phi(t)}{\partial t}$. The elements of the Hessian matrix in this case can be derived as:

$$\frac{\partial^2}{\partial \beta^2} l(\beta) = \sum_{i=1}^{n} -\kappa_i (\kappa_i + X_i\beta) X_i X_i^T \tag{4.11}$$

with the term κ being equal to $\kappa_i = \dfrac{(2y_i - 1)\phi\left[(2y_i - 1)X_i^T \beta\right]}{\Phi\left[(2y_i - 1)X_i^T \beta\right]}$.

An important aspect of both logit and probit models concerns the interpretation of the parameters, a topic which we have already discussed in Section 3.8 when dealing with spatial linear models. Indeed, in both specifications, the interpretation is not straightforward as it is in the case of the (a-spatial) linear regression model because in a non-linear model impacts are not constant over the values of the variable X, and a whole function has to be considered. In this case, the marginal effect of a unitary increase of the independent variables on the binary dependent variable is not simply expressed by the regression coefficient, and it assumes, in general, the following expression:

$$\frac{\partial E(y|X)}{\partial X} = f(X\beta)\beta \tag{4.12}$$

which, due to the non-linearity of the model, depends on the observed value of the variable X. More explicitly, for the logit model this could be expressed as:

$$\frac{\partial E(y|X)}{\partial X} = \Lambda(X\beta)\left[1 - \Lambda(X\beta)\right]\beta \tag{4.13}$$

while for the probit model it assumes the following expression:

$$\frac{\partial E(y|X)}{\partial X} = \phi(X\beta)\beta \tag{4.14}$$

4.2.2 The tobit model

A second source of non-linearity in the models can refer to the presence of censoring or truncation of the dependent variable. A general class of these models is represented by the tobit model (see *Goldberger, 1964; Tobin, 1958*). In contrast with the logit and probit specification, in a tobit model the dependent variable is censored or truncated in some way (see Greene, 2018). A latent variable linear models can then be specified, but in this case we don't observe a dependent variable, say, y^*, rather only a variable y, say, such that $y = min(y^*, c)$ if right censored, or $w = max(y^*, c)$ if left censored with c the threshold. Usually the threshold is normalized by setting c = 0. In a truncated regression, data are missing beyond a censoring point.

The simpler standard tobit model (Type I) is expressed by the following equation:

$$y^* = X\beta + \varepsilon \tag{4.15}$$

with $\varepsilon \approx i.i.d.N\left(0, \sigma_\varepsilon^2\right)$ and the usual notation for the rest. A similar notation can be used for left truncation. y^* is a latent unobservable variable, while the observable variable is defined by $y = \begin{cases} y^* : if \ y^* > c \\ 0 : if \ y^* \le c \end{cases}$. In deriving the likelihood function for variable y notice that, according to the definition given above, we have to contemplate two cases: (i) $y > 0$ and (ii) $y = 0$.

When $y > 0$ the density function for the single observation i is given by:

$$P\left(y_i > 0\right) = \frac{1}{\sigma} \phi\left(\frac{y_i - x_i\beta}{\sigma}\right) \tag{4.16}$$

with ϕ indicating again the normal probability density function.

When $y \le 0$, in contrast, the density function for the single observation i is given by:

$$P\left(y_i = 0\right) = 1 - \phi\left(\frac{x_i\beta}{\sigma}\right) \tag{4.17}$$

with ϕ the cumulative distribution function of the normal distribution. Let us now make use again of the indicator function $I_i\left(y_i^* > 0\right) = I_i$, for short. Then Equations 4.16 and 4.17 can be combined as:

$$P\left(y_i\right) = \left\{\frac{1}{\sigma} \phi\left(\frac{y_i - x_i\beta}{\sigma}\right)\right\}^{I_i} \left\{1 - \phi\left(\frac{x_i\beta}{\sigma}\right)\right\}^{1 - I_i} \tag{4.18}$$

For the hypothesis of independence from Equation 4.15 we can obtain straightforwardly the likelihood function as:

$$L\left(\beta, \sigma\right) = \prod_{i=1}^{n} \left\{\frac{1}{\sigma} \phi\left(\frac{y_i - x_i\beta}{\sigma}\right)\right\}^{I_i} \left\{1 - \phi\left(\frac{x_i\beta}{\sigma}\right)\right\}^{1 - I_i} \tag{4.19}$$

and the log likelihood as:

$$l\left(\beta, \sigma\right) = \sum_{i=1}^{n} \left[I_i ln\left\{\frac{1}{\sigma} \phi\left(\frac{y_i - x_i\beta}{\sigma}\right)\right\} + \left(1 - I_i\right) ln\left\{1 - \phi\left(\frac{x_i\beta}{\sigma}\right)\right\}\right] \tag{4.20}$$

that is used in estimation and hypothesis testing procedures.

Example 4.1

To illustrate the models presented here let us introduce a set of house-price data and house characteristics observed in Baltimore, Maryland in 1978. The data were prepared by Luc Anselin for the library spdep in R and were originally collected by Dubin (1992). The location of the houses are reported in Figure 4.1.

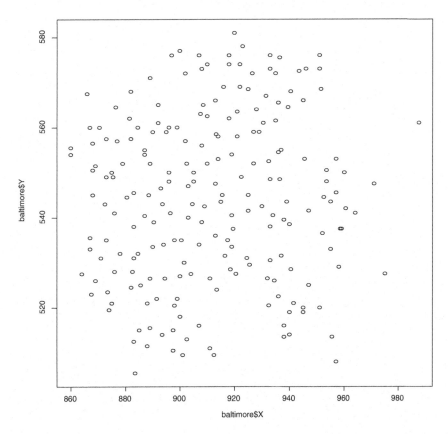

Figure 4.1 Locations of 211 houses in Baltimore.

Table 4.1 Output of a probit model explaining luxury houses in Baltimore as a function of number of storeys and square feet estimated with ML

Parameter	Estimated value	Standard error	z-test	p-value
Intercept	−1.624	0.842	−3.113	0.002
Number of storeys	−2.297	0.695	−3.308	0.001
Square feet	0.236	0.046	5.082	3.74e − 07

AIC = 96.893

Non-linear spatial models 63

Table 4.2 Output of a logit model explaining luxury houses in Baltimore as a function of number of storeys and square feet estimated with ML

Parameter	Estimated value	Standard error	z-test	p-value
Intercept	−1.584	0.455	−3.479	0.0005
Number of storeys	−1.085	0.345	−3.144	0.001
Square feet	0.118	0.022	5.310	1.1e − 07

AIC = 96.89

We estimate a probit and a logit model where a luxury house (defined as a house with a price higher than the 90th quantile) is expressed as function of two variables: square feet and number of storeys. The results obtained with the standard likelihood procedure are reported in Tables 4.1 and 4.2 for the probit and logit models (R Command: {stat}-glm.Probit). Results are obviously different in the two modeling frameworks, although the significance and the sign of the coefficients are in accordance in each model.

Example 4.2

With the same dataset, we want to explain only the price of the luxury houses (with a censoring at the 90th quantile) as a function of the number of storeys

Table 4.3 Output of a tobit model explaining the price of luxury houses in Baltimore as a function of number of storeys and square feet estimated with ML

Parameter	Estimated value	Standard error	t-test	p-value
Intercept	48.058	3.677	13.069	< 2e − 16
Number of storeys	−17.001	2.228	−7.628	2.38e − 14
Square feet	2.600	0.147	10.890	< 2e − 16

AIC = 57897.88

and square feet using a tobit model type I as shown in Table 4.3 (R command: {CensReg} CensReg).

4.3 Spatial probit and logit models

4.3.1 *Model specification*

In the spatial econometric literature the classical probit model has been adapted to account for spatial dependence in its versions as spatial lag or spatial error which we have reviewed in the case of linear models in Chapter 3. In particular,

64 *Spatial behavior of economic agents*

by analogy with the spatial lag model presented in Section 3.3, the spatial lag probit model can be expressed as:

$$y^* = \lambda Wy^* + X\beta + \varepsilon \tag{4.21}$$

with $\varepsilon \mid X \approx i.i.d.$ $N(0,1)$, W the usual non-stochastic weight matrix, y^* an n-by-1 vector of the latent variable Y, λ the spatial autoregressive coefficient, y the observed binary variable such that $y = (I(y^* > 0)$ and X the matrix of regressors. Notice that, the error variance can be normalized to 1 without loss of generality because only the sign is relevant to determine y and not the absolute value of y^*. The estimation of Equation 4.21 presents three major problems. First of all, by analogy with the case of the spatial lag specification for linear models described in Section 3.8, we have a problem of endogeneity generated by the correlation between the error and the spatially lagged value of y^*. Secondly, the standard ML estimators are also inconsistent because of the heteroscedasticity induced by spatial dependence (Case, 1992; Pinkse and Slade, 1998). Thirdly, we also observe the inefficiency of the estimators as a consequence of the neglected information in the off-diagonal terms of the variance–covariance matrix (Fleming, 2004). Equation 4.15 can be expressed in its structural form by isolating y^* in the right hand side. We have:

$$y^* = (I - \lambda W)^{-1} X\beta + (I - \lambda W)^{-1} \varepsilon = X^*\beta + \varepsilon^* \tag{4.22}$$

with $\varepsilon^* = (I - \lambda W)^{-1} \varepsilon$ and $\varepsilon \approx MVN(0,\Omega)$ and $X^* = (I - \lambda W)^{-1} X$ and assuming that all the diagonal elements of W are zero and that $\lambda < 1$.

Since ε is a spatial autoregressive process, from the results presented in Chapter 3.2 we have:

$$E(\varepsilon\varepsilon^T) = \Omega = \left[(I - \lambda W)^T (I - \lambda W) \right]^{-1} \tag{4.23}$$

In the classical probit model with no spatial effects we described the probability $P(y_i = 1)$ through the integral $\varepsilon^* = P(y_i = 1) = F(X_i, \beta) = \int_{-\infty}^{\mu_i} f(\mu) d\mu$ and $\mu = (I - \lambda W) y^* - X_i \beta$ and similarly for $P(y_i = 0)$. Similarly, in a spatial probit model, we can define the likelihood of the single observation as:

$$\begin{aligned} P(y_i = 1) &= P\left(y_i^* > 0 \mid X_i^*, w_{ij} y_i^*\right) = P\left(X^*\beta + \varepsilon^* > 0 \mid X_i^*, w_{ij} y_i^*\right) \\ &= P\left(-\varepsilon^* < X_i^* \ \beta \mid X_i^*, w_{ij} y_i^*\right) \cong \Phi\left(X^*\beta\right) \end{aligned} \tag{4.24}$$

with similar expression for $P(y_i = 0)$. The previous expression is only approximated due to the presence of heteroscedasticity. In fact, generalizing the result obtained for the a-spatial probit model (see Equation 4.6), we have:

$$P\left(y_i = 1 \mid X_i^*, w_{ij} y_i^*\right) \cong \Phi\left(\frac{X_i^*\beta}{\Omega_{ii}}\right) \tag{4.25}$$

Non-linear spatial models 65

where Ω_{ii} is the i-th diagonal element of the variance–covariance matrix reported in Equation 4.23. Equation 4.25 shows that, even if the error term ε are homeschedastic, the transformed error terms ε^* become heteroscedastic.

In the standard probit model with no spatial effects we have shown in Equation 4.3 that, due to independence, the likelihood function can be obtained as the product of the n marginal probabilities. However, when spatial effects are considered this is obviously not possible due to the lack of independence so that, in principle, the likelihood should be derived through an n-dimensional integral:

$$P(y_1 = 1, y_2 = 1, ..., y_n = 1;) = \int_{-\infty}^{\mu_1} \int_{-\infty}^{\mu_2} ... \int_{-\infty}^{\mu_n} \varphi(\mu)\, d\mu \tag{4.26}$$

with the symbol $\varphi(\mu)$, already introduced, representing the density function of an n-dimensional multivariate normal distribution $MVN(\mu, \Omega)$.

However, the integral in Equation 4.26 does not admit an analytical solution and can only be evaluated numerically.

Similarly to the specifications presented in Chapter 3.2 for linear models, it is also possible to specify a spatial probit model in the form of a spatial error model. In this case we have the following two equations:

$$y^* = X\beta + u \tag{4.27}$$

$$u = \rho W u + \varepsilon \tag{4.28}$$

In order to isolate the y^* variable on the right-hand side, Equations 4.27 and 4.28 can also be re-written in a reduced structural form as:

$$y^* = X\beta + (I - \rho)^{-1} \varepsilon \tag{4.29}$$

where $u = MVN(0, \Omega)$ and $\Omega = (I - \rho W)^{-1}(I - \rho W^T)^{-1}$.

4.3.2 Estimation

From an estimation point of view in order to estimate the parameters of spatial lag probit model (Equation 4.21), we have to solve two problems. The first relates to the presence of an endogenous error term and the second to the presence of spatial autocorrelation and of heteroscedasticity in the variance–covariance matrix. Various methods have been proposed in the literature, starting with the early contributions of McMillen (1992), Pinkse and Slade (1998) and Klier and McMillen (2008b) amongst the others (see Fleming, 2004, for a review). They can be basically traced back to the general principles of maximum likelihood and generalized method of moments.

In the standard a-spatial probit model the maximum likelihood estimators can be derived by maximizing Equation 4.6, a procedure that requires numerical optimization due to the high degree of non-linearity in the parameters. However, when considering data containing spatial dependence, if we neglect the information contained in the off-diagonal terms of the variance–covariance matrix, the

66 *Spatial behavior of economic agents*

likelihood function maximization produces estimators that are still consistent, but loose the property of efficiency. For the spatial lag probit model (Equation 4.21), with the hypothesis of normal disturbances the log likelihood function can be expressed as follows:

$$
l(\beta, \lambda | X, Wy^\star) = \sum_{i=1}^{n} y_i ln\Phi\left(\frac{\lambda \sum_{i=1}^{n} w_{ij} y_j^\star + X_i^T \beta}{\Omega_{ii}}\right)
$$
$$
+ \sum_{i=1}^{n} (1 - y_i) ln\Phi\left(1 - \frac{\lambda \sum_{i=1}^{n} w_{ij} y_j^\star + X_i^T \beta}{\Omega_{ii}}\right) \tag{4.30}
$$

However, the term $y^\bullet$ is not observable and so Equation 4.30 is not operational. In order to derive an operational version, let us use the structural form expressed in Equation 4.22. In this case the log likelihood function can be re-written in an operational form as:

$$
l(\beta, \lambda | X, Wy^\star) = \sum_{i=1}^{n} y_i ln\Phi\left(\frac{X_i^{\star T} \beta}{\Omega_{ii}}\right) + \sum_{i=1}^{n} (1 - y_i) ln\Phi\left(1 - \frac{X_i^{\star T} \beta}{\Omega_{ii}}\right) \tag{4.31}
$$

with $X^\star = (I - \lambda W)^{-1} X$. Even so, Equation 4.31 cannot be solved easily due to problems in the numerical maximization. As a solution, McMillen (1992) suggested the use of a generalization of the expectation-maximization algorithm (Dempster et al., 1977). In particular, for the spatial probit model (4.21) in the E-step of the procedure the expected value is evaluated as:

$$
E\left(y_i^\star | y = 1\right) = X_i^T \beta + E\left(\varepsilon_i | \varepsilon_i > X_i^T \beta\right) + \sigma_i \frac{\phi\left(\dfrac{X_i^{\star T} \beta}{\Omega_{ii}}\right)}{\Phi\left(\dfrac{X_i^{\star T} \beta}{\Omega_{ii}}\right)} \tag{4.32}
$$

which can be used in an M-step where the following log likelihood is maximized:

$$
l = \cos t - \frac{1}{2} \ln|\Omega| - \frac{1}{2}\left(\mu^T \mu\right) \tag{4.33}
$$

with $\Omega = (I - \lambda W)^{-1}(I - \lambda W)^{-T}$, $\mu = (I - \lambda W)\hat{y}^\star - X_i\beta$, and $\hat{y}^\star$ is the vector of the predicted values of the latent variable derived in the E-step.

Although theoretically sound, the EM approach has two drawbacks. First of all, it requires the estimation of the variance–covariance matrix Ω. The solution suggested by McMillen (1992) consisted of interpreting the probit model as a non-linear weighted least square model conditional on the spatial parameter (Amemiya, 1985), but this solution produces biased estimators (Fleming, 2004). Secondly, the estimation process can be computationally very slow and

Non-linear spatial models 67

inaccurate. Indeed, the calculation of the determinant of the matrix Ω needs to be repeated at each iteration of the M-step until convergence and in the presence of large n and dense W matrices this operation can be very long and inaccurate in that it needs to be based on approximations.

Example 4.3

Using again the dataset presented in Examples 4.1 and 4.2, we have the results shown in Table 4.4 (R command: {McSpatial}-spprobitml), where the parameter

Table 4.4 Output of a spatial lag probit model explaining luxury houses in Baltimore as a function of number of storeys and square feet estimated with ML

Parameter	Estimated value	Standard error	z-test	p-value
Intercept	-1.674	0.635	-2.635	0.008
Number of storeys	-0.558	0.323	-1.727	0.084
Square feet	0.119	0.022	5.338	0.084

$\lambda = 0.7941587$

λ is positive, and the coefficients are consistent with those found in Example 4.1 for the a-spatial probit specification.

Turning our attention to the spatial error probit model, Pinkse and Slade (1998) suggested a solution based on the generalized method of moments. Going back to Equation 4.6 the generic formulation of the log likelihood function of a probit model is:

$$l(\beta,\rho) = \ln\left[L(\beta,\rho)\right] = \sum_{i=1}^{n} y_i \left\{\ln F\left(X_i\beta\right) + (1 - y_i)\ln\left[1 - F\left(X_i\beta\right)\right]\right\}$$

which, in the hypothesis of normal disturbances, can be expressed as:

$$l\left(\beta,\rho|X,Wy^*\right) = \sum_{i=1}^{n} y_i ln\Phi\left(\frac{X_i^T\beta}{\Omega_{ii}}\right) + \sum_{i=1}^{n}(1 - y_i)ln\Phi\left(1 - \frac{X_i^T\beta}{\Omega_{ii}}\right) \tag{4.34}$$

Traditionally a GMM approach is based on the identification of a set of moment conditions based on the properties of the residuals. In this new context we introduce the notion of pseudo- (or generalized) errors, defined by:

$$\tilde{u}_i = \frac{\left\{y_i - \Phi\left(\dfrac{X_i^T\beta}{\Omega_{ii}}\right)\right\}\phi\left(\dfrac{X_i^T\beta}{\sigma_{ii}}\right)}{\Phi\left(\dfrac{X_i^T\beta}{\Omega_{ii}}\right)\left\{1 - \Phi\left(\dfrac{X_i^T\beta}{\Omega_{ii}}\right)\right\}} \tag{4.35}$$

68 *Spatial behavior of economic agents*

Let us now consider a set of k instruments arranged in a (n-by-k) matrix H. The instruments are exogenous by definition so that we can define the set of the moments condition:

$$E\left(H^T \tilde{u}\right) = 0 \qquad (4.36)$$

If we indicate with the symbol h_i the i-th row of a matrix of instruments H, the single i-th condition of Equation (4.36) can be expressed algebraically as:

$$E\left[h_i \frac{\left\{ y_i - \Phi\left(\dfrac{X_i^T \beta}{\Omega_{ii}}\right) \right\} \phi\left(\dfrac{X_i^T \beta}{\sigma_{ii}}\right)}{\Phi\left(\dfrac{X_i^T \beta}{\Omega_{ii}}\right)\left\{ 1 - \Phi\left(\dfrac{X_i^T \beta}{\Omega_{ii}}\right) \right\}} \right] = 0 \qquad (4.37)$$

so that, eventually, if we set to zero the empirical analogue of Equation 4.37, we obtain the following system of moment equations:

$$m(\beta, \rho) = \sum_{i=1}^{n} \frac{\left\{ y_i - \Phi\left(\dfrac{X_i^T \beta}{\Omega_{ii}}\right) \right\} \phi\left(\dfrac{X_i^T \beta}{\sigma_{ii}}\right)}{\Phi\left(\dfrac{X_i^T \beta}{\Omega_{ii}}\right)\left\{ 1 - \Phi\left(\dfrac{X_i^T \beta}{\Omega_{ii}}\right) \right\}} h_i = 0 \qquad (4.38)$$

If we adopt a generalized version of the method of moments, Equation 4.38 is replaced by the following minimization problem:

$$m(\beta, \rho)^T M^{-1} m(\beta, \rho) = \min \qquad (4.39)$$

M being a positive definite matrix containing the weights assigned to each sample moments $m(\beta, \rho)$. Pinkse and Slade (1998) proved that the GMM procedure provides consistent and asymptotically normal estimators and developed an explicit expression for their variance–covariance matrix using Newey and West's approach (see Newey and West, 1987).

The GMM estimator is distribution free so that we do not have to rely on the hypothesis of normality of residuals as in the maximum likelihood procedure. Furthermore, we do not need to calculate the determinant and the inverse of large n-by-n matrices, which, as noted in the previous section, constitutes the major computational problem connected with the use of the maximum likelihood procedure when estimating a spatial lag probit model. On the other side, Equation 4.35 cannot be minimized analytically, so the GMM estimators suffer from the computational problems connected with numerical optimization. Similarly to what happens when implementing the ML, this operation requires the evaluation of the variance–covariance matrix Ω repeatedly for each candidate value of the parameter ρ in a numerical search and this can become a formidable task even for moderately large sample due to the complex form of Ω.

The technique described here could be adjusted also for a spatial error logit model.

Example 4.4

With the R command: {McSpatial}-gmmprobit, we can estimate the spatial lag version of the procedure introduced by Pinkse and Slade (1998). Using again the dataset described in Example 4.1 and building up the same model, we obtain Table 4.5, which shows that, while all parameters are still significant and of the same sign as in Examples 4.1 and 4.3, now also the parameter λ is positive and significant.

Table 4.5 Output of a spatial lag probit model explaining luxury houses in Baltimore as a function of number of storeys and square feet estimated with GMM

Parameter	Estimated value	Standard error	z-test	p-value
Intercept	−1.074	0.544	−1.974	0.048
Number of storeys	−0.832	0.416	−2.001	0.045
Square feet	0.113	0.0226	5.005	5.56e−07

$\lambda = 0.7162724$ (p-value = 1.597265e − 06)

In order to estimate a spatial lag logit model, Klier and McMillen (2008a) proposed a linearized version of Pinkse and Slade's GMM approach illustrated in the previous section which avoids the problem of inverting large matrices.

Recalling Equation 4.22 the spatial lag logit model can be defined as:

$$y^* = \lambda W y^* + X\beta + \varepsilon \qquad (4.40)$$

and $\varepsilon \mid X \approx Logistic\left(0, \sigma_\varepsilon^2\right)$. In its reduced form this becomes:

$$y^* = (I - \lambda W)^{-1} X\beta + (I - \lambda W)^{-1} \varepsilon = X^* \beta + \varepsilon^* \qquad (4.41)$$

where the transformed errors ε^* are heteroscedastic with a variance–covariance matrix:

$$\hat{\Sigma} = \begin{bmatrix} \sigma_1 & 0 & 0 & 0 & 0 \\ 0 & \sigma_2 & & & 0 \\ & & & & \\ 0 & 0 & & & \sigma_n \end{bmatrix} \qquad (4.42)$$

In this context, due to the hypothesis that the errors are distributed according to the logistic law, the probability of success can be defined as:

$$P_i = P(y_i = 1) = \frac{\exp\left(X^{**}\beta\right)}{1 + \exp\left(X^{**}\beta\right)} \qquad (4.43)$$

70 Spatial behavior of economic agents

with $X^{**} = (I - \lambda W)^{-1} X \hat{\Sigma}^{-1}$ is the variable X transformed as in Equation 4.22, but also normalized to account for the heteroscedasticity.

In this setting, Klier and McMillen (2008a) define the generalized logit model as:

$$\tilde{u}_i = y_i - P_i \tag{4.44}$$

and introduced their estimation procedure, by assuming an initial value for the parameters to be estimated in Equation 4.40. Let us call them $\delta_0 = (\beta_0, \lambda_0)$.

They then use these initial values in Equations 4.39 and 4.40 to calculate the initial value of the generalized residuals, call them $\tilde{u}_0 = y_i - P_{i0}$ with an intuitive notation.

The next step involves the calculation of the gradient $G_{\delta_0} = \dfrac{\partial P_{i0}}{\partial \delta_0}$ and to regress it onto a set of instruments, say H, defined by the transformation $H = (I - \lambda W)^{-1} WX^{**}$ with X^{**} defined as before. The outcome of this operation is an estimated value for the gradient which we will call $\hat{G}_{\delta_0}$. This estimation is then employed in the following recursive expression:

$$\delta_1 = \delta_0 + (\hat{G}_0^T \hat{G}_0)^{-1} \hat{G}_0^T \tilde{u}^0 \tag{4.45}$$

which makes use of the initial value of δ_0 and of the pseudo-residuals $\tilde{u}_0$. Klier and McMillen (2008a) derived the explicit expressions for the gradients of β and λ, given by:

$$G_{\beta_i} = P_i(1 - P_i)Z_i^{**} \tag{4.46}$$

and

$$G_{\lambda_i} = P_i(1 - P_i)\left[H_i \beta - \frac{Z_i^{**} \beta}{\sigma_i^2} \Xi_{ii} \right] \tag{4.47}$$

with Ξ_{ii} the i-th diagonal element of matrix

$\Xi = (I - \lambda W)^{-1} W (I - \lambda W)^{-1} (I - \lambda W)^{-1}$.

To make the method operational and avoid the computations involved by the inversion of the matrix $(I - \lambda W)^{-1}$ Klier and McMillen (2008a) proposed linearizing Equation 4.47 by a series expansion approximation around the starting point $\lambda_0 = 0$ where no matrix inversion is required.

Following this idea, and stopping at the first linear term of the expansion, we have:

$$\tilde{u}_i \cong \tilde{u}_i^0 + G(\delta - \delta_0) \tag{4.48}$$

and let $M = (H^T H)^{-1}$. The objective function to be minimize thus becomes:

$$v^T H (H^T H) H^T v \tag{4.49}$$

Non-linear spatial models 71

where v are the transformed generalized errors defined by:

$$v_i = \tilde{u}_i^0 + G\delta_0 - G\delta \qquad (4.50)$$

In this way the procedure reduces to a two-stage least squares estimation of a standard non-spatial logit model.

In general, the linearized model provides a good approximation for estimating the true parameters although with a certain loss of efficiency. Furthermore, when the true structure of the model is captured by the model, Klier and McMillen (2008a) show that the linearization provides accurate estimates when the parameter $\lambda < 0.5$ while it produces a upward bias when $\lambda > 0.5$.

The procedure can be easily extended to deal with a spatial lag probit model instead of a logit model.

Example 4.5

Again we make use of the house price data presented in Example 4.1 to estimate a spatial lag probit model using the linearized version of the GMM procedure illustrated in this section. Results are reported in Table 4.6 for the probit model (R command: {McSpatial}-spprobit) and Table 4.7 for the logit model (R command: {McSpatial}-splogit).

Although with some difference in the absolute value, the inferential conclusions are similar for the two models. In both cases the spatial correlation parameter λ is positive and highly significant, although for the second model only the

Table 4.6 Output of a spatial lag probit model explaining luxury houses in Baltimore as a function of number of storeys and square feet estimated with a linearized version of GMM

Parameter	Estimated value	Standard error	z-test	p-value
Intercept	−0.255	0.539	−0.474	0.635
Number of storeys	−0.828	0.283	−2.923	0.003
Square feet	0.018	0.023	5.450	0.000

$\lambda = 0.95393$ (p-value = 0.000)

Table 4.7 Output of a spatial lag logit model explaining luxury houses in Baltimore as a function of number of storeys and square feet estimated with a linearized version of GMM

Parameter	Estimated value	Standard error	z-test	p-value
Intercept	0.149	1.472	0.101	0.919
Number of storeys	−1.530	0.973	−1.572	0.115
Square feet	0.171	0.074	2.296	0.021

$\lambda = 1.04116$ (p-value = 0.004)

72 *Spatial behavior of economic agents*

variable "square feet" is significant. Furthermore, comparing these results with those reported in Examples 4.1, 4.3 and 4.4, we obtain similar results in terms of the sign of the coefficients, but notice that both the absolute value and the standard errors are rather different in the three estimation methods.

4.4 The spatial tobit model

4.4.1 Model specification

Although spatial versions of the probit and logit models are probably the most commonly used non-linear models in the spatial literature, in the specific area of microeconometrics the tobit model also enjoys a certain popularity (Tobin, 1958; Amemiya, 1985). In recent years some studies (Flores-Lagunes and Schnier, 2012; Xu and Lee, 2015) extended the basic tobit model to consider spatial effects. Qu and Lee (2012) introduced into the literature, two distinct typologies of spatial lag tobit models namely: the "simultaneous spatial lag tobit model", which is expressed as:

$$y_i = max\left\{0, \lambda \sum_{i=i}^{n} w_{ij} y_j + x_i \beta + \varepsilon_i \right\} \tag{4.51}$$

and the "latent spatial lag tobit model", which is expressed through the latent variable y_i^* defined by the equation:

$$y_i = max\left\{0, y_i^* \right\} \text{ where } y_i^* = \lambda \sum_{i=i}^{n} w_{ij} y_j^* + x_i \beta + \varepsilon_i \tag{4.52}$$

It is fair to say that, compared to the latent SAR Tobit model, there are fewer studies that use the simultaneous specification, possibly because, in this case, there is still no formal proof of asymptotic properties of the ML estimators. Qu and Lee (2012) also showed that the spatial lag tobit model can be motivated by two distinct branches of microeconomic theories. The first is the literature on peer effects from an exogenous social network in which the model represents a Nash equilibrium where each individual maximizes its utility. The second is related to the standard econometric modelling in cases where a large share of data can be zero.

Apart from the Qu and Lee specification, LeSage (2000) and LeSage and Pace (2009) presented a Bayesian approach in the estimation of the latent SAR Tobit model. Similarly, Donfouet et al. (2012) and Autant-Bernard and LeSage (2011) also make us of a latent SAR Tobit model using Bayesian tools.

4.4.2 Estimation

Qu and Lee (2013) showed that the log likelihood function of the latent spatial lag tobit model (Equation 4.52) can be expressed as:

$$l(\lambda,\beta,\sigma)=\sum_{I=1}^{N}I(y_i=0)ln\Phi(z_i(\theta)-\frac{1}{2}\ln(2\pi\sigma^2)\sum_{i=1}^{n}I(y_i>0)+ln|I_2-\lambda W_{22}|$$
$$-\frac{1}{2}\sum_{i=1}^{n}I(y_i>0)z_i^2(\theta) \qquad (4.53)$$

where, in addition to the notation previously introduced, $\theta=(\lambda,\beta',\sigma)$, W_{22} represents the submatrix of W which corresponds to $y_i>0$, I_2 is the identity matrix with the same dimension and the term z_i is given by $z_i=\dfrac{(y_i-\lambda w_{ij}Y_j-x_i\beta)}{\sigma}$ where $Y=\max(0, y^*)$. Qu and Lee (2015) showed that Equation 4.53 is computationally tractable and can be maximized numerically to obtain the ML estimation. They also established the consistency and asymptotic normality of the ML estimation and proved through simulations their finite sample performance and the robustness of estimates under non-normal disturbances.

4.5 Further non-linear spatial models

Apart from the non-linear models considered in this section, in the econometric literature we find various other specifications of discrete choice models including bivariate and multivariate probit and logit, ordered probit and logit, truncation, censoring, sample selection, models for count data and duration (see Greene, 2018). Some of these topics have been treated in the spatial context (e.g. Wang and Kockelman, 2009), but the field is still largely unexplored.

From the estimation point of view in the literature, various alternatives have been introduced in an attempt to reduce the computational burden that can be very heavy even with datasets of a few thousand observations. For instance, LeSage and Pace (2009) suggest the use of a Gibbs sampler algorithm in order to estimate a spatial lag probit model. However, the approach does not eliminate the problem of the inversion of the weight matrix which is present in all the other methods. As a consequence, its use is limited to samples of few thousands of observations. They report that, in a simulation experiment with a sample size of 400 and 1,200 draws of the MCMC sampler and only $m=10$ replications of the Gibbs sampler, the estimation procedure required 20 minutes with the computational time increasing proportionally to n. Thus for instance, if we increase the sample size up to $n=10,000$, the time required increases up to about 9 hours. The procedure is obviously sensitive to m, but even reducing it to, say, $m=1$ (at the expense of accuracy) the time required is still more than 1 hour. Beron and Vijverberg (2004) proposed a further alternative based on the GHK simulator to evaluate the n-dimension integral, but without succeeding to substantially reducing the computational burden. More recently Wang et al. (2013) and Arbia et al. (forthcoming) suggest the use of a partial bivariate likelihood.

74 *Spatial behavior of economic agents*

4.6 Marginal impacts in spatial non-linear models

In Chapter 3.8 we discussed the issue of calculating the marginal impact produced on the dependent variable y of unitary changes in the dependent variables of a linear spatial regression model. In Equation 4.14 we presented the analytical expression of the analogous marginal effects in a standard probit model with no spatial dependence. It is now possible to extend this analysis to the spatial probit model. The discussion which follows draws heavily on LeSage et al. (2011) who introduced this topic in the spatial literature. Let us consider the impact on y^* in location i arising from a change in an independent variable X_k at location j (LeSage et al., 2011) By definition this is given by the derivative of the expected value of y^* that can be written as:

$$E(y^*) = S(\rho)X\beta = \eta \tag{4.54}$$

where $S(\rho) = (I - \rho W)^{-1}$ of single entry $S_{ij}(\rho)$. Let us now consider the derivative of $E(y^*)$ in location i with respect to the observation of variable X_k in location j, which can be written as $\dfrac{\partial P(y_i = 1)}{\partial X_{k,j}}$. Now remember that from Equation 4.10 we can express $P(y = 1) = F \{S(\rho)X\beta\}$ as the probability distribution function at the truncation point $S(\rho)X\beta$. Therefore we can express the marginal effect in algebraic terms as:

$$\frac{\partial P(y_i = 1)}{\partial X_{k,j}} = \left(\frac{\partial F(\eta)}{\partial \eta}\right) S_{ij}(\rho)\beta_k = f(\eta_i) S_{ij.}(\rho)\beta_k \tag{4.55}$$

where f(.) represents the probability density function $f(x) = \left(\dfrac{\partial F(x)}{\partial x}\right)$ and β_k the coefficient of variable X_k in the probit model. Notice, incidentally, that if $\rho = 0$ then $S(\rho) = I_n$ (and each entry $S_{ij}(\rho) = 0$), and Equation 4.55 expresses the marginal effect in a standard a-spatial probit model as $\dfrac{\partial P(y_i = 1)}{\partial X_{k,j}} = \left(\dfrac{\partial F(\eta)}{\partial \eta}\right)\beta_k$ where changes in the x-values of neighboring location j have no influence on location i. LeSage et al. (2011) suggested representing all the marginal effects in matrix form arranging on a diagonal matrix, the vector of the probability density function evaluated at the predictions for each observation. Let us indicate this vector as $\left[df(\eta_i)\right] \equiv \{f(\eta_i)\}$ and the diagonal matrix which contains it with the symbol D{f(η)}. By construction D is symmetric with all the non-diagonal elements equal to 0s. D is symmetric. As a consequence we can re-express Equation 4.55 for the independent variable X_k in matrix form as:

$$\frac{\partial P(y_i = 1)}{\partial X'_{\nu}} = D\{f(\eta)\}S(\rho)I_n\beta_k \tag{4.56}$$

Non-linear spatial models 75

with I_n the n-by-n identity matrix. The matrix $S(\rho)$ can be now expanded in power series as:

$$S(\rho) = I_n + \rho W + \rho^2 W^2 + \dots \tag{4.57}$$

So that Equation 4.50 becomes :

$$\frac{\partial P(y_i = 1)}{\partial X'_k} = [D\{f(\eta\} + \rho D\{f(\eta)\}W + \rho^2 D\{f(\eta)\}W^2 + \dots]\beta_k \tag{4.58}$$

We can now derive the n-by-1 vector of total effects as the row summation of the matrix expressed in Equation 4.58. This is given by:

$$\left[\frac{\partial P(y_i = 1)}{\partial X'_v}\right]\iota = [D\{f(\eta\} + \rho D\{f(\eta)\}W + \rho^2 D\{f(\eta)\}W^2 + \dots]\iota\,\beta_v \tag{4.59}$$

ι being the unitary vector of dimension n. Hence:

$$\left[\frac{\partial P(y_i = 1)}{\partial X'_v}\right]\iota = D[\{f(\eta)\iota + \rho D\{f(\eta)\}\iota + \rho^2 D\{f(\eta)\}\iota + \dots]\beta_v$$

$$= D[\{f(\eta)i] \,(I-\rho)^{-1}\,\beta_v = d[\{f(\eta)\}]\,(I-\rho)^{-1}\,\beta_v \tag{4.60}$$

In practical cases it is more useful to calculate some scalar measures which can be derived by analogy of those described in section 3.8 for linear models. In particular, the average total impact is the average of the vector of total effects, that is:

$$\text{ATI} = n^{-1}\,d\{f(\eta)\}^T\,\iota\,(I-\rho)^{-1}\,\beta_v \tag{4.61}$$

Similarly, the average direct impact is given by:

$$\frac{1}{n}tr\left[\frac{\partial P(y_i = 1)}{\partial X'_v}\right] = (\text{tr}[D\{f(\eta)\}] + \rho\text{tr}[D\{f(\eta)\}W] + \rho^2\,\text{tr}[D\{f(\eta)\}W^2] + \dots)\frac{\beta_v}{n} \tag{4.62}$$

and, obviously, the average indirect impact can be derived by:

$$\text{AII} = \text{ATI} - \text{ADI} \tag{4.63}$$

Efficient methods to derive these summary measures are described in LeSage and Pace (2009). Similar summary measures can be derived for the spatial tobit models. (See the reference manual of the R command {spatial probit}-marginal.effects).

5 Space–time models[1]

5.1 Generalities

Although there are several possible alternative statistical modelling frameworks for space–time economic data (see Cressie and Wikle, 2011), the dominant approach in econometrics considers spatial panels of individuals (Baltagi, 2008; Wooldridge, 2002). Generally speaking, the term "panel data" is used to refer to a set of repeated observations on a cross-section of economic agents such as households, firms and so on. This can be achieved by surveying a number of individual economic agents over time. Panel data models have become widespread with the increasing availability of databases, surveys and other forms of data collection containing multiple observations on individual units being continuously updated. Web scraping and crowdsourcing surveys are typical examples of this type of data. Spatial panels are a special case of panel data where we also record the geographical position of individuals. Let us start by presenting the non-spatial panel data model which forms the basis for other more sophisticated frameworks. The basic model can be expressed as follows:

$$y_{it} = \alpha + \beta^T X_{it} + \varepsilon_{it} \tag{5.1}$$

In Equation 5.1 the index $i = 1, \ldots, n$ refers to the individual economic agent, the index $t = 1, \ldots, T$ is the time index, X_{it} is a non-stochastic vector of observations of the independent variables in individual i and time t, ε_{it} the innovation term such that $\varepsilon|X \approx i.i.d.N(0, \sigma_\varepsilon^2{}_n I_n)$ and α and β parameters to be estimated. The double dimensionality of panel data allows for richer modeling possibilities with respect to the single cross-section or the single time series. Typically, microeconomic panels are characterized by a large number of cross-sectional units observed in few moments in time (short panels) or a limited number of relatively long time series (long panels). When we consider spatial panel data in particular they typically fall into the category of the short panel.

5.2 Fixed and random effects models

In microeconometrics, panel data models are used to control for "unobserved heterogeneity" related to individual-specific, time-invariant characteristics which are difficult or impossible to observe although they can lead to biased and inefficient estimates of the parameters of interest if omitted. In order to model such hidden characteristics, we can assume that the error term in Equation 5.1 can be split into two components with the first capturing individual behaviors that do not change over time. In this case Equation 5.1 becomes:

$$y_{it} = \alpha_i + \beta^T x_{it} + u_i = \alpha_i + \beta^T x_{it} + (\mu_i + \varepsilon_{it}) \qquad (5.2)$$

where the error term (called "composite error u_{it}") is split into a term μ_i, which represents the error component typical of the individual observed in location i, and a term ε_{it}, which is called the "idiosyncratic component", and it is usually assumed $\varepsilon|X \approx i.i.d.N(0, \sigma_\varepsilon^2\,{}_n I_n)$. The two components are assumed to be mutually independent. The previous framework is often referred to as the "unobserved effects model". The optimal strategy for estimating the model in Equation 5.2 is selected depending on the properties of the two error components.

We can distinguish three basic models (Baltagi, 2008).

First of all, if we do not have any individual component, we do not have estimation problems. A pooled OLS estimation is unbiased, consistent and the most efficient estimation criterion. This model is called the "pooling model" and will not be discussed in this chapter.

Secondly, if the individual-specific component μ_i is uncorrelated with the independent variables, the overall error, u_{it}, is also uncorrelated with the independent variables and the OLS criterion leads to consistent estimators. However, the presence of a common error component over individuals introduces a correlation across the composite error terms and OLS estimators become inefficient and we have to consider alternative estimators. This second situation is called in the literature "random effects". We will present these models in Section 5.3.

Finally, if the individual component μ_i is correlated with the independent variables the OLS estimators become inconsistent and we have to consider the sequence of terms μ_i as a further set of n parameters to be estimated as if we had n different intercepts, say $\alpha_{it}=\alpha_i$, one for each individual although constant over time. This model is called a "fixed effects (or within) model" and it is usually estimated using OLS after an appropriate transformation which ensures consistency. We will show how to deal with these models in Section 5.4.

5.3 Random effects spatial models

The literature has recently considered panel regression models with a spatially lagged dependent variable or spatially autocorrelated disturbances, both in the context of fixed and random effects specifications (Lee and Yu, 2010b). As noted in the previous section, in a random effects specification, the unobserved individual effects are assumed to be uncorrelated with the other explanatory variables of the model and can therefore be safely treated as components of the error term. Within the context of random effects panel data models in the literature we can have two different formalizations when the model is specified as a spatial

78 *Spatial behavior of economic agents*

error. Furthermore the random effects model can be specified in a spatial lag version (see Chapter 3).

Dealing with the spatial error version of a panel data model, in a first specification, we start by assuming that the composite error u_{it} is split into a term μ_i, which is assumed to be $\mu_i \sim$i.i.d. $N(0, \sigma\mu^2)$, and a second error term ε, which is expressed in the form of a spatial error, such that, for each $t = 1, ..., T$, we can write (Baltagi et al., 2003):

$$\varepsilon_{it} = \rho W \varepsilon_{it} + \eta_i \tag{5.3}$$

as in Section 3.2.2, with η_i a well-behaved independent normal error term $\eta \approx n.i.d.N(0, \sigma_\eta^2)$.

With respect to the standard cross-sectional models, the formalization is complicated by the presence of two instead of one indices. For this reason, before proceeding any further, we will introduce some useful notation to simplify the formalization. First of all, in order to accommodate the two indices i and t, we will make use of the Kronecker product indicated by the symbol $\otimes$ such that if $A = \begin{bmatrix} a_{11} & a_{12} \\ a_{21} & a_{22} \end{bmatrix}$ and $C = \begin{bmatrix} c_{11} & c_{12} \\ c_{21} & c_{22} \end{bmatrix}$, then

$$A \otimes C = \begin{bmatrix} a_{11}C & a_{12}C \\ a_{21}C & a_{22}C \end{bmatrix} = \begin{bmatrix} a_{11}c_{11} & a_{11}c_{12} & a_{11}c_{11} & a_{21}c_{12} \\ a_{11}c_{21} & a_{11}c_{22} & a_{21}c_{21} & a_{21}c_{22} \\ a_{12}c_{11} & a_{12}c_{12} & a_{22}c_{11} & a_{22}c_{12} \\ a_{12}c_{21} & a_{12}c_{22} & a_{22}c_{21} & a_{22}c_{22} \end{bmatrix}.$$

Secondly, we also define a matrix B such that $B=(I_n-\rho W)$, with I_n an n-by-n identity matrix, W the usual spatial weight matrix and ρ the spatial error dependence parameter. From Equation 5.3, in algebraic terms, we can write the idiosyncratic error component as $\varepsilon_{it} = (I - \rho W)^{-1} \eta_i$. Given the symbolism introduced, in matrix term this becomes:

$$\varepsilon = \left(I_T \otimes B^{-1} \right) \eta \tag{5.4}$$

with η an nT-by-1 vector of the disturbances. As a consequence, the composite error term $u_i = (\mu_i + \varepsilon_{it})$ can be written in matrix form as:

$$u = \left(i_T \otimes I_n \right) \mu \left(I_T \otimes B_N^{-1} \right) e \tag{5.5}$$

with i_T a vector of one dimension T and I_T the T-by-T identity matrix. Let us now define the matrix $J_T = i_T i_T^T$ as a T-by-T matrix constituted by ones. It can be shown that the variance–covariance matrix of u can be written as:

$$_{nT}\Omega_{nT,u} = \sigma_\mu^2 \left(J_T \otimes I_n \right) + \sigma_e^2 \left(I_T \otimes B_n^T B_n \right)^{-1} \tag{5.6}$$

From which the derivation of the likelihood is straightforward although tedious.

Space–time models 79

A second alternative specification for the spatial error was considered by Kapoor et al. (2007) where the authors assume that a spatial correlation structure could be applied not only to the idiosyncratic error, but to both error components. In this case the composite disturbance term, $u = (i_T \otimes I_n)\mu + \varepsilon$, is assumed to follow a spatial autoregressive structure (Chapter 3.2.2):

$$u = \rho(I_T \otimes W)u + \eta \tag{5.7}$$

with all symbols already introduced. Following this second specification, the variance–covariance matrix of u can now be written as:

$$_{nT}\Omega_{nT,u} = \left(I_T \otimes B^{-1}\right)\Omega_\varepsilon\left(I_T \otimes B^{-T}\right) \tag{5.8}$$

where $\Omega_\varepsilon = \sigma_\mu^2 J_T + \sigma_\eta^2 I_T \otimes I_n$ is the typical variance–covariance matrix of a one-way error component model. Although similar, the economic meaning of the two spatial error specifications are very different. In the first model only the time-varying components diffuse spatially, while in the second the spatial spillovers also display a permanent component.

Moving to a spatial lag version of a random effects panel data model, this can be written as a combination of a spatial filtering on the dependent variable y and a random effects structure for the disturbances. More formally, we have:

$$(I_T \otimes A)y = X\beta + u \tag{5.9}$$

with $A = (In - \lambda W)$, and:

$$u = (i_T \otimes \mu) + \eta \tag{5.10}$$

where the variance–covariance matrix is defined as $\Sigma = \varphi(Jt \otimes I_n) + I_n$ and the parameter φ is defined as:

$$\varphi = \frac{\sigma_\mu^2}{\sigma_\eta^2} \tag{5.11}$$

This parameter represents the ratio between the variance of the individual effect and the variance of the idiosyncratic error. From Equations 5.9 and 5.10 again, the likelihood can be easily derived.

5.4 Fixed effect spatial models

As observed in Section 5.2, if we relax the hypothesis that individual effects are uncorrelated with the independent variables then we fall into the situation known as fixed effects and the OLS strategy leads to inconsistent estimators. In this case the fixed individual effects can be eliminated using a procedure called "time-demeaning" (Wooldridge, 2002) which consist of taking the first time differences of the raw data. Following this approach we replace the original variables y and X in Equation 5.2 with the vector of the demeaned values given by:

80 *Spatial behavior of economic agents*

$$\tilde{y}_{it} = y_{it} - \bar{y}_i \tag{5.12}$$

with $\bar{y}_i = \dfrac{\sum\limits_{t=1}^{T} y_{it}}{T}$ the time mean at location i and similarly for X. This operation has the effect of removing the constant term from the regression. From a statistical point of view, the random effects hypothesis is associated to the idea of sampling individuals from an infinite population, which has led Elhorst (2009) to consider it practically irrelevant in the spatial econometric contexts. However, the current literature tends to concentrate on the statistical properties of the individual effects, which in both cases are random variables. Hence the crucial distinction becomes whether we can assume the error to be correlated with the regressors or not. The Hausman (1978) test is the standard procedure to test the hypothesis of correlation (see Lee and Yu, 2012, for a thorough discussion on this topic).

5.5 Estimation

5.5.1 Introduction

Spatial panel models expressed in terms of either random or fixed effects, can be estimated employing a maximum likelihood or a generalized method of moments approach. Generally speaking the pros and cons of the two methods are those discussed already when dealing with cross-sectional data (Section 3.2). The ML procedure is fully efficient, but is also computationally more demanding and relies on the distributional hypothesis of residual normality. On the other hand, a GMM strategy is easier computationally and does not need any distributional assumption, so estimates are more distributionally robust. In this section we will discuss with a certain detail both approaches.

5.5.2 Maximum likelihood

The standard procedures developed for ML estimation of both spatial lag and spatial error panels are a combination of the standard time-demeaning technique of non-spatial panel data (Wooldridge, 2002) and the ML framework for cross-sectional data (see Chapter 3.2). Data are transformed through time-demeaning which consists of subtracting the temporal mean from each observation in order to eliminate the individual spatial effects. After time-demeaning the standard spatial lag or spatial error estimators can be applied to the transformed data so that the first-order conditions simplify to those of OLS, with an additional spatial filter on y in the spatial lag case.

5.5.2.1 Likelihood procedures for random effect models

As mentioned in Section 5.3, the random effects spatial error can be specified in two possible ways, depending on the interaction between the spatial autoregressive effect and the individual error components.

In the first spatial error specification (Baltagi et al., 2003), only the idiosyncratic error is spatially correlated, and the model can be expressed through the following three equations:

$$y = X\beta + u \tag{5.13}$$
$$u = (i_T \otimes \mu) + \varepsilon \tag{5.14}$$

and

$$\varepsilon = \rho(i_T \otimes \mu)\varepsilon + \eta \tag{5.15}$$

with the scaled errors' covariance expressed by:

$$\Sigma_{SEM-RE} = J_T \otimes \left(T\varphi I_n + (B^T B)^{-1}\right) + E_T \otimes \left(B^T B\right)^{-1} \tag{5.16}$$

having indicated with the symbols $\bar{J}_T = \dfrac{J_T}{T}$ and $E_T = I_T - J_T$. From Equation 5.16, it follows immediately that the likelihood function can be maximized in an estimation phase.

In the second spatial error specification (Kapoor et al., 2007) the spatial model applies to both the individual and the idiosyncratic error component and can be expressed through the set of equations:

$$y = X\beta + u \tag{5.17)}$$
$$u = (i_T \otimes \mu) + \varepsilon \tag{5.18}$$

and

$$u = \rho(I_T \otimes W)u + \varepsilon \tag{5.19}$$

where the scaled errors' covariance to be substituted into the likelihood is:

$$\Sigma_{KKP} = (\varphi J_T + I_T) \otimes \left(B^T B\right)^{-1} \tag{5.20}$$

Again Equation 5.20 constitutes the basis for building up the likelihood to be maximized.

Finally, the general likelihood function for the random effects spatial lag panel model combined with any error covariance structure Σ represents the panel data version of the spatial lag cross-sectional model discussed in Section 3.2. From Equation 5.11 we have:

$$l = const - \frac{nT}{2}\ln(\sigma_\eta^2) + \frac{1}{2}\ln|\Sigma| + T\ln|A| - \frac{1}{2\sigma_\eta^2}$$
$$\frac{\left[(I_T \otimes A)y - X\beta\right]^T \Sigma^{-1}\left[(I_T \otimes A)y - X\beta\right]}{nT} \tag{5.21}$$

with Σ the composite error variance–covariance matrix. The likelihood is generally maximized using the iterative procedure suggested by Oberhofer and Kmenta (1974). Starting from an initial value for the spatial lag parameter λ and

82 *Spatial behavior of economic agents*

the error covariance parameters, we obtain estimates for β and σ_η^2 from the first order conditions:

$$\hat{\beta} = (X^T \Sigma^{-1} X)^{-1} X^T \Sigma^{-1} (I_T \otimes A) y \tag{5.22}$$

and

$$\sigma_\eta^2 = \frac{\left[(I_T \otimes A) y - X\beta \right]^T \Sigma^{-1} \left[(I_T \otimes A) y - X\beta \right]}{nT} \tag{5.23}$$

The likelihood reported in Equation 5.21 can be then concentrated and maximized with respect to the parameters contained in A and Σ. The estimated values are then used to update the expression for Σ^{-1} and the steps are repeated until convergence.

5.5.2.2 Likelihood procedures for fixed effect models

From a computational point of view, according to the framework introduced by Elhorst (2003), fixed effects estimation of spatial panel models is accomplished as a pooled estimation on time-demeaned data. Let us start by considering the panel data version of the spatial lag model described in Section 3.2. In this case, in order to estimate the parameters, we need to correct the likelihood of the pooled model by adding a spatial filtering on y using the filter $I_T \otimes A$, with $A = (I_n - \lambda W)$ and λ being, as usual, the spatial lag parameter (Elhorst, 2003). We also need to consider the explicit expression for the determinant of the spatial filter matrix $|I_T \otimes A|$ which is equal to $|A|$ raised to the power of T. The validity of Elhorst's procedures relies on a property that guarantees that $\Sigma(I_n \otimes A) y = (I_n \otimes A) \Sigma y$, for each matrix Σ, so that demeaning the spatially lagged data is equivalent to spatially lagging the demeaned data (see Mutl and Pfaffermayr, 2011; Kapoor et al., 2007).

An efficient two-step iterative estimation procedure can be obtained as follows. First of all let us consider the vector of the demeaned values for X and Y defined as in Equation 5.12. This operation has the effect of removing the constant term from the regression. Secondly, consider the residuals derived from the demeaned model with a further spatial filter on y, defined as:

$$\tilde{\eta} = (I_T \otimes A) \tilde{y} - \tilde{X}\beta \tag{5.24}$$

Thirdly, we can derive the likelihood, concentrated with respect to β and σ_η^2 :

$$l = const - \frac{nT}{2} \ln(\sigma_e^2) + T \ln|A| - \frac{nT}{2} \ln(\tilde{\eta}^T \tilde{\eta}) \tag{5.25}$$

that can be maximized with respect to λ. The value of λ thus obtained is used in a generalized least squares step, imposing the following first order conditions:

$$\hat{\beta} = \left(\tilde{X}^T \tilde{X} \right)^{-1} \tilde{X} (I_T \otimes A) \tilde{y} \tag{5.26}$$

Space–time models   83

and

$$\sigma_{\tilde{\eta}}^2 = \frac{\tilde{\eta}^T \tilde{\eta}}{nT} \tag{5.27}$$

In this way we obtain a new expression for the errors to be used in Equation 5.24. The procedure is then iterated until convergence.

The same procedure can be easily adapted to the spatial error model specification. Again, an efficient two-step procedure can be based on concentrating the likelihood with respect to β and $\sigma_{\tilde{\eta}}^2$ obtaining:

$$l = const - \frac{nT}{2}\ln(\sigma_{\tilde{\eta}}^2) + T\ln|B| - \frac{nT}{2}\ln(\tilde{\eta}^T\tilde{\eta}) \tag{5.28}$$

where the residuals from the demeaned model are now filtered using the following expression:

$$\tilde{\eta} = (I_T \otimes B)\tilde{y} - \tilde{X}\beta \tag{5.29}$$

with $B = (I - \rho W)$. Equation 5.28 can then be maximized with respect to ρ. The value of ρ obtained from the maximization of Equation 5.28 can used in a generalized least squares step, imposing the following first order conditions:

$$\hat{\beta} = \left(\tilde{X}^T \tilde{X}\right)^{-1} \tilde{X}\tilde{y} \tag{5.30}$$

and

$$\sigma_{\tilde{\eta}}^2 = \frac{\tilde{\eta}^T \tilde{\eta}}{nT} \tag{5.31}$$

obtaining new expressions for the errors to be used in Equation 5.29 and the procedure can be iterated until convergence. The methodology described can be easily extended to the SARAR specification as shown for instance by Millo and Pasini (2010).

According to Anselin et al. (2008) the operation of time-demeaning alters the properties of the joint distribution of errors, introducing serial dependence. To solve this problem, Lee and Yu (2010a) suggest a different orthonormal transformation (For a discussion and simulation results, see Lee and Yu, 2010b; Millo and Piras, 2012).

5.5.3 The generalized method of moments approach

Generalized method of moments estimators of spatial panel models use both spatial Cochrane–Orcutt transformations (Chapter 3.2), to filter out the spatial dependence, and the standard GLS or time-demeaning transformations (Section 5.5.2). The spatial Cochrane–Orcutt transformations are based on consistent estimates of the spatial parameters. Although the approach is rather general, we will follow the literature (Kapoor et al., 2007; Millo and Piras, 2012) and limit

84　*Spatial behavior of economic agents*

ourselves to the spatial error model, while referring to the existing literature for the extension to a spatial lag or a spatial SARAR version (Mutl and Pfaffermayr, 2011).

5.5.3.1　Generalized method of moments procedures for random effects models

Kapoor et al. (2007) extended to the panel case the generalized moment estimator suggested in Kelejian and Prucha (1999) for a cross-sectional model presented in Section 3.2.2. The authors present an estimation procedure which enables the estimation of the spatial parameter ρ of the error process and of the two variance components of the disturbance term, respectively $\sigma_1^2 = \sigma_\mu^2 + \sigma_\eta^2$ and σ_η^2. They then introduce the following moment conditions:

$$
E\begin{bmatrix}
\dfrac{1}{n(T-1)}\varepsilon^T Q_0 \varepsilon \\[2mm]
\dfrac{1}{n(T-1)}\bar{\varepsilon}^T Q_0 \bar{\varepsilon} \\[2mm]
\dfrac{1}{n(T-1)}\bar{\varepsilon}^T Q_0 \varepsilon \\[2mm]
\dfrac{1}{n(T-1)}\varepsilon^T \varepsilon \\[2mm]
\dfrac{1}{n(T-1)}\bar{\varepsilon}^T \bar{\varepsilon} \\[2mm]
\dfrac{1}{n(T-1)}\bar{\varepsilon}^T \varepsilon
\end{bmatrix}
=
\begin{bmatrix}
\sigma_\eta^2 \\[2mm]
\sigma_\eta^2 \dfrac{1}{n} tr(W^T W) \\[2mm]
0 \\[2mm]
\sigma_1^2 \\[2mm]
\sigma_1^2 \dfrac{1}{n} tr(W^T W) \\[2mm]
0
\end{bmatrix}
\tag{5.32}
$$

where, $Q_0 = \dfrac{I_T - J_T}{T}$ and I_N is the (time-)demeaning matrix, so that $Q_0 y = \tilde{y}$ (see previous section). Furthermore, we define $\varepsilon = u - \rho\bar{u}$, $\bar{\varepsilon} = \bar{u} - \rho\bar{\bar{u}}$, $\bar{u} = (I_T \otimes W_n)u$ and $\bar{\bar{u}} = (I_T \otimes W_n)\bar{u}$.

The estimator implied by Equation 5.32 is based on the fact that in a random effects model without a spatial lag of the dependent variable, the OLS estimator of β is consistent, therefore the OLS residuals can be employed in the GMM procedure.

While a first set of GMM estimators is based only on the first three equations assigning equal weights to them, a second set of estimators make use of all of the moment conditions and an optimal weighting scheme: the inverse of the variance covariance matrix of the sample moments at the true parameter values under the assumption of normality (see Kapoor et al., 2007). A third set of estimators can also be defined making use of all moment conditions but with a simplified weighting scheme and can be used when computational difficulties arise in calculating the elements of the asymptotic variance covariance matrix of the sample moments.

While the first estimator can be used to perform a spatial Cochrane–Orcutt transformation in order to eliminate individual effects, the data are further pre-multiplied by $I_{nT} - \left(\dfrac{1-\sigma_\nu}{\sigma_1}\right)Q_0$ using a standard approach in the panel data literature. In this case the feasible GLS estimator reduces to an OLS calculated on the "doubly" transformed model. Finally, small sample inference can be based on the following expression for the parameter's variance–covariance matrix:

$$\Gamma = (X^{*T}\Omega_\varepsilon^{-1}X^*)^{-1} \tag{5.33}$$

where the variables X^* are the result of a spatial Cochrane–Orcutt transformation of the original model, and both X^* and Ω_ε^{-1} are dependent on the estimated values of ρ, σ_μ^2 and σ_1^2.

5.5.3.2 Generalized method of moments procedures for fixed effects models

If we choose to adopt a fixed effects model, we can exploit a modification of the above procedure. Mutl and Pfaffermayr (2011) noted that, under the fixed effects assumption, OLS estimators of the regression equation are no longer consistent and suggested replacing the OLS residuals with the spatial two-stage least squares within residuals. In the spatial error case, a simple within-estimator will produce consistent estimates of the model parameters. Following this idea, we can reformulate the first three moments conditions of Kapoor et al. (2007) replacing the residuals with the within residuals and then estimate the spatial parameter using the GMM restricted to the first three moments conditions. The model parameters are then obtained by OLS after a further spatial Cochrane–Orcutt transformation of the within transformed variables.

5.6 A glance at further approaches in spatial panel data modeling

The literature on spatial panel data models has grown rapidly in recent years and the largest number of theoretical and applied papers published in spatial econometrics are now related to this topic (see Arbia, 2012 for a review). The basic frameworks presented here are only a small description of a much larger field of research and applications. Excellent survey papers in this area are provided by Baltagi and Pesaran (2007), the review article by Lee and Yu (2010b) and the book by Elhorst (2014) to which we refer the reader for more details. Furthermore, we limit ourselves to what are referred to in the literature as static panel data models which do not include any time lag. When a time lag is included we deal with what are termed "dynamic spatial panel data models". This large class of models are further distinguished into "stable" and "unstable" models and include the discussion of important issues such as spatial unit roots, spatial co-integration and explosive roots. Despite the interest in these models they are not included in this book where we want to keep the discussion as simple as possible. Furthermore, for this class of models, no pre-defined package is currently available in the language R. (For an exhaustive review of these topics see Lee and Yu, 2011; Baltagi et al., 2013; Bai and Li, 2018;,Li et al., 2019; Orwat-Acedańska, 2019.)

Example 5.1: Insurance data

Although there is great interest in the current scientific debate on spatial panel data for micro-data, it is still difficult to find freely available datasets to test the methods discussed in this chapter referring to the single individual agent, because most of the applications so far are still confined to regional aggregated data. However, just to give the reader a taste of the possible applications, in this example we will make use of regional data, but treating them as if they were individuals, considering the coordinates of the centroids of each area as point data. The dataset {splm}Insurance contains data on insurance consumption in the 103 Italian provinces from 1998 to 2002 and contains different variables among which the "real per capita gross domestic product" and the "real per capita bank deposit". In what follows we will build up a model where we explain the per capita bank deposit as a function of per capita GDP. The locations of the 103 centroids are given in Figure 5.1.

We start by estimating a pooled model with no spatial components with OLS obtaining the results in Table 5.1. We then estimate the different specifications of spatial panel data models. In all cases we used a k-nearest neighbor setting k = 3. We start considering the results of a random coefficient models. Remember that in the case of random coefficients, we have an extra parameter φ described in Equation 5.11 which is the ratio between the variance of the individual effect and the variance of the idiosyncratic error.

The first model is a panel model without spatial effects which leads to the results estimated with maximum likelihood in Table 5.2, where all parameters including φ are significant.

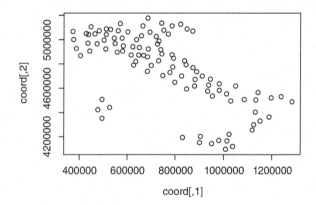

Figure 5.1 Centroids of the 103 Italian provinces.

Space–time models 87

The second model is a spatial lag random effects model estimated with maximum likelihood which leads to the results in Table 5.3. Notice that in this specification the spatial correlation parameter is positive and significant.

The third model is a spatial error random effects model with the specification of Baltagi et al. (2003) estimated with maximum likelihood which leads to the results in Table 5.4.

Table 5.1 Output of a pooled regression with no spatial components of the per capita bank deposit expressed as a function of per capita GDP in the 103 Italian provinces. Estimation method: maximum likelihood

Parameter		Standard error	t-test	p-value
Intercept	−2088.1	424.46	−6.436	1.822e − 010
Real per capita GDP	0.615	0.0179	34.235	2.2e − 16

$R^2 = 0.69556$

Table 5.2 Output of a panel data random effect model with no spatial components of the per capita bank deposit expressed as a function of per capita GDP in the 103 Italian provinces. Estimation method: maximum likelihood

Parameter		Standard error	t-test	p-value
Intercept	1346.5	999.68	13.4689	2.2e − 16
Real per capita GDP	0.272	0.052	−5.217	1.816e − 07

$\varphi = 28.6664$ (0.0001)

Table 5.3 Output of a spatial lag panel data random effect model of the per capita bank deposit expressed as a function of per capita GDP in the 103 Italian provinces. Estimation method: maximum likelihood

Parameter		Standard error	t-test	p-value
Intercept	2078.1	756.98	2.745	0.0006
Real per capita GDP	0.1027	0.0456	2.541	0.011

$\varphi = 14.627$ (0.0002); $\lambda = 0.546$ (p-value < 2.2e − 16)

Table 5.4 Output of a spatial error panel data random effect model of the per capita bank deposit expressed as a function of per capita GDP in the 103 Italian provinces. Specification of Baltagi et al. (2003). Estimation method: maximum likelihood

Parameter		Standard error	t-test	p-value
Intercept	−186.733	608.442	−0.306	0.758
Real per capita GDP	0.506	0.033	15.219	<2e − 16

$\varphi = 4.592$ (p-value = 2.393e − 07); $\rho = 0.663$ (p-value < 2.2e − 16)

88 *Spatial behavior of economic agents*

The fourth model is a spatial error, random effects model with the specification of Kapoor et al. (2007) estimated with maximum likelihood which leads to the results in Table 5.5. In these last two models the spatial error correlation parameters are positive and significant and of comparable absolute values in the two specifications.

Remaining in the area of random effects we have a last case of spatial error, but using GMM as estimation method giving the results in Table 5.6. In all models except the last, the estimated variance of the individual effect is much bigger than that of the idiosyncratic error, the latter showing substantial spatial correlation. This is a strong evidence in favor of a spatial process in the errors.

We now move to consider the case of a fixed effect. Notice that in this case we do not have an intercept to the model due to the operation of demeaning described in Equation 5.12. We start with spatial lag, random effects model using maximum likelihood, which gives the results in Table 5.7.

Finally, for the case of a fixed effect, with spatial error, random effects model, using maximum likelihood we have Table 5.8. If we adopt a random effect approach notice that the estimates of the parameters β are not too different in the

Table 5.5 Output of a spatial error panel data random effect model of the per capita bank deposit expressed as a function of per capita GDP in the 103 Italian provinces. Specification of Kapoor et al. (2007). Estimation method: maximum likelihood

Parameter		Standard error	t-test	p-value
Intercept	403.618155	759.860	0.531	0.5953
Real per capita GDP	0.4659	0.036	12.84	<2e – 16

φ = 5.452 (p-value = 3.852e – 07); ρ = 0.611333 (p-value < 2.2e – 16)

Table 5.6 Output of a spatial error panel data random effect model of the per capita bank deposit expressed as a function of per capita GDP in the 103 Italian provinces. Estimation method: GMM

Parameter		Standard error	t-test	p-value
Intercept	–208.971	716.670	–0.292	0.771
Real per capita GDP	0.500	0.034	14.659	<2e – 16

φ = 0.785; ρ = 0.623

Table 5.7 Output of a spatial lag panel data fixed effect model of the per capita bank deposit expressed as a function of per capita GDP in the 103 Italian provinces. Estimation method: maximum likelihood

Parameter		Standard error	t-test	p-value
Real per capita GDP	–0.3466	0.049	–7.024	2.152e – 12

λ = 0.448 (p-value < 2.2e – 16)

Table 5.8 Output of a spatial error panel data random effect model of the per capita bank deposit expressed as a function of per capita GDP in the 103 Italian provinces. Estimation method: maximum likelihood

Parameter		Standard error	t-test	p-value
Real per capita GDP	−0.274	0.062	−4.393	1.117e − 05

ρ = 0.477 (p-value < 2.2e − 16)

various specifications and from those obtained with a non-spatial specifications. Notice also, however, that looking at the standard errors, those related to the pooled estimators are the smallest so that we can think they are underestimating the true values and provide a less reliable estimate biased towards the rejection of the null hypothesis.

In the two cases of the fixed effects models, in contrast, the β coefficients become negative with similar absolute values. Spatial correlation is always positive and significant in all specifications confirming the need to introduce these corrections in the case examined.

Note

1 We are thankful to Giovanni Millo for collaborating in the writing of this chapter.

Part III

Modeling the spatial locational choices of economic agents

6 Preliminary definitions and concepts in point pattern analysis

This chapter introduces various important spatial concepts relating to points whose spatial location is considered to be random. It introduces the general concept of a point pattern, of complete spatial randomness (to be used as a benchmark) and the ideas of cluster and inhibitory point patterns. It further presents various indices of spatial randomness and statistical testing procedures to verify the significance of the departure from the complete spatial randomness (CSR) case (quadrat counting and the Clarke–Evans test)

6.1 Spatial point patterns of economic agents

The aim of this chapter is to introduce the necessary framework, definitions and concepts to identify the spatial location patterns of economic agents. The typical dataset providing the micro-geographical distribution of economic events and activities in a given study area consists of a set of spatial coordinates indicating their locations. In the terminology of spatial statistics, if the observed locations of economic agents (such as firms' establishments and customers' houses) have a negligible physical size with respect to the geographical dimension of the whole study area, the set of their geographical coordinates is called a "spatial point pattern".

Spatial point patterns, like any other types of data, can be analyzed using statistical methods designed to assess why the observed points are arranged in a given pattern. This can be of importance for two main reasons: firstly, an analysis of the spatial distribution of points can be a valid approach to identifying the behavioral models in all those cases where we have prior knowledge of the underlying data generating mechanisms. This is the case, for example, of the spatial distribution of firms over a given area, where economic theories may point to the existence of certain particular configurations, as we shall see a little later on. Secondly, when our knowledge of the phenomenon is rather limited, as in the case of a preliminary exploratory analysis, the evidence gathered from an analysis of the point pattern may constitute the initial phase of the description and formalization of the phenomenon itself.

Figure 6.1 shows the spatial point pattern of the 164 start-up firms in the tourism and hospitality sector in the main island of Sicily in 2010. When observing

94 Locational choices of economic agents

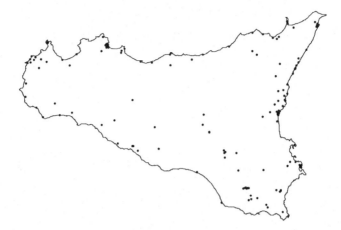

Figure 6.1 Locations of start-up firms in the tourism and hospitality sector in Sicily, 2010.

this map, the first question that comes to mind is whether or not the economic activities are purely randomly scattered in space or whether, on the contrary, they follow a regular pattern which may be regarded as having some economic importance. For example, firms may tend to cluster, or to localize, in particular locations, such as the seaside. As it is often the case in econometric analysis, the first step towards the identification of any interesting regularities involves a process of abstracting the phenomenon we wish to study from any disturbing factors. In this context, we can proceed by considering the economic activities as if they were located in a homogeneous space. This process can only be partially legitimized in that it invariably eliminates other factors which may prove to be of importance in our analysis of localization processes (such as, for example, the presence of useful infrastructure or proximity to communication routes). However, it does enable us to make a start.

6.2 The hypothesis of complete spatial randomness

Figure 6.2 illustrates three different artificial examples of spatial point patterns in a square area. In particular, the first shows local aggregations of points, which could be due to some form of clustering mechanism or to territorial variation within the considered area. Figure 6.2b depicts a pattern where points are distributed approximately regularly over the area, suggesting that a mechanism may have favored inhibition amongst points' locations and encouraged an even spatial distribution.

The pattern in Figure 6.2c does not show any kind of systematic structure and might be considered a completely random pattern. The basic key concept, which represents the starting point for the analysis of any spatial point pattern, is the hypothesis of complete spatial randomness (Diggle, 2003; Cressie, 1993).

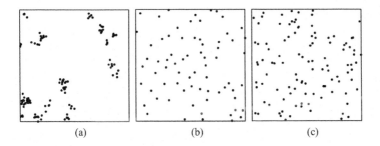

Figure 6.2 Paradigmatic examples of spatial point patterns: (a) aggregated pattern; (b) regular pattern; (c) random pattern.

This benchmark hypothesis for a spatial point pattern asserts, heuristically, that the points have been generated under two specific conditions:

i "stationarity", the constant propensity to host points within the pattern: that is, the area of the pattern is homogeneous;
ii "independence", the absence of spatial interactions amongst points: that is, each point's location is independent of the other points' locations.

Generally, the first step in the inferential analysis of a spatial point pattern consists of deciding whether the observed pattern is consistent with the CSR hypothesis. As in other branches of statistics, inferential analysis is primarily conducted by relying on formal stochastic mechanisms generating data. In this specific context, stochastic processes are labelled as spatial point processes.

6.3 Spatial point processes

A spatial point process is a stochastic process that generates objects in the plane forming a countable set of points $x_i = (x_{1i}, x_{2i}) : i = 1, 2, ...$, in which x_{1i} and x_{2i} are, respectively, the horizontal and vertical spatial coordinates of the ith object (Diggle, 2003). Point processes can be used to analyze spatial point pattern data within a model-based perspective, through comparisons between the theoretical properties of an assumed underlying point process model and their empirical counterparts estimated on the observed data.

The main properties of a generic spatial point process are the theoretical summary descriptions called "first-order" and "second-order" intensity functions. The first-order intensity function can be formally defined as follows (Diggle, 2003; Cressie, 1993):

$$\lambda(x) = \lim_{|dx| \to 0} \left\{ \frac{E[N(dx)]}{|dx|} \right\} \qquad (6.1)$$

96   Locational choices of economic agents

To clarify the notation here employed (borrowed from Diggle, 2003), dx is an infinitesimally small spatial region containing the generic point x, $N(dx)$ represents the number of points located in it and $|dx|$ denotes its area.

Equation 6.1 can be interpreted as the expected number of points per unit located within an infinitesimal region centered on the generic point x. Therefore, heuristically, $\lambda(x)dx$ expresses the probability of finding a point around the location x. If the first-order intensity is constant throughout the space, that is if $\lambda(x) = \lambda$, it represents the expected number of events per unitary area and the point process is stationary (Diggle, 2003).

The second-order intensity function can be similarly defined as follows (Diggle, 2003; Cressie, 1993):

$$\lambda_2(x,y) = \lim_{|dx|,|dy| \to 0} \left\{ \frac{E\left[N(dx) N(dy) \right]}{|dx||dy|} \right\}, \qquad (6.2)$$

where x and y denote two distinct generic events in the area. Informally, $\lambda_2(x,y)$ can be interpreted as the expected number of points located in locations x or y and hence $\lambda_2(x,y)dxdy$ can be interpreted as the probability that two points locate in two infinitesimal regions centered in x and y and with surface areas dx and dy respectively (Diggle et al., 2007). Therefore, Equation 6.2 is the appropriate theoretical summary description of the spatial dependence amongst points.

If a process is stationary we have $\lambda_2(x,y) \equiv \lambda_2(x-y)$; furthermore, if a process is stationary and also isotropic, $\lambda_2(x,y)$ depends only on the distance, say d, between x and y and hence $\lambda_2(x,y) = \lambda_2(d)$ (Diggle, 2003).

6.3.1 Homogeneous Poisson point process

Over the years, the spatial statistics literature has proposed a number of spatial point processes that can be used to model and analyze various kinds of point patterns. All of them are somewhat rooted in the homogeneous Poisson point process, which can essentially be seen as the basic framework for the building of more complex models. Moreover, it can be used as the reference benchmark model, since it properly represents the CSR hypothesis. Indeed, following Diggle (2003), the homogeneous Poisson process in a finite region A, with area $|A|$, and characterized by a first-order intensity $\lambda > 0$ can be defined as fulfilling the following two conditions:

i   The number of points, say n, that can be generated in A follows a Poisson distribution with mean $\lambda|A|$.
ii   Given n, the n points are generated *i.i.d.* according to the uniform distribution on A.

It can be easily noted that these conditions mirror closely the definition of CSR hypothesis. On one hand, condition i implies that the intensity is constant, and

Preliminary definitions and concepts 97

hence it corresponds exactly to the stationarity condition of CSR hypothesis; on the other, condition ii parallels the independence condition of CSR hypothesis, as it prescribes that the points are generated independently to each other.

In order to generate a point pattern as a realization of the homogeneous Poisson process on A, given λ, two simulation steps can be followed. First, the simulation of the n number of points from the Poisson distribution with mean proportional to the chosen value of λ is carried out. Secondly, once the random value n is returned, the n points are generated independently according to a uniform distribution on A. Figure 6.3 shows two possible realizations of the homogeneous Poisson process in a unit square, with λ parameter equal to, respectively, 50 and 100.

Alternatively, instead of referring to a random value of n, we might be interested in carrying out simulations that are conditional on a fixed number of points. As we will see in Chapter 7, conditional simulated patterns have a crucial importance in inferential analysis because they can represent useful hypothetic theoretical counterfactuals of observed patterns. Conditional simulations can be carried out following the second step of the procedure mentioned above with n as a chosen constant. By way of illustration, Figure 6.4 shows two possible

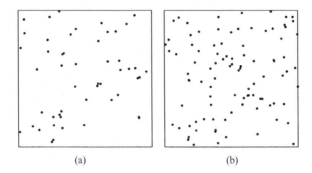

Figure 6.3 Two realizations of a homogeneous Poisson process in a unit square: (a) with parameter $\lambda = 50$; (b) with parameter $\lambda = 100$.

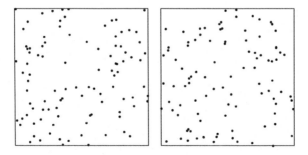

Figure 6.4 Two realizations of a homogeneous Poisson process conditional on 100 points in a unit square.

98 *Locational choices of economic agents*

partial realizations of a homogeneous Poisson process conditional on 100 points in a unit square.

The homogeneous Poisson process can act as a unique benchmark model because any other point process would necessarily generate point patterns that are more aggregated (as in Figure 6.2a) or more regular (as in Figure 6.2b) than a CSR pattern. Therefore, point processes can be loosely classified into "aggregated processes" and "regular processes".

6.3.2 *Aggregated point processes*

The most frequent violation of the CSR hypothesis that can occur in the context of economic data is probably that due to aggregation. Aggregation of points can essentially arise because of "true contagion" of one point by another or because of "apparent contagion" between points (Arbia and Espa, 1996). When dealing with point patterns of firms, apparent contagion may arise if exogenous factors lead to the location of firms in certain specific geographical zones. For instance, firms may cluster locally in order to exploit favorable conditions within the area, such as the presence of useful infrastructure, proximity to communication routes or the possibility of benefiting from public incentives by locating in specific areas outside residential centers. On the other hand, true contagion may occur when the presence of one event in a given area stimulates the presence of other events nearby. For instance, the presence of "leader" firms could encourage the settlement of "followers" in the same area because of the working of knowledge spillovers.

Apparent contagion is related to the violation of the CSR condition of stationarity; true contagion to that of independence. Two of the main classes of models that generate aggregated point patterns are the inhomogeneous Poisson processes, leading to apparent contagion, and the Poisson cluster processes, leading to true contagion.

6.3.2.1 *Inhomogeneous Poisson point processes*

Apparent contagion is the result of relaxing the condition of stationarity of the homogeneous Poisson process. The lack of stationarity implies that the first-order intensity is no longer constant throughout the territory. It may be higher in certain sub-regions of the area and lower in others. As a consequence, there will be zones with a relatively high intensity of points and others with a relatively low intensity of points, and this will produce an aggregated pattern.

Apparent contagion will thus occur as a result of the fact that, although each point is located independently of each other, the presence of some zones that are more suited to accommodating points than others leads to aggregations (Arbia and Espa, 1996).

A class of point processes that describe aggregated point patterns due to apparent contagion is the class of inhomogeneous Poisson processes which can be simply defined by replacing the constant first-order intensity λ of the homogeneous

Poisson point process with a non-negative function $\lambda(x)$ that varies on space. Therefore, following Diggle (2003), an inhomogeneous Poisson process in a finite region A, with area $|A|$, and characterized by a spatially varying first-order intensity $\lambda(x)$ is such that:

i The number of points, say n, that can be generated in A follows a Poisson distribution with mean $\int_A \lambda(x)\,dx$.

ii Given n, the n points are generated *i.i.d.* on A according to a distribution with probability density function proportional to $\lambda(x)$.

A common computational algorithm to simulate inhomogeneous Poisson processes was first suggested by Lewis and Shedler (1979). It is based on "thinning", that is: first of all it generates a homogeneous Poisson process of intensity λ_0 equal to the maximum value of the function $\lambda(x)$ on the study region A; then it deletes each point, independently of other points, with deletion probability $\lambda(x)/\lambda_0$. By way of example, Figure 6.5 shows two partial realizations of an inhomogeneous Poisson process in a unit square, with spatially varying intensity function $\lambda(x) = 100\exp(-3x_1)$, where x_1 is the horizontal coordinate.

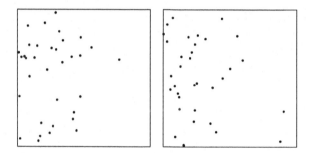

Figure 6.5 Two realizations of an inhomogeneous Poisson process in a unit square with intensity $\lambda(x) = 100\exp(-3x_1)$ bounded by 100.

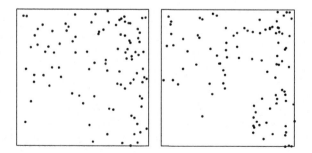

Figure 6.6 Two realizations of an inhomogeneous Poisson process conditional on 100 points in a unit square with intensity $\lambda(x_1, x_2) = x_1^2 + x_2^2$.

100 *Locational choices of economic agents*

If we are interested in simulations conditional on a fixed number of points n, we can follow a similar algorithm which consists of generating a point $x_i = (x_{i1}, x_{i2})$ from the uniform distribution on A and then accepting (or rejecting) it with probability $\lambda(x_i)/\lambda_0$. The algorithm repeats this step continuously and stops when n points have been accepted. Figure 6.6 shows two realizations of a conditional inhomogeneous Poisson process, with 100 points, characterized by $\lambda(x_1, x_2) = x_1^2 + x_2^2$.

6.3.2.2 Cox processes

Another class of point processes characterized by apparent contagion that can be useful in the context of economic applications is represented by the Cox processes. They represent a natural extension of the inhomogeneous Poisson processes where the source of spatial inhomogeneity, that is the intensity function $\lambda(x)$, rather than being deterministic, is stochastically driven by a random process. Therefore, these processes are "doubly stochastic" (Cox, 1955; Grandell, 1976; Daley and Vere-Jones, 2003) and allow explicit modeling of spatial intensity endogenously rather than exogenously.

Formally, following Diggle (2003), a Cox process in a finite region A can be defined as follows,

i The first-order intensity is generated by a non-negative random function $\Lambda(x)$ on A.

ii Given $\Lambda(x) = \lambda(x)$, the points are generated following an inhomogeneous Poisson process with intensity function $\lambda(x)$ (see Section 6.3.2.1).

Provided that $\Lambda(x)$ is stationary, the first-order and second-order intensity functions of the point process are, respectively, given as

$$\lambda = E\big[\Lambda(x)\big] \text{ and } \lambda_2(x, y) = E\big[\Lambda(x), \Lambda(y)\big].$$

Cox processes can be straightforwardly simulated by first generating $\lambda(x)$ from $\Lambda(x)$ and then generating the points using the algorithm for simulating inhomogeneous Poisson processes as described in Section 6.3.2.1. Figure 6.7 shows a partial realization of a Cox process in which $\Lambda(x)$ is a Gaussian random field with mean $\mu = 100$, variance $\sigma^2 = 0.25$ and correlation function $\rho(d) = \exp\{-d/0.25\}$ with d indicating the distance between locations. Also shown is the underlying intensity surface $\lambda(x) = \Lambda(x)$ as a grey-scale image, where the lighter areas have higher intensities.

A particularly attractive subclass of Cox processes is the so-called log-Gaussian Cox process (Møller et al., 1998). According to this type of model, $\Lambda(x) = exp\{S(x)\}$, where $\{S(x)\}$ is a Gaussian process with mean μ_S, variance σ_S^2 and correlation function $\rho_S(d)$. The log-Gaussian specification is attractive because explicit expressions can be derived for the properties of the point process.

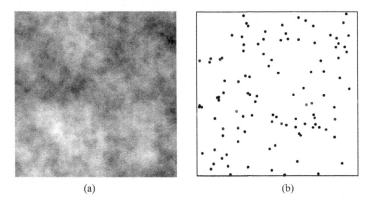

Figure 6.7 A realization of a Gaussian Cox process in a unit square with mean $\mu = 100$, variance $\sigma^2 = 0.25$ and correlation function $\rho(d) = \exp\{-d/0.25\}$: (a) the generated underlying intensity surface (grey-scale image); (b) the generated point pattern.

Indeed, exploiting the moment generating function of a log-Gaussian distribution, the first-order intensity of a log-Gaussian Cox process can be written as:

$$\lambda = E[\Lambda(x)] = E[\exp(S(x))] = \exp(\mu_S + 0.5\sigma_S^2).$$

For the covariance structure we have that $\Lambda(x)\Lambda(y) = \exp\{S(x) + S(y)\}$. Since $S(x) + S(y)$ is also Gaussian with mean $m = 2\mu_S$ and variance $v = 2\sigma_S^2[1 + \rho_S(d)]$ then $E[\Lambda(x)\Lambda(y)] = \exp(m + v/2)$ and hence:

$$\lambda_2(x, y) = E[\Lambda(x)\Lambda(y)] = \lambda^2 \exp\{\sigma_S^2 \rho_S(d)\}.$$

6.3.2.3 Poisson cluster point processes

A class of point processes that describe aggregated point patterns due to true contagion is the class of Poisson cluster processes. It was introduced by Neyman and Scott (1958) as a class of models that allow the modeling of dependence among points and hence the incorporation of an explicit form of spatial clustering (Diggle, 2003). An interesting schematic way of visualizing the occurrence of an aggregated point pattern by means of a Poisson cluster process is the "leader–follower" framework proposed by Arbia and Espa (1996). Let us consider a finite region and let us suppose that a certain number of leader firms are located within its boundaries. Then let us fix a threshold distance for local related activities and, according to this threshold, define an area of influence for each leader. For ease of simplicity we consider that this area has the same extension for all leader firms. Now let us fix a certain number of followers for each leader as the realization of a random variable. Finally, allocate the followers to the leader firms on the basis of a given bivariate distribution. For example, a bivariate uniform distribution may be used in those cases where the probability within the area of influence can be taken to be constant or, alternatively, we may consider a bivariate normal distribution if we assume that the probability of locating the followers decreases exponentially with an increase in the distance from the leader. The resulting process is the Poisson cluster process shown in Figure 6.8.

More formally, Diggle (2003) defines a Poisson cluster process in a finite region A as fulfilling:

i   The leader points are spatially distributed in A according to a homogeneous Poisson process with first-order intensity ρ.
ii The numbers of followers per leader are generated *i.i.d.* according to a given probability distribution (typically Poisson).
iii the locations of the followers are generated *i.i.d.* around their respective leaders' locations according to a given bivariate probability density function (typically normal or uniform).

Like the homogeneous Poisson process, the Poisson cluster processes are stationary and are characterized by a first-order intensity $\lambda = \rho\mu$, where μ is the mean number of followers per leader.

If a Poisson cluster process is specified using a Poisson distribution with mean μ for the random number of followers per leader and a radially symmetric normal distribution with standard deviation σ for the location of followers around their leaders, it is said to be a Thomas cluster process (Thomas, 1949). If, instead, the dispersion of followers with respect to their leaders' locations follows a uniform distribution inside a circle of radius R centered on the leader point, we have a Matérn cluster process (Matérn, 1986). The dispersion parameters σ and R represent the spatial extension of the area of influence for each leader.

Figure 6.9 shows two realizations of a Poisson cluster process in a unit square with $\rho = 25$ and $\mu = 4$. In Figure 6.9a the location of each follower relative to its

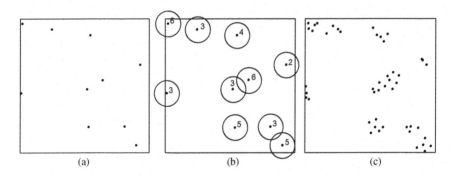

Figure 6.8 The genesis of a Poisson cluster process: (a) location of leaders; (b) setting the dimensions of the areas of influence of local related activities and location of the followers; (c) the resulting point process.

leader is realized following the uniform distribution on a random circular disc with maximum radius $R = 0.025$. In Figure 6.9b, instead, followers are dispersed around their leaders according to a radially symmetric normal distribution with $\sigma = 0.025$.

In Figure 6.9a, it can be clearly seen that the dispersion of followers within the cluster is homogeneous across all the area of influence. In contrast, the pattern represented by Figure 6.9b suggests that the followers intensity tends to diminish as the distance from the cluster center increases.

Conditioning on the number of leader points and number of followers per leader is straightforward. Rather than specifying the parameters of random variables, we simply need to fix constant values. By way of illustration, Figure 6.10 shows realizations of a Poisson cluster process conditional on fixed quantities. In Figure 6.10a the 25 groups of four followers are clearly identifiable. The visual identification of clusters is less straightforward in Figure 6.10b due to the coalescence between nearby clusters.

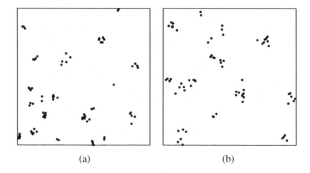

Figure 6.9 Two realizations of a Poisson cluster process in a unit square with $\lambda = 25$ and $\mu = 4$: (a) uniform dispersion of followers, with maximum radius 0.025; (b) radially symmetric normal dispersion of followers, with $\sigma = 0.025$.

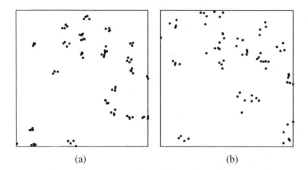

Figure 6.10 Two realizations of a Poisson cluster process in a unit square with 25 leader points and 4 followers per leader: (a) uniform dispersion of followers, with maximum radius 0.025; (b) radially symmetric normal dispersion of followers, with $\sigma = 0.025$.

 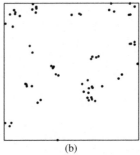

(a) (b)

Figure 6.11 Two realizations of a Poisson cluster process in a unit square with 100 followers randomly assigned amongst 25 leader points: (a) uniform dispersion of followers, with maximum radius 0.025; (b) radially symmetric normal dispersion of followers, with $\sigma = 0.025$.

For identification purposes, in order to recreate specific paradigmatic situations, we might be interested in performing simulations conditional on the total number of events on the study region. Indeed, when the number of followers per leader is randomly generated according to a Poisson distribution, the point process can be simulated by randomly allocating a fixed number of events amongst the leader points. This is illustrated in Figure 6.11 which shows two simulated patterns where the 100 followers are randomly assigned amongst the 25 leader points.

6.3.3 Regular point processes

A probably less frequent, but still relevant, form of violation of the CSR hypothesis in the context of economic data is the spatial "inhibition" that leads to regular or dispersed point patterns. Regularity in the location of economic activities, such as stores, can occur, for example, because the presence of a store in a given geographical area forces back competing stores due to the locally differentiated monopolistic or oligopolistic nature of the market. In a case like this, a store "inhibits" the location of other stores within the surrounding area. A common theoretical inhibitory model in the field of economic geography is the "central place" model introduced by Christaller (1933) and subsequently used by Lösch (1954), Isard (1956) and others in more recent years.

The first statistical formulation of an inhibitory process is historically traced back to Matérn (1960), who suggested constructing an inhibitory process starting from a realization of a homogeneous Poisson process with given intensity ρ and then deleting all pairs of generated points that are separated by a distance less than a specified threshold δ, defined as "inhibition distance". The remaining points represent a realization of the Matérn model I inhibition process.

Matérn (1960) has also proposed a somewhat "dynamic" version of this process in which the points generated by the homogeneous Poisson process are marked with "birth times", obtained as independent realizations of a uniform distribution in [0,1]. Each point is then removed if it is located within a distance δ of another point that was born earlier, whether or not the latter has itself previously been retained or removed. The remaining points constitute a realization of the Matérn model II inhibition process. Figure 6.12 shows two realizations of, respectively, Matérn model I and Matérn model II in a unit square both with $\rho = 50$ and $\delta = 0.08$. To make the two realizations directly comparable, the same random number seed has been used. It can be noted that Matérn model II tends to have a higher final first-order intensity for the same parameter values.

A further natural variation of the scheme of Matérn inhibition processes is the simple sequential inhibition (SSI) process (Diggle, 2003) which is based on the rationale that a point that has been removed cannot inhibit the occurrence of newer points. Specifically, the SSI process generates points sequentially one-by-one until a given number n of points has been reached. Each point is generated according to the uniform distribution in the region of interest independently of the previously generated points. If the newly generated point is located within a distance δ of an existing point, then it is removed; otherwise, it is retained. In order to illustrate the sequential nature of the SSI process, Figure 6.13 shows three phases of the building of a realization in a unit square with $n = 50$ and $\delta = 0.08$.

Matérn model I, Matérn model II and SSI are sometimes labelled "hard-core" inhibition processes since they strictly prevent the occurrence of points located at

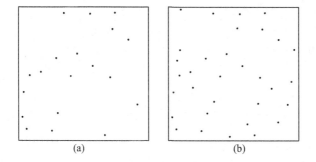

Figure 6.12 Two realizations of Matérn inhibition processes in a unit square with $\rho = 50$ and $\delta = 0.08$: (a) Matérn model I; (b) Matérn model II.

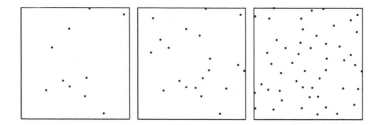

Figure 6.13 Three phases of the development of a simple sequential inhibition process in a unit square with $n = 50$ and $\delta = 0.08$.

a distance smaller than the inhibition distance. This lack of flexibility makes the hard-core processes unrealistic in describing many empirical patterns. Indeed, to describe properly numerous regular patterns, especially those of economic phenomena, a less strict inhibition criterion, be it static or dynamic, may be necessary. For example, in real circumstances it is not uncommon to find two or more stores competing with each other but being located very close to one another.

The inhibition processes that are more flexible in this respect are often labelled "soft-core" processes in that they generate patterns where the number of neighbor points within the inhibition distance δ tends to be smaller with respect to CSR patterns, but it is not zero. A popular soft-core process is the Strauss process (Strauss, 1975; Kelly and Ripley, 1976), which is characterized by three parameters, namely the spatial intensity β, the inhibition distance δ and the interaction parameter γ. A Strauss process generates n points of a pattern, say $x_1,...,x_n$, according to the following probability density function:

$$f(x_1,...,x_n) = \alpha \beta^n \gamma^s$$

where s represents the number of distinct pairs of points that are separated by a distance lower than δ and α is a normalizing constant. In practice, the Strauss process generates CSR patterns with given first-order intensity β, but in which the points have a probability equal to $1-\gamma$ of being deleted if they are located closer than δ to other points.

The parameter γ regulates the level of strictness of the inhibition mechanism, higher values of γ imply more flexibility. In particular, if $\gamma=0$ the inhibition process is hard-core as it does not allow distances among points that are lower than δ; on the other hand, if $\gamma=1$ it reduces to a homogeneous Poisson process with first-order intensity β. It is necessary to respect the condition $\gamma \leq 1$ in order to avoid the process exploding and generating an infinite number of points (Kelly and Ripley, 1976). Figure 6.14 illustrates the role of γ by showing three realizations, obtained using the same random number seed, of a Strauss process in a unit square with $\beta=50$, $\delta=0.08$ and $\gamma=0.1, 0.5$ and 0.8, respectively. The increase in the level of flexibility is clear.

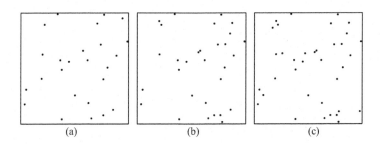

Figure 6.14 Three realizations of the Strauss process in a unit square with $\beta=50, \delta=0.08$ and (a) $\gamma=0.1$; (b) $\gamma=0.5$; (c) $\gamma=0.8$.

6.4 Classic exploratory tools and summary statistics for spatial point patterns

Traditional techniques for performing preliminary analysis of spatial point patterns consist essentially of graphical exploratory tools and formal tests for the hypothesis of complete spatial randomness. They can be subdivided into two general classes of methods: (i) quadrat-based methods and (ii) distance-based methods.

6.4.1 Quadrat-based methods

The quadrat-based approaches to the preliminary analysis of a spatial point pattern of interest, observed in a rectangular study region A, involve the partition of A into contiguous rectangular sub-regions of the same area called "quadrats". The frequencies, or counts, of points falling in the quadrats can be used to compute useful statistics or to perform tests. To begin with, if we suspect that the intensity of the underlying point process is not constant over A, we can obtain a simple estimate of the first-order intensity function by dividing the quadrat counts by the areas of their corresponding quadrats (Baddeley et al., 2015). See Figure 6.15 for an illustrative example. Let us suppose that the left panel displays a spatial point pattern of business units in a 100-kilometer-by-100-kilometer region. In order to estimate the varying intensity function of this pattern, first of all, the region is partitioned into quadrats forming a 5-by-5 grid of rectangles with an area of 400 square kilometers each; secondly, the average intensity, that is the ratio between counts and area, in each quadrat is computed. The central panel of Figure 6.15 displays the partition into quadrats and reports the corresponding intensity estimates. Since, for example, the upper-left quadrat hosts nine business units in an area of 400 square kilometers, its average intensity is $9 / 400 = 0.022$ business units per square kilometer. The pixel image of the quadrat intensities displayed in the right panel of Figure 6.15 represents an estimate of the first-order intensity function. Figure 6.15 shows that the intensity is not constant across the quadrats, as it varies from a minimum of 0.005 to a maximum of 0.038 units per square kilometer.

Strong differences among quadrat intensities provide evidence against the CSR hypothesis and hence against the assumption that the data generating process is a homogeneous Poisson point process. A Pearson's chi-squared test based on quadrat counts can be used to assess if the observed differences in intensity are strong enough to reject the (null) CSR hypothesis. Let us consider the partition of A into m quadrats of equal area a, and the let $n_1, n_2, \ldots, n_i, \ldots, n_m$ be the observed quadrat counts. If the CSR hypothesis is true then each n_i is a realization of an independent Poisson random variable with mean λa, where λ is the (unknown) first-order intensity corresponding to the expected number of points per unitary area. Considering that the natural estimate of λ is $\hat{\lambda} = n / (ma)$, where n is the total number of points observed in A and ma gives the total area

108 *Locational choices of economic agents*

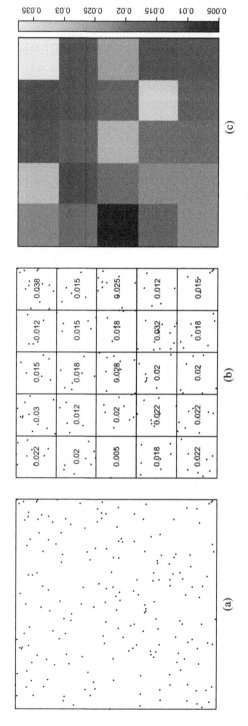

Figure 6.15 Quadrat-based estimation of intensity for a hypothetical pattern of business units: (a) point pattern; (b) quadrat average intensities (business units per square kilometer); (c) estimated intensity function.

of A, the expected count for quadrat n_i under CSR is $e_j = \hat{\lambda}a = n / m$. Therefore, the proper chi-square statistic is

$$\chi^2 = \sum_{i=1}^{m} \frac{(n_i - e_i)^2}{e_i} = \sum_{i=1}^{m} \frac{(n_i - n / m)^2}{n / m}.$$

Provided that n / m is greater than 5, if the CSR hypothesis is true then χ^2 follows approximately a χ^2_{m-1} distribution. Consequently, significantly great or small values of χ^2 indicate that the observed point pattern in A tends to be, respectively, more aggregated or more regular than a CSR pattern.

For the point pattern of business units depicted in Figure 6.15, $\chi^2 = 23.97$ with a two-sided p-value = 0.927 which imply that the CSR hypothesis cannot be rejected, and hence that the observed differences amongst the quadrat average intensities are likely due to chance.

The results of quadrat-based methods depend strongly on the size of the quadrats and hence on the partition of A. Unfortunately, the choice of the partitioning scheme is usually arbitrary and an optimal criterion to guide this choice is not available. In light of this, Grieg-Smith (1952) proposed an approach to verifying the robustness of results with respect to the size of quadrats. The approach is based on the use of different alternative partitions of A characterized by differing quadrats' size. In particular, Grieg-Smith (1952) suggests starting with a given grid of quadrats, such as a 32-by-32 one, and then obtain a series of other less granular grids by progressively aggregating the adjacent quadrats into 2-by-2, 4-by-4, 8-by-8 and so on, blocks. For each grid, it is convenient to compute the "index of dispersion" of the quadrat counts, which corresponds to the ratio between the sample variance and the sample mean of quadrat counts. If we let $\bar{n} = n / m$ indicating the sample mean of quadrat counts, the sample variance can be computed as:

$$s^2 = \frac{1}{m-1} \sum_{i=1}^{m} (n_i - \bar{n})^2$$

and hence the index of dispersion is given by:

$$\frac{s^2}{\bar{n}} = \frac{m}{n(m-1)} \sum_{i=1}^{m} (n_i - \bar{n})^2.$$

As already discussed, under CSR the quadrat counts are independent realizations of the same Poisson random variable. Since the mean and variance of a Poisson random variable are the same, the index of dispersion of a CSR pattern should be approximately equal to 1. Therefore, plotting the values of the index of dispersion for the different grids against the corresponding block size allows us to assess how the results of the quadrat-based methods are affected by the spatial scale, that is by the way the study area is partitioned. Figure 6.16 shows a plot of the index of dispersion versus block size (k-by-k) for the point pattern of

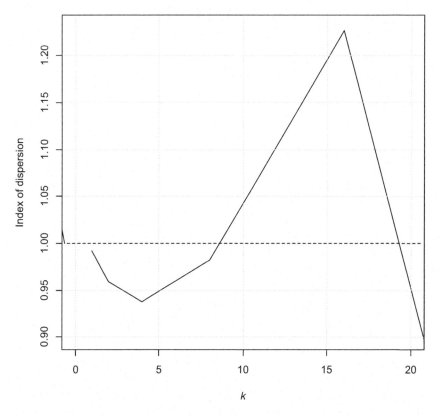

Figure 6.16 Behavior of the index of dispersion with respect to the block size (k-by-k) for the artificial data depicted in Figure 6.15.

business units depicted in Figure 6.15. The values of the index observed for each block size fluctuate around 1 thus providing evidence that the observed pattern is consistent with the CSR hypothesis at any spatial scale.

6.4.2 Distance-based methods

Distance-based approaches assess the characteristics of a spatial point pattern of interest through the analysis of the distribution of the distances among the points without subdividing the study region A coarsely into discrete sub-areas. They have the important advantage, over the quadrat-based methods, of exploiting the precise information on the location of units and not depending on the arbitrary choice of quadrat size. Indeed, while the Grieg-Smith (1952) approach allows the measurement of how the arbitrary partition of space into quadrats affects the results, it is not completely satisfactory since the index of dispersion detects only coarse discrete differences in the spatial scale.

Preliminary definitions and concepts 111

A particularly convenient kind of distance that can be used to summarize the characteristics of a spatial point pattern is the nearest-neighbor distance. If d_{ij} indicates all the pairwise distances between any generic pair of points i and j observed in the pattern, then the nearest-neighbor distance for point i is given by $d_i = \min\{d_{ij}, \forall j \neq i\}$, which represents the distance between point i and its nearest neighbor.

The distribution of the d_i values for all the points $i = 1, \ldots, n$ of an observed point pattern can give insights about the characteristics of the distribution of points. In particular, an aggregated point pattern tends to have relatively small d_i values (smaller than those of a CSR pattern); while a regular pattern tends to have relatively large d_i values (larger than those of a CSR pattern). In light of this, Clark and Evans (1954) suggested that evidence that a point pattern is not completely random can be detected through the comparison between the average of its nearest-neighbor distances d_i and the expected average nearest-neighbor distance under the hypothesis of CSR. However, since the nearest-neighbor distances among very close points can be statistically dependent, they suggested taking into consideration a random sample of the observed points and proposed the following index:

$$R = \frac{\bar{d}_O}{\bar{d}_E} \tag{6.3}$$

where $\bar{d}_O = \sum_{i=1}^{m} d_i$ is the average of the nearest-neighbor distances for m randomly selected points of the observed pattern and $\bar{d}_E$ is the expected mean nearest-neighbor distance of a homogeneous Poisson process.

Clark and Evans (1954) shown that, under a homogeneous Poisson process with first-order intensity λ, the mean nearest-neighbor distance is $1 / (2\sqrt{\lambda})$. As we have seen previously, the natural estimate of λ is $\hat{\lambda} = n / |A|$, where $|A|$ is the area of A, and hence $\bar{d}_E = 1 / (n / |A|)$.

Therefore, an observed point pattern can be considered as a realization of a homogeneous Poisson process and hence treated as a completely random pattern when $R = 1$. On the other hand, if R is significantly greater (or lower) than 1 we have evidence that the observed pattern is more regular (or more aggregated) than a CSR pattern.

The Clark–Evans index can then be used to perform a test for the CSR hypothesis. Clark and Evans (1954) derived the approximated sampling distribution of R under CSR. They found that if the underlying point process is a homogeneous Poisson process then R follows approximately a normal distribution with mean $\mu = 1$ and variance equal to $s^2 = (1 / \pi - 1 / 4) / (m\hat{\lambda})$. Therefore, two-tailed or one-tailed tests of complete spatial randomness can be conducted using the test statistic $z = (R - 1) / s^2$ and the standard normal distribution.

Donnelly (1978) has shown, however, that R can be positively biased due to edge effects, which can occur because the observed points located near the boundary of A may have an actual nearest neighbor located outside the boundary

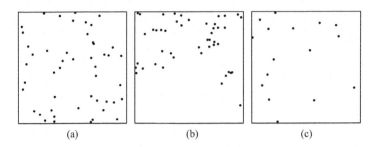

Figure 6.17 Three simulated spatial point patterns: (a) realization of a homogeneous Poisson process; (b) realization of a Poisson cluster process; (c) realization of a Matérn inhibition process.

of A. For these points it is not possible to compute the actual nearest-neighbor distance. Equation 6.3 does not account for this circumstance and hence tends to overestimate the nearest-neighbor distance and leads to positively biased estimates. Donnelly (1978) provided a formula for $\bar{d}_E$ that is adjusted for edge effects that can be used in the context of a rectangular study region. Another popular approach to edge correction consists on identifying a smaller subarea of A, say a "buffer" area, and computing $\bar{d}_O$ taking only the nearest-neighbor distances of the observed points located within the buffer area.

As an example, let us consider the three spatial point patterns depicted in Figure 6.17: the pattern on the left is a realization of a homogenous Poisson process and hence is consistent with CSR; the central pattern is a realization of a Poisson cluster process and hence is aggregated; the pattern on the left is a realization of a Matérn inhibition process and hence is regular. The Clark-Evans test has the ability to differentiate between the three paradigmatic point patterns since for the random pattern $R = 1.0957$ with a (two-tailed) p-value $= 0.1954$; for the aggregated pattern $R = 0.7256$ with a (lower-tailed) p-value $= 0.0002$; and for the regular pattern $R = 1.4229$ with an (upper-tailed) p-value $= 0.0006$.

Distance-based methods, such as the Clark–Evans index and the Clark–Evans test, have the advantage of being simple and intuitive but have also the disadvantage that they do not allow inspection of spatial location patterns at varying spatial scales simultaneously. Chapter 7 will introduce a more sophisticated approach that overcomes this limitation.

7 Models of the spatial location of individuals

This chapter introduces the exploratory tool known as the "K-function" to characterize a univariate homogeneous point pattern. It discusses the behaviour of the K-function in the benchmarking case of complete spatial randomness and in the two major violations related to clustering and inhibition. It also introduces the "Monte Carlo procedure" to test the significance of the departure from the complete spatial randomness benchmark.

7.1 Ripley's K-function

The methods used to identify the spatial location patterns of economic agents described in Chapter 6, both the quadrat-based methods and the Clark–Evans test, rely on zoning and hence require the arbitrary selection of a partitioning scheme. Therefore, they do not allow for the inspection of spatial location patterns at varying spatial scales simultaneously. In light of this, Ripley (1976; 1977) introduced the idea that a single number (as given by an index or a test statistic) cannot summarize the observed pattern at different spatial scales, and, by extending the work of Bartlett (1964), he proposed a functional statistic able to overcome the problem. The importance of this statistic, the K-function, lies in its dual role as a summary descriptive measure of the spatial characteristics of the observed pattern and as a tool that can be used for parameter estimation and goodness-of-fit testing of the point pattern generating process. It is, indeed, not an exaggeration to say that Ripley's K-function is the most common basic tool used to analyze the spatial distribution of dimensionless events on a continuous space. In particular, it has proved a powerful tool for testing for the presence of spatial dependence or interaction within a micro-geographical pattern. As a result, since its introduction, the K-function has been widely applied in various fields such as ecology, epidemiology and, more recently, economics (Arbia, 1989; Arbia and Espa, 1996; Barff, 1987; Feser and Sweeney, 2000; Sweeney and Feser, 1998; Marcon and Puech, 2003).

Formally, the K-function is an alternative description, with respect to the second-order intensity function $\lambda_2(x, y)$ introduced in Chapter 6, of the second-order properties of a spatial point process that can be adopted under the

114 *Locational choices of economic agents*

assumption of stationarity and isotropy (Diggle, 2003). A stationary and isotropic spatial point process is such that $\lambda_2(x, y) = \lambda_2(d)$, where $d = \|x - y\|$ is the Euclidean distance between the typical locations x and y. A process of this kind is therefore characterized by the fact that the spatial interactions among points (that may identify the locations of a certain kind of economic agents) depend only on their distance and not on their specific positions. As a consequence, the second-order properties of a stationary and isotropic point process can also be properly described by the K-function, which can heuristically be defined as follows:

$$K(d) = \lambda^{-1} E \text{ [number of further points falling at a distance } \leq d$$
$$\text{from a typical point]} \tag{7.1}$$

where λ denotes the intensity (that is constant because of the stationarity assumption), corresponding to the mean number of events per unitary area. Therefore, $\lambda K(d)$ indicates the expected number of further points up to a distance d of a typical point (Ripley, 1977). In the empirical economic analyses where the data-generating point process is stationary and isotropic (that is when the territory is essentially homogeneous), the K-function quantifies properly the mean (global) level of spatial interactions between the economic agents (such as firms or consumers) up to each distance d.

Under the further tenable assumption that the point process is orderly, which essentially implies that each location cannot host more than one point, Ripley (1976) has shown that the link between $K(d)$ and $\lambda_2(d)$ is:

$$\lambda K(d) = 2\pi\lambda^{-1} \int_0^d \lambda_2(u) u \, du. \tag{7.2}$$

The link between the two functions lies in the fact that both describe the distribution of the distances between pairs of points in a point pattern, where $K(d)$ is related to the cumulative distribution function and $\lambda_2(d)$ to the probability density function (Diggle, 2003). In the context of practical applications, however, it is more convenient to work with the K-function rather than with the second-order intensity function, as the former can be more straightforwardly estimated from the observed dataset (Diggle, 2003). It is because of this important practical advantage that the K-function has become the most popular statistic used to detect the presence of spatial dependence, positive or negative, in a spatial point pattern.

7.2 Estimation of Ripley's K-function

The denominator of Equation 7.1 is the parameter λ, the mean number of events per unitary area. A natural and common estimator for λ is $\hat{\lambda} = n/|A|$, where n is the number of observed points and $|A|$ is the total surface of the study area A. Borrowing the notation from Diggle (2003), the numerator of $K(d)$ can be

Models of spatial location of individuals 115

similarly estimated by the non-negative and non-decreasing function $\tilde{E}(d)$ computed at given chosen distances d. This function is defined as follows:

$$\tilde{E}(d) = n^{-1}\sum_{i=1}^{n}\sum_{j \neq i} I\left(d_{ij} \leq d\right),$$

where d_{ij} is the spatial distance between the ith and the jth observed points and $I\left(d_{ij} \leq d\right)$ represents the indicator function such that $I = 1$ if $d_{ij} \leq d$ and 0 otherwise. In practical applications d_{ij} is usually computed as the simple Euclidean distance, but virtually any other definition can be employed as well. For example, alternative definitions may include a distance based on the time required to reach the ith point from the jth point or on the economic cost involved in the trip. Some authors have envisaged the use of social distances (Doreian, 1980) or a broader definition of economic distance (Case et al., 1993; Conley and Topa, 2002). Distances computed according to the empirically observed flows (Murdoch et al., 1997) or to trade-based interaction measures (Aten, 1996; 1997) could also be employed in empirical economic research.

The function $\tilde{E}(d)$ is a measure of the count of all pairs of points separated by a distance $d_{ij} \leq d$ from each other and hence it can properly estimate the expected number of further points up to a distance d of a typical event. However, because of the usual arbitrary bounded nature of the area of the observed point pattern, edge effects can arise that make $\tilde{E}(d)$ negatively biased. The observed points located near the boundary of the study area may, in fact, be close to unobserved points located outside the study area. Therefore, for these points, it may not be possible to count the actual number of further points located up to a distance d. The estimator $\tilde{E}(d)$ does not account for this circumstance and hence tends to underestimate the actual degree of spatial interaction and can lead to negatively biased estimates. The literature has proposed so far many methods to correct for this kind of bias (see e.g. Cressie, 1993; Ilian et al., 2008). The most frequently used method is due to Ripley (1976) and essentially consists of increasing $I\left(d_{ij} \leq d\right)$, for the ith and jth points affected by edge effects, by an amount equal to the proportion of the circumference with radius d which cannot be observed because of the boundaries of the study area. According to this method, an unbiased estimator for $E[.]$ in Equation 7.1 is

$$\hat{E}(d) = n^{-1}\sum_{i=1}^{n}\sum_{j \neq i} w_{ij}^{-1} I\left(d_{ij} \leq d\right) \tag{7.3}$$

where the weight w_{ij} is the proportion of the circumference of the circle centred on the ith point, passing through the jth point, which lies within the study area. Diggle (2003) provided explicit formulas for w_{ij} that can be used in the context of rectangular and circular study areas and Goreaud and Pélissier (1999) extended them to the case of areas with relatively simple irregular shapes. The edge-correction weights become intractable for complex arbitrary polygonal

116   *Locational choices of economic agents*

areas, such as the administrative geographical units that the economic researchers have to typically deal with (e.g. countries, regions or cities). For these cases, for example, splancs and spatstat packages for R (Rowlingson and Diggle, 2015; Baddeley and Turner, 2005) incorporate computational algorithms, rather than explicit formulas, for calculating w_{ij} that allow the handling of study areas of any complex shape.

In the end, using Equation 7.3 and $\hat{\lambda} = n/|A|$ to estimate λ, we obtain the original Ripley's (1976) estimator for $K(d)$,

$$\tilde{K}(d) = n^{-2} |A| \sum_{i=1}^{n} \sum_{j \neq i} w_{ij}^{-1} I\left(d_{ij} \leq d\right).$$

Many authors (e.g. Cressie, 1993; Diggle, 2003) have subsequently suggested estimating λ by $(n-1)/|A|$ rather than $n/|A|$, leading to a slightly different form of the estimator:[1]

$$\hat{K}(d) = \frac{|A|}{n(n-1)} \sum_{i=1}^{n} \sum_{j \neq i} w_{ij}^{-1} I\left(d_{ij} \leq d\right), \tag{7.4}$$

which is now the most commonly used formula.

$\hat{K}(d)$ is approximately unbiased for each given value of d. However, as d increases, the bias can increase because the value of w_{ij} can become large and, eventually, unbounded. In order to avoid the bias becoming too serious, it is common practice to restrict d to a value smaller than the extension of the study area. For example, for an approximately rectangular area, Ripley (1976) suggests using d values lesser than $1/4$ of the smaller side length of the area; while Diggle (2003) found that for a unit square area the theoretical upper limit of d is $\frac{1}{2}\sqrt{2}$.

7.3 Identification of spatial location patterns

For several data-generating point processes, that can be of interest in modelling the spatial behaviour of economic agents, it is possible to compute the expectation on the right-hand side of Equation 7.1, so that $K(d)$ can be written in a closed form (Dixon, 2002). This makes the K-function a useful tool to develop procedures for identifying the data-generating point processes based on the comparison between the theoretical form of the function and its empirical counterpart estimated on the observed data. In this section, we show the main K-function-based methods for parameter estimation and goodness-of-fit testing of data-generating point processes.

7.3.1 The CSR test

The most popular use of the K-function is to test the hypothesis of complete spatial randomness. As anticipated at the beginning of this chapter, unlike the quadrat-based tests presented in Chapter 6, the CSR test based on the K-function does not require the discretization of the space into sub-areas and hence is robust against modifiable areal unit problem effects. Moreover, it has the advantage of better characterizing and quantifying the deviations from CSR towards clustering or dispersion.

We have already seen in Chapter 6 that, theoretically, a complete spatial random point pattern is a pattern generated by a homogeneous Poisson process. Therefore, in order to test if an observed spatial point pattern is consistent with the CSR hypothesis, it is possible to verify if the observed points follow a homogeneous Poisson process. As shown by Ripley (1976), the theoretical form of the K-function for this process can be analytically evaluated using Equation 7.2. We recall that, under the homogeneous Poisson process assumption, points are uniformly and independently distributed over the study area. Under uniformity, the first-order intensity of the process is constant, $\lambda(d) = \lambda$, and, because of independence, the second-order intensity is

$$\lambda_2(d) = \lambda^2, \, d > 0. \tag{7.5}$$

Therefore, substituting Equation 7.5 into Equation 7.2 we obtain

$$K(d) = \pi d^2, \, d > 0. \tag{7.6}$$

Equation 7.6 can properly represent the null hypothesis of CSR and can be used as a benchmark to develop formal tests. Significant deviations from this benchmark indicate the alternative hypothesis of either spatial heterogeneity or spatial dependence, or both. In particular, if $K(d) > \pi d^2$ there are more points within a distance d, from each points, than expected under CSR. In case the observed point pattern represents the spatial distribution of economic agents in an homogeneous space, this circumstance implies that positive spatial interactions among agents, and hence clustering, are detected. On the other hand, if $K(d) < \pi d^2$ there are less than expected points within a distance d from each points implying, for example, negative spatial interactions among economic agents that tend to repulse each other up to a distance d.

To favor an easier interpretation, Besag (1977) proposed the linear transformation of $K(d)$:

$$L(d) = \sqrt{K(d)/\pi}$$

where the linearization is obtained by dividing by π and computing the square root. Under this normalization, the null hypothesis of complete spatial randomness is represented by a straight line because it is satisfied when $L(d) = d$. Other similar normalizations have followed since Besag (1977), such as $\tilde{L}(d) = \sqrt{K(d)/\pi} - d$ (see e.g. Marcon and Puech, 2003) that makes the CSR hypothesis represented by 0.

118 *Locational choices of economic agents*

The sampling distribution of $\hat{K}(d)$ under CSR is analytically tractable only in the cases of simple study areas A. In particular, Lang and Marcon (2013) developed an analytical global test for $K(d)$ against the CSR hypothesis that can be used for point patterns observed in a square A, while Marcon et al. (2013) extended it to a rectangular A. In cases of arbitrarily shaped study areas, it is common practice to make inferences about the CSR hypothesis by estimating the sampling distribution of $\hat{K}(d)$ by direct Monte Carlo simulations of the homogeneous Poisson process. Moreover, as compared with global tests, the Monte Carlo simulations approach has the advantage of detecting deviations from CSR at each distance d. As illustrated by Besag and Diggle (1977), this simple inferential procedure consists, firstly, of generating m point patterns according to the homogeneous Poisson process conditional on the same number of points of the observed pattern under analysis. Secondly, for each of the m simulated patterns, a different $\hat{K}(d)$ (or a transformation of it, such as $\hat{L}(d)$ or $\tilde{\hat{L}}(d)$) can be computed. With the m resulting estimated functions, it is then possible to obtain the approximate $m/(m+1) \times 100\%$ confidence envelopes from the highest and lowest values of the $\hat{K}(d)$ (or $\hat{L}(d)$ and $\tilde{\hat{L}}(d)$) functions computed from the m CSR simulated patterns. The graph of the estimated function and its corresponding confidence envelopes against d can represents a proper significant test. Indeed, if the observed curve of $\hat{K}(d)$ (or $\hat{L}(d)$ and $\tilde{\hat{L}}(d)$) lies outside – above or below – the simulation envelopes at some distances d, we have indications of significant departures from CSR at those distances.

As a way of illustrating the Monte Carlo-simulated confidence envelopes approach to testing the CSR hypothesis, Figure 7.1 shows the performance of the test in different paradigmatic empirical circumstances. In particular, the graphs in the figure depict the behavior of $\hat{L}(d)$ on the vertical axis and the distance d on the horizontal axis. In each graph, the solid line represents the observed function, while the shaded area is bounded by the corresponding upper and lower confidence envelopes for 999 realizations of a homogeneous Poisson process. It can be clearly noted that (unlike the quadrat-based CSR tests that are conditioned on the arbitrary choice of a specific spatial scale) the K-function-based tests identify significant deviations from CSR (toward clustering or inhibition) at varying spatial scales simultaneously. In particular, this distance-based approach allows the detection of differing, even opposite, spatial patterns co-occurring within the same dataset. For example, the empirical situation depicted in Figure 7.1 is characterized by clustering at small distances and inhibition at relatively higher distances due to the presence of small clusters of units located far apart from each other. Conversely, Figure 7.1d exhibits inhibition at small distances and clustering at relatively higher distances due to the presence of a large concentration of units in the east part of the geographical area in which they are located distancing each other.

Models of spatial location of individuals 119

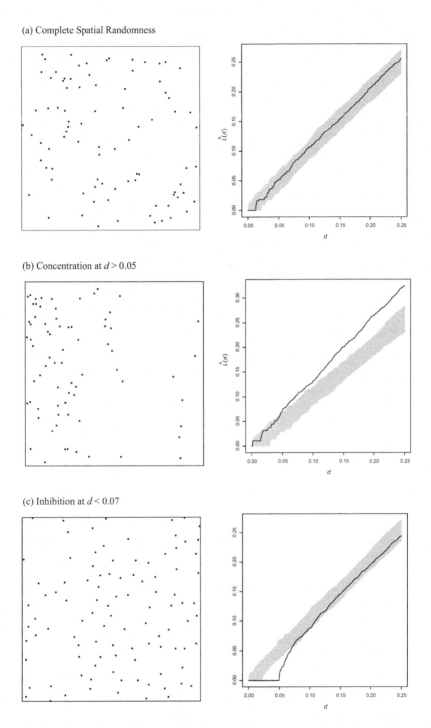

Figure 7.1 Performance of the *K*-function-based CSR test in different paradigmatic empirical circumstances.

120 *Locational choices of economic agents*

(d) Clustering at $0.08 < d < 0.17$

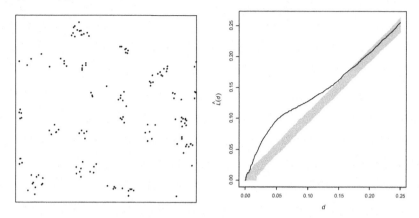

(e) Concentration at $0.015 < d < 0.06$ and inhibition at $0.10 < d < 0.12$

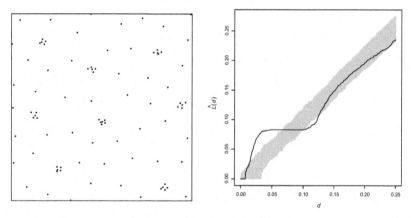

(f) Inhibition at $d < 0.075$ and concentration $d > 0.140$

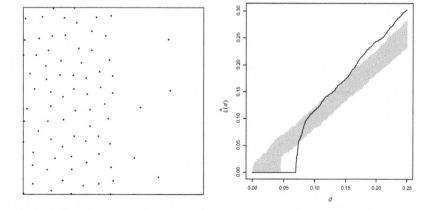

Figure 7.1 (Continued)

7.3.2 Parameter estimation of the Thomas cluster process

As we have seen in Chapter 6, the Thomas model (1949) is a Poisson cluster process that firstly generates a set of leader points according to a homogeneous Poisson process with intensity ρ and then, around each leader point, generates a random number of follower points. This process is characterized by the fact that the number of followers of each leader is a Poisson random variable with mean μ and the dispersion of followers with respect to their leaders' locations follows a radially symmetric normal distribution with standard deviation σ. Moreover, because of the assumption of stationarity, the theoretical first-order intensity of the process is $\lambda = \rho\mu$.

Diggle (2003) shows that the theoretical K-function for the Thomas process is

$$K(d) = \pi d^2 + \frac{1}{\rho}\left(1 - \exp\left(-\frac{d^2}{4\sigma^2}\right)\right). \tag{7.7}$$

The process parameters, that is ρ, μ and σ, can then be estimated from the observed data by finding the optimal parameters' values that ensure the closest match between the theoretical K-function, as expressed by Equation 7.7, and the empirical K-function estimated from the observed data. In order to find the optimal values, Diggle and Gratton (1984) proposed the "method of minimum contrast", subsequently generalized by Møller and Waagepetersen (2003), which essentially consists of minimizing the following general discrepancy criterion:

$$D(\theta) = \int_0^{d_0}\left[\hat{K}(u)^q - K(u;\theta)^q\right]^p du \tag{7.8}$$

where θ is the set of parameters to be estimated, $\hat{K}(u)$ indicates the observed value of the K-function computed from the data, $K(u;\theta)$ denotes the theoretical expected value of the K-function, and d_0, q and p are constants that need to be chosen. According to this method, θ is estimated as the value $\hat{\theta}$ that minimizes the criterion $D(\theta)$.

A detailed discussion on how to specify the values for q, p and d_0 depending on the empirical situation under study is given by Diggle (2003). A typical choice for the first two constants is $q = 1/4$ and $p = 2$ so that $D(\theta)$ corresponds to the integrated squared difference between the fourth roots of the two K-functions (Waagepetersen, 2007).

With respect to d_0, Diggle (2003) recommends that, for theoretical and practical reasons, its value should be substantially smaller than the spatial extension of the observed study area. We can then estimate the values of $\theta = (\rho, \sigma)$ of a Thomas process through the method of minimum contrast by using Equation 7.7 and hence minimizing

$$D(\theta) = \int_0^{d_0}\left[\hat{K}(u)^{1/4} - \left(\pi u^2 + \rho^{-1}\left[1 - \exp\left(-u^2/\left(4\sigma^2\right)\right)\right]\right)^{1/4}\right]^2 du. \tag{7.9}$$

Once the optimal value of $\theta = (\rho, \sigma)$ is obtained, the remaining mean number of followers, parameter μ, can be derived from the estimated first-order intensity $\hat{\lambda}$.

Example 7.1: The spatial location pattern of new pharmaceutical and medical device manufacturing firms in Veneto (Italy)

Let us consider an example of the K-function-based method for parameter estimation of a Thomas cluster process. The data we are using consists of the observed micro-geographical pattern of firm entries into the pharmaceutical and medical device manufacturing industry in Veneto, a region situated in the north-east of Italy with an area of 18,399 km^2. This dataset is a subset of an internationally comparable database of Italian firm demographics, managed by the Italian National Institute of Statistics (ISTAT), and contains the (normalized) geographical coordinates of the 333 newly created firms during the period between years 2004 and 2009.

Figure 7.2 reports the spatial distribution of firms. As can be noted, new businesses seem to concentrate in some specific geographical areas thus violating the CSR hypothesis. This is confirmed by the CSR test depicted in Figure 7.3.

For simplicity, let us suppose that the industrial territory of Veneto is substantially homogeneous and that a theoretical economic model suggests that new firms in the pharmaceutical and medical device manufacturing sector should follow a leader–follower location pattern. A Thomas cluster process can then be

Figure 7.2 Locations of the 333 new firms in the pharmaceutical and medical device manufacturing sector in Veneto, 2004–2009.

Models of spatial location of individuals 123

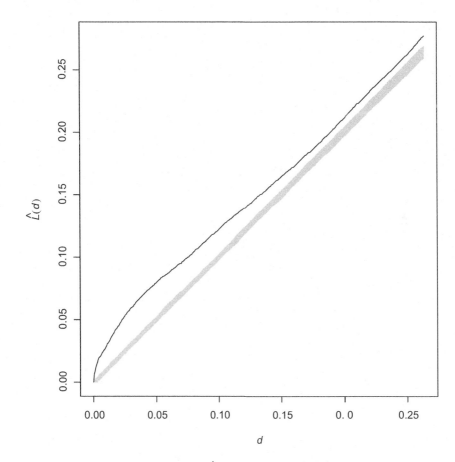

Figure 7.3 Behavior of the empirical $\hat{L}(d)$ (continuous line) and the corresponding 99.9 per cent CSR confidence bands (shaded area) for the 333 new firms in the pharmaceutical and medical device manufacturing sector in Veneto, 2004–2009.

plausible as a data-generating model, which can be fitted using the method of minimum contrast and, in particular, solving the minimum optimization problem specified by Equation 7.9 through least squares estimation. The obtained estimates are $\hat{\rho} = 76.0$, $\hat{\sigma} = 0.012$ and $\hat{\mu} = 8.4$. As a simple goodness-of-fit examination, we can rely on the graphical summary, depicted in Figure 7.4, that compares the behavior of $\hat{L}(u)$ (solid line) with confidence envelops for 99 realizations of the fitted Thomas process (shaded area). The graph indicates that the fit is statistically adequate and that the observed data are compatible with the estimated model.

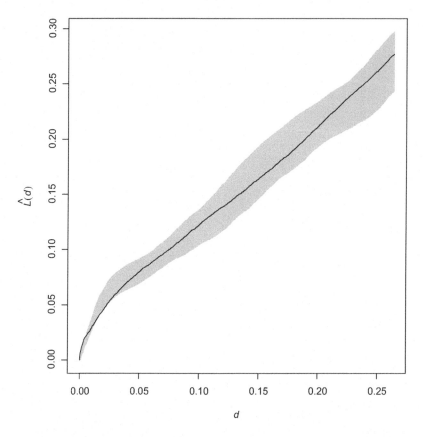

Figure 7.4 Goodness-of-fit of a Thomas process to the pharmaceutical and medical device manufacturing firms data using the empirical (continuous line) and confidence envelopes from 99 simulations of the fitted model (shaded area).

7.3.3 Parameter estimation of the Matérn cluster process

As we have seen in Chapter 6, the Matérn cluster process (Matérn, 1986) is a Poisson cluster process that, like the Thomas model, firstly generates a set of leader points according to an homogeneous Poisson process with intensity ρ and then, around each leader point, generates a random number of follower points. This process is characterized by the fact that the number of followers of each leader is a Poisson random variable with mean μ and the location of followers with respect to their leaders' locations are independently and uniformly distributed inside a circle of radius R centered on the leader point. Even in this case, because of the assumption of stationarity, the theoretical first-order intensity of the process is $\lambda = \rho\mu$.

Møller and Waagepetersen (2003) show that the theoretical K-function for the Matérn cluster process is

$$K(d) = \pi d^2 + \frac{1}{\rho} h\left(\frac{d}{2R}\right) \qquad (7.10)$$

where

$$h(z) = \begin{cases} 2 + \dfrac{1}{\pi}\left[(8z^2 - 4)\arccos(z) - 2\arcsin(z) + 4z\sqrt{(1-z^2)^3} - 6z\sqrt{1-z^2}\right] & \text{if } z \leq 1 \\ 1 & \text{if } z > 1 \end{cases}$$

The process parameters, ρ and R, can be estimated from the observed data through the method of minimum contrast by using Equation 7.10 as the discrepancy criterion expressed by Equation 7.8. In turn, the remaining estimate of parameter μ can be derived from the estimated first-order intensity $\hat{\lambda}$.

Example 7.2: The spatial location pattern of new pharmaceutical and medical device manufacturing firms in Veneto (continued)

In this example we try to assess whether the observed micro-geographical pattern of new firms in the pharmaceutical and medical device manufacturing

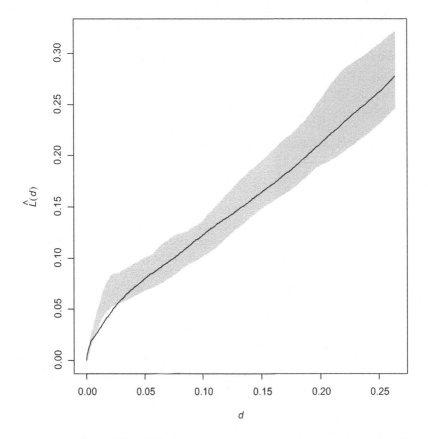

Figure 7.5 Goodness-of-fit of a Matérn cluster process to the pharmaceutical and medical device manufacturing firms data using the empirical $\hat{L}(d)$ (continuous line) and confidence envelopes from 99 simulations of the fitted model (shaded area).

126 *Locational choices of economic agents*

industry, presented in Example 7.1, can be better described by the Matérn cluster process than the Thomas model. In other words, we examine whether the dispersion of firms around the cluster centers follows a uniform rather than a normal distribution.

The least squares estimation of the Matérn cluster process using Equation 7.8, with Equation 7.10 for specifying $K(u;\theta)$, gives estimates $\hat{\rho}=76.5$, $\hat{R}=0.024$ and $\hat{\mu}=8.3$. The goodness-of-fit inspection, depicted in Figure 7.5, that compares the behavior of $\hat{L}(u)$ (solid line) with confidence envelops for 99 realizations of the fitted Matérn cluster process (shaded area), indicates rejection of the model at small distances. This implies that the spatial distribution of the pharmaceutical and medical device manufacturing firms within the clusters is better modelled by the normal distribution.

7.3.4 *Parameter estimation of the log-Gaussian Cox process*

The K-function can also be exploited, through the method of minimum contrast, to fit a different class of aggregated point processes. In particular, it has been proven to be especially efficient in estimating the parameters of a log-Gaussian Cox process. We recall from Chapter 6 that, essentially, this class of point processes assumes that the first order intensity is a non-negative-valued process, $\{\Lambda(x):x\in\mathbb{R}^2\}$, such that $\Lambda(x)=\exp\{S(x)\}$, where $S(x)$ is a stationary Gaussian random field with mean μ, variance σ^2 and covariance function $\gamma(d)$. If we specify the covariance function according to a correlation function $\rho(d)$, then $\lambda=\exp(\mu+0.5\sigma^2)$ and $\gamma(d)=\exp(\sigma^2\rho(d))$ (Møller et al., 1998). As shown by Møller and Waagepetersen (2003), for the log-Gaussian Cox process the theoretical expected K-function takes the form

$$K(d)=2\pi\int_0^d u\gamma(u)\,du.$$

In order to fit the process, a parametric covariance function needs to be specified. A common choice is the exponential covariance function $\gamma(d)=\sigma^2\exp(-d/\alpha)$, where α is a parameter that controls the scale of the spatial autocorrelation.

In this framework, the method of minimum contrast is first used to find optimal values of the process parameters, σ^2 and α. Secondly, the remaining estimate of parameter μ can be derived from the estimated first-order intensity $\hat{\lambda}$.

Note

1 This formula is preferable because of technical aspects related to the fact that the unbiased estimator for λ^2 is $n(n-1)/(|A|)^2$ (Illian et al., 2008). This difference is obviously irrelevant if n is large.

8 Points in a heterogeneous space

This chapter extends the modeling framework presented in the previous chapter to the case of a heterogeneous economic space. It introduces the concepts of D-function, inhomogeneous K-function, K-density and M-function and illustrates the differences with the previous approach and its empirical relevance in practical cases.

8.1 Diggle and Chetwynd's D-function

As discussed in Chapter 7, Ripley's K-function statistic is a proper summary measure of the spatial characteristics of an observed point pattern dataset and a suitable inferential tool to test for the presence of spatial dependence, only under the assumption that the data-generating point process is stationary, say $\lambda(x) = \lambda$: that is, only if the territory can be considered essentially homogeneous. However, in real-case situations, the space where economic agents operate, and hence locate, is rarely homogeneous. For instance, firms may not locate in some areas due to the presence of legal and geophysical limitations or may locate in certain zones because of the influence of exogenous factors such as the presence of useful infrastructures, proximity to communication routes or more advantageous local taxation systems. In other words, referring to the statistical categories introduced in Chapter 6, the K-function cannot distinguish between apparent and true contagion.

In order to relax the assumption of spatial homogeneity, Diggle and Chetwynd (1991) proposed a method, which is based on the K-function and the use of a case-control design setting, to detect the presence of significant actual spatial dependence while controlling for the spatial heterogeneity of the study area. Let us consider a set of cases located in a given study area, such as the firms belonging to a specific industry or the firms that exit the market within a given time period. Let us also consider a reference set of controls located in the same study area, such as the firms belonging to all other industries or all firms that still operate in the market. Under the working assumption that the unobserved exogenous factors of spatial heterogeneity affecting the location of cases and controls are substantially the same, we can detect positive (negative) spatial interactions among cases if the cases are more spatially concentrated (dispersed) than the controls. In order to measure the over-concentration (over-dispersion) of cases

128   *Locational choices of economic agents*

with respect to controls, Diggle and Chetwynd (1991) defined the D-function statistic, that is:

$$D(d) = K_{cases}(d) - K_{controls}(d) \tag{8.1}$$

where $K_{cases}(d)$ and $K_{controls}(d)$ are the K-function for the cases and controls patterns respectively. In this setting, the controls represent the reference pattern capturing spatial heterogeneity and hence $D(d) = 0$ can properly represents the null hypothesis of absence of spatial interactions within an inhomogeneous space. Therefore, if at a given distance d, $D(d) > 0$, the cases are relatively more spatially concentrated than the controls, implying the presence of actual spatial interactions among cases. However, if at a given distance d, $D(d) < 0$, the cases are relatively less spatially concentrated than the controls, indicating spatial dispersion among cases.

$D(d)$ can be straightforwardly estimated from the observed case-control data with $\hat{D}(d) = \hat{K}_{cases}(d) - \hat{K}_{controls}(d)$, where $\hat{K}_{cases}(d)$ and $\hat{K}_{controls}(d)$ are the empirical K-function, computed using Equation 7.4, for the cases and controls patterns respectively. In order to assess if $\hat{D}(d)$ is significantly greater (lower) than zero and to test the null hypothesis of absence of relative spatial interaction, Diggle and Chetwynd (1991) refer to the hypothesis of "random labelling", introduced by Cuzick and Edwards (1990). Under this hypothesis, the observed points are labelled randomly as cases or controls. Since the hypothesis of random labelling is consistent with the hypothesis of no spatial interactions between cases, $D(d) = 0$ can be tested with a simple Monte Carlo procedure which consists on generating m simulations, in each of which the observed "labels" identifying the cases and controls are randomly permuted amongst the observed locations. For each of the m simulated patterns, a different $\hat{D}(d)$ can be computed. With the m resulting estimated functions, it is then possible to obtain the approximate $m/(m+1) \times 100\%$ confidence envelopes from the highest and lowest values of the $\hat{D}(d)$ functions computed from the m randomly labelled patterns. The graph of the estimated function and its corresponding confidence envelopes against d can represent a proper significant test. Indeed, if the observed curve of $\hat{D}(d)$ lies outside – above or below – the simulation envelopes at some distances d, we have indications of significant departures from random labelling, and hence from the hypothesis of no spatial interactions, at those distances.

As a way of illustration of the Monte Carlo-simulated confidence envelopes approach to testing the no spatial interactions hypothesis under spatial heterogeneity, Figure 8.1 shows the performance of the test in different paradigmatic empirical circumstances. In particular, the graphs in the figure depict the behavior of $\hat{D}(d)$ on the vertical axis and the distance d on the horizontal axis. In each graph, the solid line represents the observed function, while the shaded area is bounded by the corresponding upper and lower confidence envelopes for 999 randomly labelled patterns. Figure 8.1a depicts a hypothetical empirical situation where the level of spatial interactions among cases is not significantly different from that among the controls and hence the D-function-based test detects no

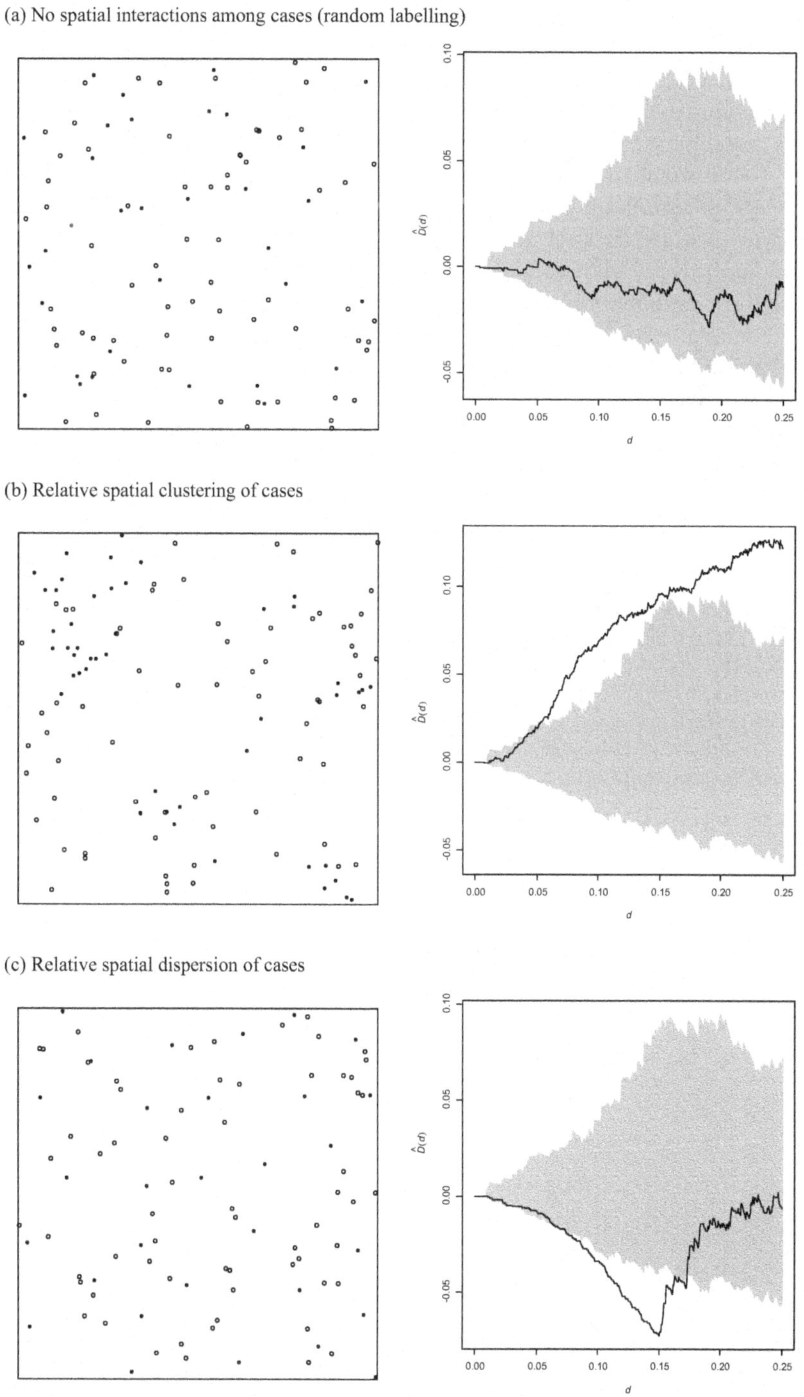

Points in a heterogeneous space 129

(a) No spatial interactions among cases (random labelling)

(b) Relative spatial clustering of cases

(c) Relative spatial dispersion of cases

Figure 8.1 Performance of the D-function-based test of spatial interactions in different paradigmatic case-control settings. The locations of the cases are represented by solid circles and the locations of the controls are represented by empty circles.

spatial clustering or dispersion of cases. In Figure 8.1b the cases are significantly more concentrated than the controls, indeed the D-function-based test detects significant relative spatial clustering. Figure 8.1c shows the opposite situation, in which the cases are significantly more dispersed than the controls, leading the D-function to deviate downwards from the null hypothesis of random labelling thus revealing the presence of relative spatial dispersion among cases.

It is important to note that the D-function can only be used to test for the presence of significant relative spatial concentration/dispersion but cannot be used to measure its level, as the values of the function cannot be meaningfully interpreted (Marcon and Puech, 2003). The D-function, in its original or slightly modified form, has been used widely in empirical economic studies. For example, Sweeney and Feser (1998) used this approach to assess whether the spatial distribution of firms in North Carolina depended upon their size; Feser and Sweeney (2000) focused on the spatial clustering of firms' industrial linkages; Marcon and Puech (2003) evaluated the geographical concentration of industries in France; Arbia et al. (2008) detected the existence of knowledge spillovers analyzing the spatial pattern of patents and Kosfeld et al. (2011) studied the conditional concentration of German industries.

Example 8.1: The spatial location pattern of firms' exits from the hospitality market on the main island of Sicily

Let us consider an example of the use of the D-function to test for the presence of interactions in the spatial distribution of failed hospitality businesses on the main island of Sicily. The number of such businesses established in 2010 was 164 and we observed whether or not they ceased to operate during the period 2011

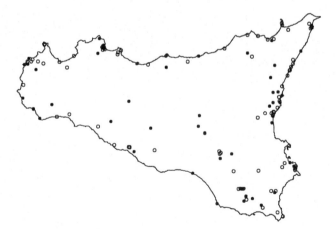

Figure 8.2 Locations of the 164 hospitality businesses established in Sicily, 2010. The firms that survived until 2015 are represented by empty circles; the 55 that did not are represented by solid circles.

to 2015. The businesses consisted of the following types of accommodation: hotels, resorts, youth hostels, mountain retreats, holiday homes, farm stays, campgrounds, and holiday and other short-stay accommodation.[1] Data provided by the Italian National Institute of Statistics (ISTAT).

Figure 8.2 shows the spatial distribution of the 164 hospitality firms and distinguishes between the 109 that survived until 2015 (empty circles) and the 55 that failed (solid circles). As the map clearly suggests, the territory is highly heterogeneous as hospitality firms tend to be located near the seaside. As a consequence, the spatial intensity of firms' locations cannot be realistically considered as constant.

Suppose we are interested in assessing whether there is some spatial dynamic, such as a contagious effect or a local competition phenomenon, in the failure of firms. Since the spatial intensity of firms' locations is not constant, we cannot

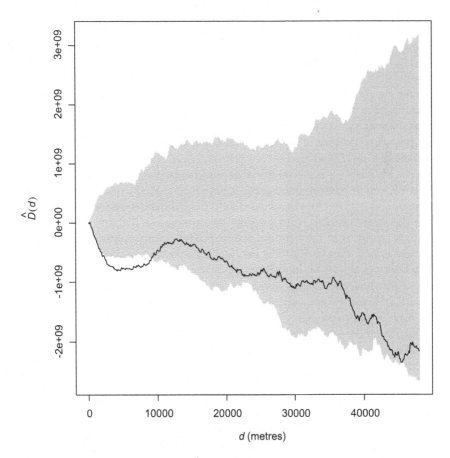

Figure 8.3 Behavior of the empirical $\hat{D}(d)$ (continuous line) and the corresponding 99.9 per cent random labelling confidence bands (shaded area) for the 55 failed hospitality firms in Sicily, 2011–2015.

use the K-function to detect spatial dependence among firms' failures as we may obtain spurious results in which spatial interactions are confounded with spatial heterogeneity. Under the reasonable assumption that the location of firms which survived and the location of firms that failed was affected by the same spatial variation factors, we can detect significant spatial dependence in the death processes of firms while verifying whether failed firms are more spatially concentrated or dispersed than survived firms. We can then perform the D-function-based test treating the firms that exited the market and the firms that survived as cases and controls, respectively. Figure 8.3 shows the results of the test revealing that, at small distances (below 9 km), failed firms are relatively spatially dispersed. This evidence suggests that failure in the hospitality industry in Sicily is not contagious, as failures tend to occur relatively far apart from each other. We have then a preliminary indication that the death process of firms is characterized by spatial local competition where the failure of a firm positively affects the survival of the other firms located nearby.

8.2 Baddeley, Møller and Waagepetersen's K_{inhom}-function

Despite its effectiveness as a tool to assess the statistical significance of spatial interactions in a case-control setting, the D-function has some relevant limitations. First of all, its values are not straightforwardly interpretable and hence do not provide a measure of the degree of spatial dependence. Secondly, and more importantly, the D-function detects relative, not absolute, spatial interactions. It detects, a positive (or negative) spatial dependence between cases when cases' locations are seen to be more aggregated (or dispersed) than the trend in the controls' pattern. This implies that the results of different D-functions cannot be compared, over the same distances, if the controls' patterns are not the same; indeed, if the controls change then the benchmark distribution capturing spatial heterogeneity changes as well, thus invalidating any comparisons (Marcon and Puech, 2017).

Baddeley et al. (2000) introduced a function that overcomes these limits and allows the detection and measurement of absolute spatial dependence, within a spatially heterogeneous setting, while allowing comparisons between different datasets. In particular, they derived an inhomogeneous version of Ripley's K-function, called K_{inhom}, which can be seen as a generalization of the traditional measure, which is limited to homogeneous point processes, to the case of a general kind of inhomogeneous point processes.

In Chapter 6 we have seen that an inhomogeneous point process is essentially a homogeneous Poisson process where the constant first-order intensity λ is replaced by a first-order intensity function varying over the space (say $\lambda(x)$). According to Baddeley et al. (2000), an inhomogeneous Poisson process is also, in particular, "second-order intensity-reweighted stationary" if:

$$\lambda_2(x, y) = \lambda(x)\lambda(y)g(x - y)$$

where $g(x - y)$ is a function that accounts for the level of spatial dependence between the x and y arbitrary events. In this kind of setting, the second-order

Points in a heterogeneous space 133

intensity of the inhomogeneous Poisson process, at the point locations x and y, is the product of the first-order intensities at x and y multiplied by a spatial correlation factor. If there is no spatial interaction between the points of the process at locations x and y then $\lambda_2(x,y) = \lambda(x)\lambda(y)$ and $g(x-y) = 1$. As a consequence, when $g(x-y) > 1$, we have attraction, while if $g(x-y) < 1$, we have repulsion (or inhibition) between the two locations (Møller and Waagepetersen, 2007).

If we further assume isotropy, $g(\cdot)$ depends only on the distance between points, $d = \|x-y\|$, and hence $\lambda_2(x,y) = \lambda(d)$ and $g(x-y) = g(d)$. The scaled quantity $g(d) = \lambda_2(x,y)/\lambda(x)\lambda(y)$ is sometimes referred to as the "pair correlation function" (Ripley 1976, 1977).

If $\lambda(x)$ is bounded away from zero, the K_{inhom}-function of a second-order intensity-reweighted stationary and isotropic spatial point process is given by:

$$K_{inhom}(d) = 2\pi \int_0^d u g(u) \mathrm{d}u, \text{ with } d > 0 \tag{8.2}$$

(Baddeley et al. 2000; Diggle 2003).

In the empirical economic analyses where the data-generating point process is inhomogeneous, the K_{inhom}-function quantifies properly the mean (global) level of spatial interactions between the economic agents (such as firms or consumers) up to each distance d, while controlling for the presence of spatial heterogeneity, as modelled by $\lambda(x)$. In particular, if the data-generating point process is an inhomogeneous Poisson process without spatial interactions between agents, we have $K_{inhom}(d) = \pi d^2$. In contrast, when $K_{inhom}(d) > \pi d^2$ (or $K_{inhom}(d) < \pi d^2$) the underlying point process tends to generate point patterns of agents that are relatively more aggregated (or more dispersed) than the ones that an inhomogeneous Poisson process with first-order intensity $\lambda(x)$ and no spatial interactions would generate (Diggle et al. 2007).

To ease the interpretation, we can exploit the same linear transformations proposed for Ripley's K-function, such as $L_{inhom}(d) = \sqrt{K_{inhom}(d)/\pi}$ or $\tilde{L}_{inhom}(d) = \sqrt{K_{inhom}(d)/\pi} - d$ that make the null hypothesis of no spatial interactions represented by d and 0, respectively.

8.2.1 Estimation of K_{inhom}-function

Baddeley et al. (2000) have shown that, if $\lambda(x)$ is known, a proper edge-corrected unbiased estimator of $K_{inhom}(d)$ is given by:

$$\hat{K}_{inhom}(d;\lambda(d)) = \frac{1}{|A|} \sum_{i=1}^{n} \sum_{j \neq i} \frac{w_{ij} I(d_{ij} \leq d)}{\lambda(x_i)\lambda(x_j)} \tag{8.3}$$

where $|A|$ is, as usual, the total surface of the study area, the term d_{ij} is still the Euclidean spatial distance between the ith and the jth observed points, and $I(d_{ij} \leq d)$ continues to represent the indicator function such that $I = 1$ if $d_{ij} \leq d$ and 0 otherwise. As with the estimator of the homogeneous K-function

134   *Locational choices of economic agents*

(see Section 7.2), due to the presence of edge effects arising from the bounded nature of the study area, we still need to introduce the adjustment factor w_{ij} in order to avoid potential biases in the estimates close to the boundary.

In practical applications $\lambda(x)$ is unknown, and usually we do not have a theoretical economic model that specifies a given functional form for it. Therefore, it has to be estimated. The literature has proposed both parametric and nonparametric approaches to the estimation. In case the nonparametric estimation is preferable, a popular method in this context is the kernel smoothing technique (see Silverman, 1986). Baddeley et al. (2000) proposed the use of a slightly modified version of the Berman and Diggle's kernel estimator (1989) of $\lambda(x)$, that is:

$$\hat{\lambda}_h(x_i) = \sum_{i \neq j} h^{-2} k\left(\frac{x_j - x_i}{h}\right) \bigg/ C_h(x_j), \tag{8.4}$$

where $k(\cdot)$ is a radially symmetric bivariate probability density function (typically chosen to be Gaussian), h represents the bandwidth (i.e. the parameter controlling the smoothness of the intensity surface) and $C_h(x_j) = \int k_h(x_j - u) du$ is a factor that allows correction of the presence of edge effects.

Baddeley et al. (2000) show that, with a careful, proper, choice for the bandwidth h, the estimator of the K_{inhom}-function, $\hat{K}_{\text{inhom}}\left(d; \hat{\lambda}(d)\right)$, that incorporates Equation 8.4 into Equation 8.3, can provide an approximately unbiased estimation of the inhomogeneous K-function. However, Diggle et al. (2007) showed that non-parametrically estimating both $\lambda(x)$, which represents the spatial heterogeneity of the data-generating process, and $K_{\text{inhom}}(d)$, which expresses the spatial interactions among events, using the same observed point pattern data may lead to spurious estimates. Indeed, we cannot really distinguish the contributions due to spatial heterogeneity or spatial dependence phenomena unless we rely on some assumptions about the nature of the underlying data-generating process. In some microeconomic applications, for example, it may be plausible to assume that the spatial scale of the first-order intensity is larger than the spatial scale of the second-order intensity. This assumption may then imply that the heterogeneity of the geographical space operates at a larger scale than the one characterizing spatial interactions amongst economic agents, and, as a consequence, these two characteristics of the underlying data-generating point process are separable (Diggle et al. 2007). This specific assumption may be realistic if prior knowledge or theoretical indications about the geographical extent of spatial interactions amongst economic agents is available, as may be the case, for example, when analyzing spatial competition among retailers (see e.g. Arbia et al., 2015b).

Alternatively, following the example of Diggle (2003) among others, in those empirical circumstances where $\lambda(x)$ can be considered as a function of exogenous geographically referenced variables expressing spatial heterogeneity, the values of $\lambda(x)$ can be estimated using a parametric regression model. For example, in the context of micro-geographical location patterns of firms, these variables, which represent common factors shared by the firms located in the same area, could be the geographical coordinates of communication routes, the locations of useful

Points in a heterogeneous space 135

infrastructures or the positions of firms of different vertically related industries. A convenient specification of the model for $\lambda(x)$, that describes the probability that an economic agent locates in x as a consequence of heterogeneous conditions, is the log-linear model:

$$\lambda(x) = \exp\left\{\sum_{j=1}^{k} \beta_j z_j(x)\right\} \tag{8.5}$$

where $z_j(x)$ is one of k geographically referenced explanatory variables and β_j is the associated regression parameter.

While assuming that the observed locations of the economic agents are the realization of an inhomogeneous Poisson process with intensity function $\lambda(x)$, the model in Equation 8.5 can be fitted to the data using likelihood-based methods. Because of advantages in the computational implementation, the model is commonly fitted by maximizing its pseudo-likelihood (Besag, 1975) through the Berman–Turner approximation (Berman and Turner, 1992). A clear and detailed discussion of the method is given by Baddeley and Turner (2000). As shown by Strauss and Ikeda (1990), maximum pseudo-likelihood of a Poisson model is equivalent to maximum likelihood.

This equivalence makes it possible to test for goodness-of-fit of the model expressed in Equation 8.5 using standard formal likelihood ratio criteria based on the χ^2 distribution.

8.2.2 Inference for K_{inhom}-function

Since the sampling distribution of $\hat{K}_{\text{inhom}}\left(d; \hat{\lambda}(d)\right)$ is unknown, in order to assess the statistical significance of the test of $K_{\text{inhom}}(d)$ against the hypothesis of no spatial interactions, we need to rely on Monte Carlo-simulated confidence envelopes. In particular, we can rely on an inferential procedure that consists, firstly, on generating m point patterns according to an inhomogeneous Poisson process conditional on the same number of points of the observed pattern under analysis and with $\lambda(x)$ estimated parametrically or non-parametrically using Equation 8.4 or Equation 8.5. Secondly, for each of the m simulated patterns, a different $\hat{K}_{\text{inhom}}(d)$ (or a transformation of it, such as $\hat{L}_{\text{inhom}}(d)$ or $\tilde{L}_{\text{inhom}}(d)$) can be computed. With the m resulting estimated functions, it is then possible to obtain the approximated $m/(m+1)\times100\%$ confidence envelopes from the highest and lowest values of the $\hat{K}_{\text{inhom}}(d)$ (or $\hat{L}_{\text{inhom}}(d)$ and $\tilde{L}_{\text{inhom}}(d)$) functions computed from the m patterns simulated according to the null hypothesis. The graph of the estimated function and its corresponding confidence envelopes against d can represent a proper significant test. Indeed, if the observed curve of $\hat{K}_{\text{inhom}}(d)$ (or $\hat{L}_{\text{inhom}}(d)$ and $\tilde{L}_{\text{inhom}}(d)$) lies outside – above or below – the simulation envelopes at some distances d, we have indications of significant departures from hypothesis of no spatial interactions at those distances.

Example 8.2: Local competition of supermarkets in the municipality of Trento (Italy)

To illustrate the use of the K_{inhom}-function we refer to an example in which the aim is to verify the presence of a relevant pattern of spatial competition in the location of supermarkets within the city of Trento in 2004 (Figure 8.4a). The spatial intensity of the location process of supermarkets cannot be reasonably assumed to be constant as stores tend to locate as close as possible to the potential market demand, which is obviously not regularly distributed in the area of the city. Let us suppose that in this empirical circumstance we can use the number of households by census tract in 2004 (Figure 8.4b), which is the finest available level of spatial resolution for this variable, as a proxy for the spatial distribution of potential customers in the city of Trento.

To assess the nature and level of spatial interactions among supermarkets while controlling for the spatial heterogeneity of the potential market demand and hence of the retail location opportunities, the K_{inhom}-function-based test can be performed by estimating $\lambda(x)$ parametrically according to Equation 8.5 and using the number of households by census tract as a useful covariate capturing spatial heterogeneity. The resulting estimated spatial intensity is therefore given by the following estimated equation:

$$\hat{\lambda}(x) = \exp\{-15.033 + 0.007 h(x)\}$$

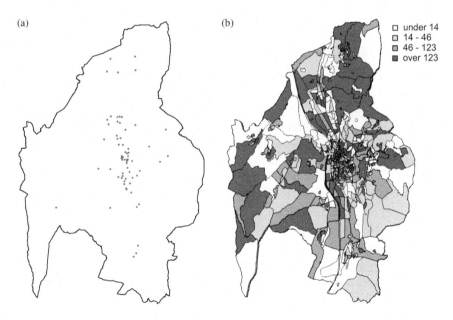

Figure 8.4 (a) locations of the 82 supermarkets in Trento in 2004; (b) quartile distribution of the number of households by census tract in 2004. Source: Italian National Institute of Statistics.

in which $h(x)$ represents the number of households in the census tract where point x is located. The estimated model coefficient for $h(x)$ is positive and significant (at the 5% level both according to the Wald and likelihood ratio tests), thus implying that supermarkets tend to locate in the relatively more populated areas of the city. Having derived an estimate of $\lambda(x)$ we can then estimate $\hat{K}_{\text{inhom}}(d)$ (and hence $\hat{L}_{\text{inhom}}(d)$) using Equation 8.3. Figure 8.5 displays $\hat{L}_{\text{inhom}}(d)$ along with the confidence envelopes referred to the null hypothesis of absence of spatial dependence at a 99.9% significance level. The graph seems to reveal a complex location phenomenon for the supermarkets in Trento which occurs at different spatial scales. In particular, a significant upward deviation of the estimated function is evident, relative to the confidence bands at small distances (below 1.5 km), while a significant strong downward deviation occurs after 2.5 km. This suggests

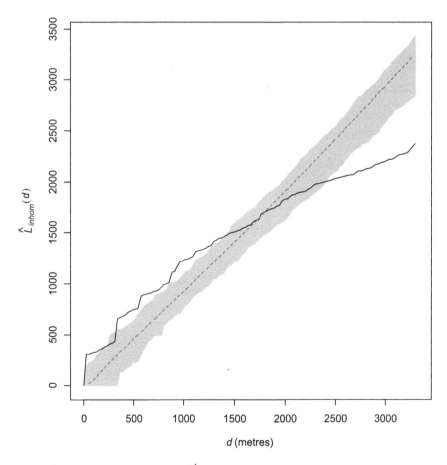

Figure 8.5 Behavior of the empirical $\hat{L}_{\text{inhom}}(d)$ (continuous line) and the corresponding 99.9 per cent confidence bands under the null hypothesis of absence of spatial interactions (shaded area) for the 82 supermarkets in Trento, 2004.

138   *Locational choices of economic agents*

that once we control for the spatial distribution of potential market demand, we find both positive and negative spatial externalities at play which lead to small-scale spatial clusters of supermarkets (with an extension within 1.5 km) that tend to form at not less than 2.5 km from other clusters of supermarkets.

In this example the K_{inhom}-function has helped to empirically disentangle spatial heterogeneity from the spatial dependence observed in the pattern of the supermarkets in Trento. The L_{inhom}-function reported in Figure 8.5 clearly shows how strong the tendency is for stores to locate in isolated small clusters because of a genuine interaction amongst economic agents and not just because of a tendency to concentrate in the most populated areas. In other words, the L_{inhom}-function identifies situations of over-concentration at small distances and over-dispersion at relatively higher distances as opposed to a non-constant underlying intensity. In this way, it clearly quantifies the level of spatial interactions which cannot simply be put down to exogenous factors which change smoothly over space such as the potential market demand.

8.3 Measuring spatial concentration of industries: Duranton–Overman K-density and Marcon–Puech M-function

Following the increasing availability of economic micro-geographical data, a growing stream of literature in the field of spatial economics and regional sciences has been focusing on developing distance-based measures of spatial concentration of industries that can overcome the methodological limits of the more traditional indices, such as the "location quotient" or "Ellison–Glaeser index" (Ellison and Glaeser, 1997), which are based on discrete areal-level data. The most established and used distance-based measures of spatial clusters of firms are probably the K-density and M-function, that have been developed, respectively, by Duranton and Overman (2005) and Marcon and Puech (2010). Both measures have been proposed as adaptations of Ripley's K-function to the empirical contexts of industrial agglomeration. In particular, they have been developed in order to meet the methodological requirements formalized by Duranton and Overman (2005) which state that an ideal measure of spatial concentration of firms' plants should (i) allow comparison of the level of concentration among different industries, (ii) control for industrial concentration, (iii) control for spatial heterogeneity as represented by the spatial distribution of the whole manufacturing, (iv) provide the statistical significance of the estimated values and (v) be robust with respect to spatial scale of data aggregation. As a matter of fact, Ripley's K-function does not meet, in particular, property iii, because, as we have discussed in this section, it detects actual spatial clustering only under the assumption of spatial homogeneity. This assumption, however, does not hold as the spatial intensity of firms' locations cannot be realistically considered as constant. The K-density and M-function are two alternative relative measures of spatial concentration of firms located in a heterogeneous space within the same industry.

8.3.1 Duranton and Overman's K-density

Duranton and Overman's K-density (2005), say $\hat{K}_{density}$, is conceptually similar to the second-order intensity function $\lambda_2 \left(\|x - y\| \right)$, introduced in Chapter 6, as it represents an estimator of the density distribution of the distances between pairs of firms' locations. As pointed out by Marcon and Puech (2017), $\hat{K}_{density}$ can also be viewed as an estimator of the probability density function of finding another firm located at a given distance d from a typical reference firm. Indeed, essentially, it computes the observed average number of pairs of firms at each distance and then applies a smoothing in order to obtain a continuous function that sums to 1. More precisely, $\hat{K}_{density}$ can be defined as:

$$\hat{K}_{density}\left(d\right) = \frac{1}{n\left(n-1\right)} \sum_{i=1}^{n} \sum_{j \neq i} k\left(d_{ij}, d; h\right),$$

where

$$k\left(d_{ij}, d; h\right) = \frac{1}{h\sqrt{2\pi}} \exp\left(-\frac{\left(d_{ij} - d\right)^2}{2h^2}\right)$$

is a Gaussian kernel smoother à la Silverman (1986) such that it reaches the maximum value when $d_{ij} = d$ while it decreases, as d_{ij} deviates from d, following a Gaussian distribution with a given standard deviation h, namely the bandwidth. Duranton and Overman (2005) suggest choosing the value of the bandwidth h according to the criterion proposed by Silverman (1986; see Section 3.4.2; Equation 3.31).

Following a similar approach to that of random labelling for the D-function (see Section 8.1), to assess the statistical significance of $\hat{K}_{density}$, its values are compared to the confidence interval of the null hypothesis that firms are randomly reassigned to the actual observed firms' locations. This implies that the function does not have a closed-form benchmark value for the null hypothesis of absence of spatial clustering, which is instead derived by means of a Monte Carlo approach. In practice, at each simulation, the firms of a single sector of activity (or of any specific typology of interest) are randomly assigned over the locations of all firms of all sectors (or of all the possible typologies). The null hypothesis of absence of spatial interactions among the firms of the same sector (or the same typology) is then represented by the center of the Monte Carlo-simulated confidence envelopes. In this respect, similarly to the D-function, K-density allows for the detection of relative, rather than absolute, spatial concentration of firms of a specific typology. Duranton and Overman (2005) have also proposed a weighted version of the function that also accounts for the size of firms, as measured for example by the number of employees, the value-added, the capital, and so on. See Duranton and Overman (2005) for more details.

140 *Locational choices of economic agents*

In the last few years K-density has been used quite extensively in the field of spatial economics and regional sciences. We can cite, among the most notable empirical works, Duranton and Overman (2008), Klier and McMillen (2008b), Koh and Riedel (2014), Kerr and Kominers (2015) and Behrens and Bougna (2015).

8.3.2 *Marcon and Puech's* M-*function*

Marcon and Puech (2010)'s M-function can be viewed as a distance-based version of the popular location quotient of regional industrial specialization. Indeed, in a framework where firms belong to different typologies (e.g. different industries), it consists of a function of the distance d that provides the relative frequency of firms of a specific typology of interest (e.g. a particular industry) that are located within d of a typical reference firm of the same type, compared to the same ratio computed with respect to all firms of all types. If the typical firm is indicated by i, another firm of the same type is denoted by j^c and another firm of any typology is represented by j, then the M-function can be estimated by:

$$\hat{M}(d) = \sum_{i=1}^{n} \frac{\sum_{j^c \neq i} I(d_{ij} \leq d) w_{j^c}}{\sum_{j^c \neq i} I(d_{ij} \leq d) w_j} \bigg/ \sum_{i=1}^{n} \frac{W_c - w_{j^c}}{W - w_j}$$

where w_{j^c} and w_j are weights associated to firms j and j^c, respectively. Analogously, W_c and W are the total weight of firms j^c and the total weight of all firms in the dataset, respectively. The weights can be specified using any useful variable representing the size of firms. If the size is not taken into consideration, the weights are all set to 1.

As with the location quotient, $\hat{M}(d)$ has a benchmark value of 1 for any distance. Therefore, if at a given distance d, $\hat{M}(d)$ is significantly greater than 1, we detect significant relative spatial concentration of firms of the chosen typology of interest if compared to all other firms. However, if at a given distance d, $\hat{M}(d)$ is significantly lower than 1, we detect significant relative spatial dispersion of firms of the chosen typology of interest if compared to all other firms. The confidence interval for the null hypothesis of 1 can be derived through Monte Carlo simulations based on random reassignments of firms' typologies.

Some notable empirical works that employed the M-function to analyze the spatial patterns of firms are those of Jensen and Michel (2011) and Moreno-Monroy and García (2016).

Example 8.3: The spatial pattern of single-plant metallurgy manufacturing firms in the province of Trento

As an example of the application of the *K*-density and *M*-function measures of spatial concentration, and their associated tests, let us suppose that we are interested in analyzing the spatial pattern of a set of micro-data on single-plant firms in the metallurgy manufacturing industry in the province of Trento. This dataset was collected in 2009 by the Italian National Institute of Statistics. The dataset reports, in particular, the full address and the five-digit activity sector reference – according to the Nace Rev. 2 European industrial classification system – of the 1,007 single-plant manufacturing firms operating in the area. On the basis of such information we can identify the 98 single-plant firms belonging to the metallurgy sector. Figure 8.6 shows the spatial distribution of these plants.

In order to detect the genuine spatial concentration generated by the interactions among metallurgical firms, while controlling for the heterogeneity of their geographical territory, we use the $\hat{K}_{density}$ and $\hat{M}(d)$ functions, which consider the spatial distribution of all manufacturing (Figure 8.6a) as the null distribution. Figure 8.7 show the behavior of the two estimated functions, along with the 99% confidence level simulation-based envelopes referring to the null hypothesis of absence of spatial dependence. Both measures reveal a significant strong tendency of metallurgical single-plant firms to cluster until at least 25 km. As a cumulative function which detects spatial interactions up to a certain distance, $\hat{M}(d)$ is better at identifying the global pattern of spatial clustering.

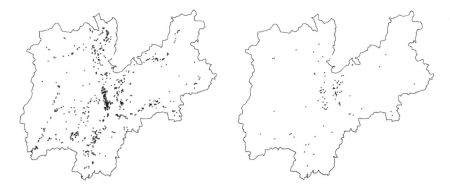

Figure 8.6 Location of the 1,007 single-plant manufacturing firms in the province of Trento, 2009: (a) all manufacturing plants (1,007 observations); (b) plants from the metallurgy sector (98 observations). Source: Italian National Institute of Statistics.

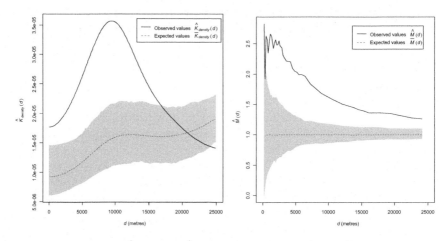

Figure 8.7 Behavior of $\hat{K}_{density}$ and $\hat{M}(d)$ and the corresponding 99% confidence bands for the metallurgy sector in Trento, 2009.

However, as a density function which detects spatial interactions specifically at a certain distance, $\hat{K}_{density}$ is better at detecting the presence of local density of firms. Marcon and Puech (2010) show that $\hat{K}_{density}$ and $\hat{M}(d)$ are complementary rather than alternative approaches to measuring spatial clustering of economic activities and, as a consequence, both measures should be used to provide a complete picture of the spatial pattern of interactions. See Marcon and Puech (2010) for an interesting discussion of this issue.

Note

1 The relevant NACE codes are I55100, I55201, I55202, I55203, I55204, I55205, I55300, I55902.

9 Space–time models

This chapter extends the modeling framework presented in Chapters 7 and 8 to the case of a dynamic point pattern. It introduces the concept of a spatio-temporal K-function which allows the separation of the spatial and temporal dynamics and their interactions. Its use is demonstrated in the context of firm demography.

9.1 Diggle, Chetwynd, Häggkvist and Morris' space–time K-function

Ripley's K-function and its various variants and extensions, presented in Chapters 7 and 8, can be conveniently used to perform an essentially static analysis of the spatial distribution of economic agents on a continuous space. For some microeconomic phenomena of interest, however, analyzing a micro-geographical pattern of events as it is observed in a given single moment of time can be limiting or, worse, misleading. The importance of considering the temporal dynamics in the analysis of spatial patterns of events is well explained by Getis and Boots' seminal work (1978) which defines a useful "framework for viewing spatial processes". The proposed conceptualization illustrates that without looking at the temporal evolution of a phenomenon of interest it is not possible to clearly detect the mechanism generating its spatial structure. More precisely, it is shown that even very different spatio-temporal point processes can lead to spatial patterns that look exactly the same. This implies that only phenomena with no increase or decrease of points over time can be represented as pure spatial processes (Getis and Boots, 1978) and, therefore, can be successfully analyzed while neglecting their time dimension.

Diggle et al. (1995) proposed a dynamic extension of Ripley's K-function which allows the characterization of the second-order properties of a general homogeneous spatio-temporal point process. Let us consider that the observed dataset of interest is a "time-labelled spatial point pattern" where each point location has also a label indicating its time of occurrence. Let us also consider that this dataset is a realization of a spatio-temporal point process that generates countable sets of points (s_i, t_i) where $s_i \in \mathbb{R}^2$ is, following the notation used in Chapter 6, the spatial location of the ith event and $t_i \in \mathbb{R}$ represents its time of

144 *Locational choices of economic agents*

occurrence. If the spatio-temporal point process is homogeneous both in space and time, that is if it is characterized by a constant first-order intensity λ_{ST}, defined as the mean number of events per unitary spatial area per unit time interval, Diggle et al. (1995) suggest that its second-order properties can be defined by the space-time K-function:

$$K(d,t) = \lambda_{ST}^{-1} \, E \, [\text{number of further points falling at a distance} \leq d$$
$$\text{and a time} \leq t \text{ from a typical point}]. \qquad (9.1)$$

In Chapter 7, in the context of static analysis, we have seen that under the null hypothesis of complete spatial randomness, that is if the generating spatial point process is a homogeneous Poisson process, the static K-function can be written in a closed form and, in particular, $K(d) = \pi d^2$. Analogously, Diggle et al. (1995) show that under the null hypothesis of complete spatio-temporal randomness, that is if the locations and the corresponding times of occurrence are generated, respectively, by two independent homogeneous Poisson processes on $\mathbb{R}^2$ and $\mathbb{R}$ then

$$K(d,t) = 2\pi d^2 t. \qquad (9.2)$$

Equation 9.2 can be used as a benchmark to develop formal tests of absence of spatio-temporal interactions among economic agents. Alternatively, under the consideration that in practice the underlying spatio-temporal point process is observed in a finite spatial region, say A, and within a finite time interval, say $(0, T)$, Diggle et al. (1995) suggest that the absence of spatio-temporal interactions among events is also consistent with the independence between the spatial and temporal component processes and hence with the following factorization of the space–time K-function:

$$K(d,t) = K_S(d) \, K_T(t) \qquad (9.3)$$

In Equation 9.3, $K_S(d)$ is Ripley's K-function, as defined in Equation 7.1, that we recall here for convenience:

$$K_S(d) = \lambda_S^{-1} \, E \, [\text{number of further points falling at a distance} \leq d \text{ from a}$$
$$\text{typical point}]$$

and $K_T(t)$ is the K-function of the temporal component process, which is defined as:

$$K_T(t) = \lambda_T^{-1} \, E \, [\text{number of further points falling at a time interval} \leq t \text{ from}$$
$$\text{a typical point}]$$

where λ_S represents the constant spatial intensity, i.e. the mean number of points per unitary area, and similarly λ_T denotes the constant temporal intensity; that is, the mean number of points per unit time.

9.1.1 Estimation of space–time K-function

Diggle et al. (1995) found an approximately unbiased estimator for $K(d,t)$ by extending Ripley's (1976) estimator for static spatial point processes – see Equation 7.4 – to the case of spatio-temporal point processes. In particular, referring to a time-labelled point pattern with (s_i, t_i): $i = 1, 2, ..., n$ locations and corresponding time labels, observed within a spatial region A and a time interval $(0,T)$, the approximately unbiased estimator for $K(d,t)$ is:

$$\hat{K}(d,t) = \frac{|A|T}{n(n-1)} \sum_{i=1}^{n} \sum_{j \neq i} w_{ij}^{-1} v_{ij}^{-1} I(d_{ij} \leq d) I(t_{ij} \leq t) \tag{9.4}$$

where, as usual, d_{ij} is the spatial distance between the ith and the jth observations and $I(d_{ij} \leq d)$ represents the indicator function such that $I = 1$ if $d_{ij} \leq d$ and 0 otherwise. Analogously, t_{ij} is the time interval between the ith and the jth observations and $I(t_{ij} \leq t)$ represents the indicator function such that $I = 1$ if $t_{ij} \leq t$ and 0 otherwise. In addition, as in Equation 7.4, w_{ij} is an edge-effect correction factor corresponding to the proportion of the circumference of the circle centered on s_i, passing through s_j, which lies within the study region A. By analogy, in order to correct also for the potential temporal edge effects, v_{ij} is introduced and consists on the time segment starting from t_i, passing through t_j, lying within the observed total duration time between 0 and T.

Following the same logic, edge-effect adjusted approximately unbiased estimators for $K_S(d)$ and $K_T(t)$ are, respectively,

$$\hat{K}_S(d) = \frac{|A|}{n(n-1)} \sum_{i=1}^{n} \sum_{j \neq i} w_{ij}^{-1} I(d_{ij} \leq d)$$

and

$$\hat{K}_T(t) = \frac{T}{n(n-1)} \sum_{i=1}^{n} \sum_{j \neq i} v_{ij}^{-1} I(t_{ij} \leq t)$$

(Diggle et al., 1995).

9.1.2 Detecting space–time clustering of economic events

With microdata regarding the occurrences of single economic events in space and time, such as the establishment of new firms or the sale of real estate, and under the assumption that the data-generating spatio-temporal point process is homogeneous, the space-time K-function can be used to detect and measure space-time clustering. Since the null hypothesis of complete spatio-temporal randomness can be expressed in terms of independence between the spatial and temporal component processes, and hence by Equation 9.3, one possible

146 *Locational choices of economic agents*

diagnostic tool for space–time clustering of economic agents can be the function proposed by Diggle et al. (1995):

$$\hat{D}(d,t) = \hat{K}(d,t) - \hat{K}_S(d)\,\hat{K}_T(t) \tag{9.5}$$

This empirical summary statistic is proportional to the increased numbers of economic events occurred within spatial distance d and time interval t with respect to a process which is characterized by the same temporal and spatial characteristics but no space–time interaction. Therefore, the presence of space–time interactions can be detected by the emergence of peaks on the 3-dimensional surface of $\hat{D}(d,t)$ plotted against d and t.

Diggle et al. (1995) have also proposed the following transformation of Equation (9.5) that provides relative quantities rather than absolute numbers:

$$\hat{D}_0(d,t) = \hat{D}(d,t) \big/ \left\{ \hat{K}_S(d)\,\hat{K}_T(t) \right\} \tag{9.6}$$

Equation 9.6 is indeed proportional to the relative increase in the occurrence of economic events within spatial distance d and time interval t with respect to a process with the same temporal and spatial characteristics, but no space–time interaction, and, in some empirical circumstances, can ease the interpretation. Likewise $\hat{D}(d,t)$, also $\hat{D}_0(d,t)$ can be plotted in a 3-dimensional graph against d and t to visualize and detect the interaction between the spatial and temporal component processes.

It can be noted that, for any d and t, both $\hat{D}(d,t)$ and $\hat{D}_0(d,t)$ have a benchmark value of 0 representing the null hypothesis of no space–time interactions between economic events. Since the sampling distribution of $\hat{D}(d,t)$ is intractable, Diggle et al. (1995) have introduced a Monte Carlo simulation procedure to assess the statistical significance of the deviations of $\hat{D}(d,t)$ from 0. The procedure consists of performing a number of, say m, simulations in each of which the observed time "labels" are randomly permuted amongst the observed locations. For each of the m resulting simulated spatial–temporal point patterns, a different $\hat{D}(d,t)$ can be computed, thus obtaining $\hat{D}_i(d,t)$: $i = 1,2,...,m$ estimates. The variance of the distribution of these m estimates, say $\hat{V}(d,t)$, provides an unbiased estimate of the variance of $\hat{D}(d,t)$ under the null hypothesis of no space–time interaction (Diggle et al., 1995). The following standardized statistic:

$$\hat{R}(d,t) = \hat{D}(d,t) \big/ \sqrt{\hat{V}(d,t)} \tag{9.7}$$

can then be used as an inferential tool that allows the visualization of deviations from the null hypothesis. In particular, Diggle et al. (1995) suggest that the plot of Equation 9.7 against $\hat{K}_S(d)\,\hat{K}_T(t)$ can be viewed analogously to the plot of the regression model's standardized residuals against model predicted values. Indeed, if there is no significant dependence between the spatial and temporal

Space–time models 147

component processes then approximately 95% of the values of $\hat{R}(d,t)$ would lie within two standard errors (Diggle et al., 1995). As a consequence, a relevant amount of values of $\hat{R}(d,t)$ outside the interval $(-2, 2)$ would indicate a significant deviation from the null hypothesis and hence would reveal a potentially interesting form of space–time interactions among economic agents that could be better interpreted through the examination of the plot of $\hat{D}(d,t)$, or $\hat{D}_0(d,t)$, against d and t.

Finally, Diggle et al. (1995) also proposed a simple global Monte Carlo test for space–time interaction that consists of taking the actual observed sum of the $\hat{R}(d,t)$ values, that is:

$$u = \sum_d \sum_t \hat{R}(d,t)$$

and rank it with respect to the m analogous sums $u_i = \sum_d \sum_t \hat{R}_i(d,t)$: $i = 1, 2, ..., m$ computed for the m Monte Carlo simulated spatio-temporal point patterns. A particularly extreme value of u among the $u_1, ..., u_m$ values would constitute evidence of overall space–time interaction. For example, if u is ranked above (or below) 95 out of 100 values of u_i then the probability that the observed space–time interaction occurred by pure chance is less than 5%.

As a way of illustration of this approach to the analysis and testing of space–time interactions among events, Figures 9.1, 9.2 and 9.3 show the behavior of $\hat{D}(d,t)$ and $\hat{R}(d,t)$ and the performance of the associated Monte Carlo test in the three different paradigmatic empirical circumstances of no space-time interactions, spatio-temporal clustering and spatio-temporal inhibition. In all figures, the first graph (a) depicts a spatio-temporal point pattern where the events' locations are represented by circles with size proportional to the time of occurrence of the events; the second graph (b) is the plot of $\hat{D}(d,t)$ against d and t; and the third graph (c) is the plot of $\hat{R}(d,t)$ against $\hat{K}_S(d)\hat{K}_T(t)$. In particular, Figure 9.1 refers to a stylized fact where economic agents tend to locate independently of where and when the other actors locate. Indeed, Figure 9.1b shows that $\hat{D}(d,t)$ fluctuates randomly around 0, and Figure 9.1c shows that almost all values of $\hat{R}(d,t)$ lie between -2 and 2. Figure 9.2 describes instead the case of space–time clustering where, as depicted by the map, the economic agents that form spatial clusters tend also to have similar times of occurrence. In this case, function $\hat{D}(d,t)$ reveals a strong positive peak around $d = 0.12$ and $t = 0.10$ and the plot of $\hat{R}(d,t)$ indicates that a large amount of values are greater than 2 indicating statistically significant spatio-temporal interactions. On the other hand, Figure 9.3 describes the situation of space–time inhibition where, as it is suggested by graph (a), economic agents tend to locate distancing each other both in space and time. We can indeed observe a significant steep negative peak in the plot of $\hat{D}(d,t)$.

148 *Locational choices of economic agents*

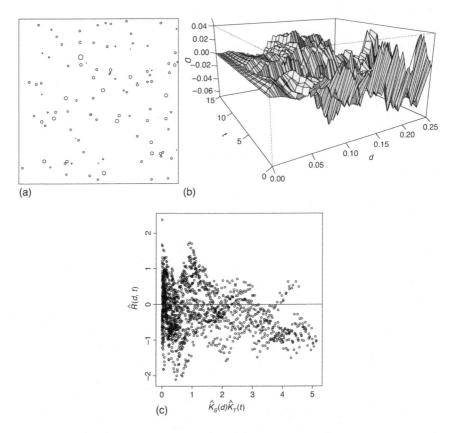

Figure 9.1 Performance of the space–time K-function approach under complete spatio-temporal randomness (*p*-value test Monte Carlo = 0.816).

The space–time K-function has been used in some empirical economic related studies. For example, Arbia et al. (2010) used this approach to detect the existence of space–time clustering of ICT firms in Rome; Kang (2010) analyzed the spatio-temporal distribution of firms in the Columbus metropolitan area (Ohio); Conrow et al. (2015) studied the spatio-temporal relationship between alcohol sellers' locations and crime events in Buffalo, New York.

9.2 Gabriel and Diggle's *STIK*-function

Diggle et al.'s space–time K-function (1995) can properly describe and detect the spatio-temporal characteristics of an observed time-labelled point pattern dataset under the assumption that the data-generating spatio-temporal process is homogeneous, both in space and time. Nevertheless, the associated Monte Carlo test for space–time interaction, which is based on random permutations of

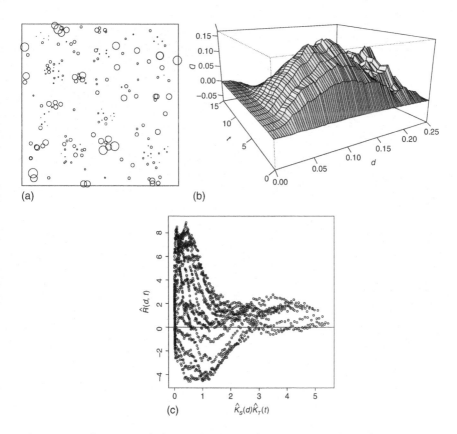

Figure 9.2 Performance of the space–time *K*-function approach under space-time clustering (*p*-value test Monte Carlo = 0.001).

the time labels t_i: $i = 1, 2, ..., n$, still provides valid inference even if the underlying data-generating process is inhomogeneous (Diggle et al., 1995).

However, in order to deal explicitly with spatio-temporal inhomogeneity, Gabriel and Diggle (2009) proposed an extension of the space–time *K*-function to the context of inhomogeneous spatio-temporal point processes. Their proposed space–time inhomogeneous *K*-function (*STIK*-function) formally is a reduced measure of the second-order properties of an inhomogeneous spatio-temporal point process and, as we will show, can be efficiently used to measure and detect spatio-temporal clustering of economic events (e.g. firm entries or exits) while controlling for the heterogeneity of the territory and/or time period under study.

Let us continue to assume that the observed time-labelled point pattern (s_i, t_i): $i = 1, 2, ..., n$ is a realization of a spatio-temporal point process. Let us consider, however, that now this process is inhomogeneous. Analogously to what we have seen for purely spatial point processes in Chapter 6, an inhomogeneous spatio-temporal point process is characterized by a non-constant first-order

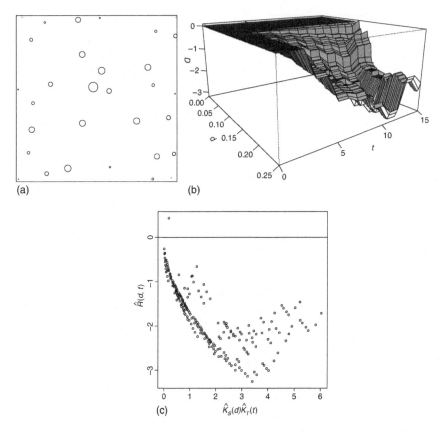

Figure 9.3 Performance of the space–time K-function approach under space-time inhibition (p-value test Monte Carlo = 0.001).

intensity function, $\lambda(s,t)$, that in a spatio-temporal setting can be defined as follows (Gabriel and Diggle, 2009):

$$\lambda(s,t) = \lim_{|ds \times dt| \to 0} \frac{E[N(ds \times dt)]}{|ds \times dt|} \tag{9.8}$$

where $ds \times dt$ is an infinitesimally small spatio-temporal region containing the point (s,t), $N(ds \times dt)$ represents the number of points located in it and $|ds \times dt|$ is the volume of $ds \times dt$. Equation 9.8 can therefore be interpreted as the expected number of points located within an infinitesimal region centered on the point (s,t). As a consequence, a relatively high (low) value of $\lambda(s,t)$ implies a relatively high (low) expected concentration of points located around (s,t).

In the context of the study of economic phenomena, $\lambda(s,t)$ may describe spatio-temporal heterogeneity which occurs because exogenous factors lead economic agents to locate in certain geographical areas and during certain times.

Space–time models 151

For example, firms may not locate in some areas and period of times due to the presence of legal and geophysical limitations or may locate in certain zones during given periods because of the influence of exogenous factors such as the timely presence of useful infrastructures, the proximity to communication routes or more advantageous local taxation systems.

According to Gabriel and Diggle (2009), the second-order intensity function can be generalized from the context of a purely spatial point process to the setting of a spatio-temporal point process using the following function:

$$\lambda_2\left((s,t),(s',t')\right) = \lim_{|ds\times dt|,|ds'\times dt'|\to 0} \frac{E\left[N\left(ds\times dt\right)N\left(ds'\times dt'\right)\right]}{|ds\times dt||ds'\times dt'|}$$

where (s,t) and (s',t') denote two distinct generic events in the spatio-temporal domain. Informally, $\lambda_2\left((s,t),(s',t')\right)$ can be interpreted as the expected number of point events located in s' and occurred in time t' or located in s and occurred in time t.

In the context of the analysis of the spatio-temporal distribution of economic agents, $\lambda_2\left((s,t),(s',t')\right)$ may describe, for example, the spatio-temporal dependence occurring when the presence of an economic activity in an area, because of the working of spatial externalities, attracts other firms to locate in the same area relatively rapidly.

In reality, space–time clusters of economic activities may be due to the joint action of spatio-temporal heterogeneity and spatio-temporal interactions among economic agents. However, in many empirical applications, although it is important to measure the agglomeration of economic activities properly, it is often important to disentangle heterogeneity from interactions or, in other words, to distinguish between exogenous and endogenous formation of clusters of economic agents.

The *STIK*-function (which represents a different and more tractable measure, with respect to $\lambda_2\left(\cdot\right)$, of the second-order properties of a spatio-temporal point process), can be used to identify the endogenous effects of the spatio-temporal interactions among economic agents after adjusting for the exogenous effects of the spatio-temporal characteristics of the region under observation.

It is useful to first introduce the pair correlation function (Gabriel and Diggle, 2009):

$$g\left((s,t),(s',t')\right) = \frac{\lambda_2\left((s,t),(s',t')\right)}{\lambda(s,t)\lambda(s',t')}$$

which can be heuristically interpreted as a measure of the spatio-temporal association between (s,t) and (s',t'). Indeed, in the case of no spatio-temporal interactions between (s,t) and (s',t') we have $\lambda_2\left((s,t),(s',t')\right) = \lambda(s,t)\lambda(s',t')$ and hence $g\left((s,t),(s',t')\right) = 1$. On the other hand, if $\lambda_2\left((s,t),(s',t')\right) > \lambda(s,t)\lambda(s',t')$ and $g\left((s,t),(s',t')\right) > 1$ we detect some form of attraction, while if $\lambda_2\left((s,t),(s',t')\right) < \lambda(s,t)\lambda(s',t')$ and $g\left((s,t),(s',t')\right) < 1$ we have some form of repulsion, or inhibition, between (s,t) and (s',t').

152 *Locational choices of economic agents*

While extending the concept of second-order reweighted stationarity introduced by Baddeley et al. (2000) (see Chapter 8) from a pure spatial context to a spatio-temporal setting, Gabriel and Diggle (2009) define a spatio-temporal point process as second-order intensity reweighted stationary and isotropic if $\lambda(s,t)$ is bounded away from zero and if $g\left((s,t),(s',t')\right)$ depends only on the spatial distance u, between s and s', and the time interval v, between t and t'.

In the light of these concepts and definitions, the *STIK*-function of a second-order intensity reweighted stationary and isotropic spatio-temporal point process can be written as (Gabriel and Diggle, 2009):

$$K_{ST}(u,v) = 2\pi \int_{-v}^{v} \int_{0}^{u} g(u',v') u' \mathrm{d}u' \mathrm{d}v' \tag{9.9}$$

with $g(u,v) = \lambda_2(u,v) / \left(\lambda(s,t) \lambda(s',t') \right)$.

Gabriel and Diggle (2009) show that the *STIK*-function can be used to develop a formal test for the presence of spatio-temporal concentration because, under the null hypothesis of no spatial temporal interactions, it is possible to compute the integral in the right-hand side of Equation 9.9 and hence writing $K_{ST}(u,v)$ in a closed form. The inhomogeneous spatio-temporal Poisson process is the process which represents the benchmark of no spatio-temporal interactions in a heterogeneous environment, where the spatio-temporal heterogeneity is specified by a known first-order intensity function $\lambda(s,t)$ (see Diggle, 2007). Gabriel and Diggle (2009) show that if the observed points (s_i,t_i) : $i = 1,2,...,n$ are a realization of an inhomogeneous spatio-temporal Poisson process with given $\lambda(s,t)$, then

$$K_{ST}(u,v) = \pi u^2 v, \text{ with } u > 0 \text{ and } v > 0 \tag{9.10}$$

Equation 9.10 can properly represent the null hypothesis of no spatio-temporal interactions among events. Therefore, significant deviations from this benchmark indicate the alternative hypothesis of spatio-temporal dependence. In particular, if $K_{ST}(u,v) > \pi u^2 v$ we detect positive dependence and then spatio-temporal clustering (a situation where events tend to attract each other both in time and space); in contrast, when $K_{ST}(u,v) < \pi u^2 v$ we have, as usual, evidence of negative dependence and hence inhibition (in which events tend to distance each other both spatially and in time).

9.2.1 Estimation of STIK-function and inference

A significance test to verify whether economic agents tend to interact in space and time may consist of assessing if, for some u and v, the function $K_{ST}(u,v) - \pi u^2 v$, estimated on the observed spatio-temporal distribution of the economic agents $(s_i,t_i) : i = 1,2,...,n$ within a spatial region A and a time interval $(0,T)$, is significantly greater than 0. Diggle and Gabriel (2009) have shown that an approximately unbiased estimator for $K_{ST}(u,v)$ is

$$\hat{K}_{ST}(u,v) = \frac{1}{|A|T} \frac{n}{n_v} \sum_{i=1}^{n_v} \sum_{j>i}^{n_v} \frac{1}{w_{ij}} \frac{1}{\lambda(s_i,t_i)\lambda(s_j,t_j)} I\left(u_{ij} \le u\right) I\left(t_{ij} \le v\right) \quad (9.10)$$

which has to be computed with the (s_i, t_i) sorted so that $t_i < t_{i+1}$. The notation in Equation 9.10 is coherent with that used for Equation 9.4. The new term n_v refers to the number of point for which $t_i \le T - v$. The introduction of n/n_v allows to adjust for the temporal edge effects (Diggle and Gabriel, 2009).

We already know from Chapter 8 that in practical applications $\lambda(s,t)$ in Equation 9.10 is unknown and that, in general, it is difficult to identify a theoretical economic model that specifies a given functional form for it. In most cases it has then to be estimated. In this respect, Gabriel and Diggle (2009) suggest using the working assumption that $\lambda(s,t)$ can be factorized into the product of the separated spatial intensity, say $m(s)$, and temporal intensity, say $\mu(t)$: that is, that $\lambda(s,t) = m(s)\mu(t)$. According to this assumption, the separable effects are considered of first-order kind, and hence generated by the spatio-temporal heterogeneity, while the non-separable effects are considered of second-order kind, and hence as a consequence of spatio-temporal interactions among events (Gabriel and Diggle, 2009). As in the purely spatial context considered in Chapter 8, both parametric and nonparametric approaches to the estimation of $m(s)$ and $\mu(t)$ are available. In case the nonparametric estimation is preferable, a suitable procedure is that of kernel smoothing. Alternatively, if suitable additional information is available one can still rely on parametric regression models where $m(s)$ and $\mu(t)$ are specified as functions of a set of, respectively, geographically and temporally referenced variables capturing the effects of spatio-temporal heterogeneity. These variables should represent common contextual factors shared by the economic agents located in the same area during the same period of time. This would allow the inclusion of both individual traits and the context where the economic agents operate within a unified framework.

In order to evaluate the statistical significance of the deviations of $\hat{K}_{ST}(u,v) - \pi u^2 v$ from 0 we can rely on Monte Carlo simulated tolerance envelopes (Gabriel and Diggle, 2009). In particular, we can rely on an inferential procedure that consists on generating counterfactual spatio-temporal point patterns according to an inhomogeneous spatio-temporal Poisson process with first-order intensity $\hat{\lambda}(s,t) = \hat{m}(s)\hat{\mu}(t)$, conditional upon the number of the observed events.

Example 9.1: Long run spatial dynamics of ICT firms in Rome, 1920–2005

Let us consider an example that illustrates the use of the *STIK*-function approach to the analysis of the spatio-temporal clustering of firms in the ICT sector in Rome. The data we are using consist of the locations of new ICT firms in Rome observed over a fairly long period, 1920 to 2005. In particular, the dataset reports the full address and the year of establishment of the 169 plants currently

154 *Locational choices of economic agents*

operating in the area, thus disregarding the firms that exited the market before 2005. Figure 9.4 displays the spatial and temporal distribution of these firms. As can be noted, the economic activity seems to concentrate in some specific geographical areas (namely the main urban areas of the city) and in the most recent years.

Due to the unavailability of other variables proxying for the contextual spatial and temporal heterogeneity, we may find it proper to estimate the separate temporal intensity $\mu(t)$ of the establishment of new firms using standard kernel density smoothing. As we already know from Chapter 8, the separate spatial intensity $m(s)$, can be properly estimated using the spatial kernel estimator proposed by Baddeley et al. (2000) (see Equation 8.4). Figure 9.5 displays the resulting estimates for the spatial and temporal intensity functions.

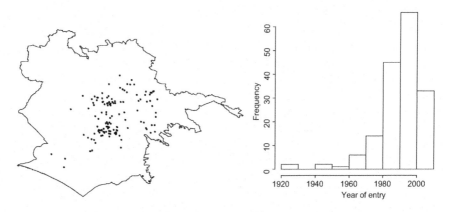

Figure 9.4 Spatial (a) and temporal (b) distribution of the 169 new firms in the ICT sector in Rome, 1920–2005. Source: Industrial Union of Rome (UIR).

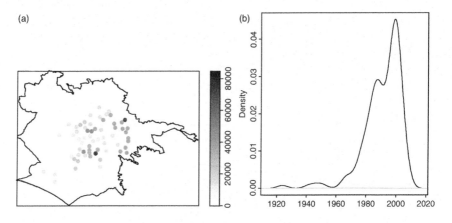

Figure 9.5 Estimated spatial intensity (a) and temporal intensity (b) for new firms in the ICT sector in Rome, 1920–2005.

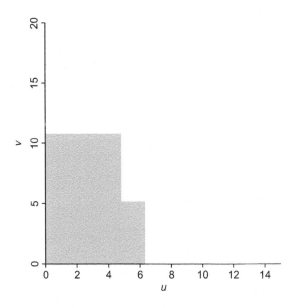

Figure 9.6 Plot of the function $\hat{K}_{ST}(u,v) - \pi u^2 v$ for new firms in the ICT sector in Rome, 1920–2005, compared with the tolerance envelopes under the null hypothesis of no spatio-temporal interactions: shaded areas are those leading to rejection of the null hypothesis.

Now that we have an estimate of $\hat{\mu}(t)$ and $\hat{m}(s)$ we can obtain $\hat{K}_{ST}(u,v) - \pi u^2 v$ and perform the test for spatio-temporal interactions among new firms while adjusting for an underlying spatial and temporal trend. According to Gabriel and Diggle (2009) the results of the test can be usefully visualized as in Figure 9.6. In particular, this kind of graph summarizes the comparison between the behavior of $\hat{K}_{ST}(u,v) - \pi u^2 v$, which refers to the observed data, and the tolerance envelopes simulated according to the null hypothesis of no spatio-temporal interactions among economic agents: the shaded areas identify the values of spatial distance u and temporal distance v for which the empirical $\hat{K}_{ST}(u,v) - \pi u^2 v$, describing the observed firm entries data, is above the 95th percentile of the $\hat{K}_{ST}(u,v) - \pi u^2 v$ (thus rejecting the null hypothesis) computed on 1,000 simulations of an inhomogeneous Poisson process with first-order intensity $\hat{\lambda}(s,t) = \hat{m}(s)\hat{\mu}(t)$.

Significant spatio-temporal clusters of ICT firms occur with a time lag of approximately 10 years up to a distance of basically 5 km. This provides evidence of a phenomenon of space–time clustering which cannot be explained merely by spatio-temporal heterogeneity (an exogenous characteristic of the observed area and of the observed period, as described by $\hat{\mu}(t)$ and $\hat{m}(s)$), but it is also due to some form of genuine interaction amongst economic agents.

Part IV

Looking ahead

Modeling both the spatial location choices and the spatial behavior of economic agents

10 Firm demography and survival analysis

10.1 Introduction

Part II of this book was devoted to methods and techniques for analyzing the spatial behavior of individual economic agents taking their locations as exogenously given. Part III was devoted to the methodologies used to study the locational choice of economic agents and their joint locations with respect to other agents. The scope of the growing field of spatial microeconometrics makes use of both streams of literature to build up a new modeling strategy which treats location as endogenous and takes into account simultaneously both individuals' locational choices and their economic decisions in the chosen location. The literature in this area is still relatively in its infancy (Dubé and Legros, 2014; Arbia et al., 2016) and rather scattered in a few articles. The aim of this chapter is to show through case studies how it is possible to join together within a unified framework the lessons learnt in the first chapters of this book and produce models in this direction.

A first example of a spatial microeconometric model can be found in the literature related to firm demography and firm survival. The current state-of-the-art in this area includes a vast variety of contributions and empirical methodologies mainly for data aggregated at macro- or meso-territorial levels, in which the typical observations consist of administrative units such as regions, counties or municipalities. Comparatively less attention has been devoted to the development of a systematic approach to the analysis of individual micro-data where the observations are represented by the locations of each individual firm. This approach strongly limits the possibility of obtaining robust evidences about economic dynamics for two main reasons. The first is related to the modifiable areal unit problem (Arbia, 1989) mentioned in Chapter 1: with regional data we do not observe the dynamics of the single individual but only the dynamics of variables within arbitrary partitions of the territory. The second reason is that theoretical models of firm demography are based on behavioral models of single individual economic agents (Hopenhayn, 1992; Krueger, 2003; Lazear, 2005 among others), so that if we base our conclusions on regional aggregates we support the theoretical model only if we are ready to admit the restrictive and unrealistic assumption of the homogeneity of each firm's behavior

160   *Looking ahead*

within the region. In the few remarkable cases where a genuine micro-approach was adopted, the results confirm the relevance of neighborhood effects that reveal interesting scenarios for future researches. For instance, Igami (2011) shows that the introduction of a new large supermarket in one area increases the chance of failure for larger stores in the neighborhood, but increases the probability of survival of smaller incumbents. Analyzing a set of data collected in the food retailing sector, Borraz et al. (2014) show that the establishment of a supermarket in the neighborhood of a small store significantly increases the probability of the small store going out of business in the same year. A good way of overcoming these limitations is to simply remove the boundaries and analyze the economy of a continuous space. Economists often see that economic activities are located in a continuous space and that "there is no particular reason to think that national boundaries define a relevant region" (Krugman 1991a; 1991b). So why should a regional boundary define a relevant region? Obviously we are not saying that boundaries should be ignored altogether but only that we need to distinguish between the meanings of boundaries in different situations. In some instances boundaries can be classified as significant borders, that is, places where the economic conditions change abruptly because of some change, for example, in the tax system or transport costs. In other instances borders are irrelevant, where nothing actually happens from an economic standpoint. Starting from these considerations, we think that the shift of emphasis from a meso- to a micro-level is likely to bear interesting fruit. Krugman (1991a) has remarked that "if we want to understand differences in national growth rate, a good place to start is by examining differences in regional growth". Here we assert that a good way to understand regional economics is to begin by examining the micro-behavior of economic agents in the economic space, and so explore the micro-foundations of regional economics. After a model has been identified at the micro spatial level, we can always superimpose an administrative grid and examine the implied meso-scenario.

In fact, phenomena in nature are encountered in continuous space and are developed over continuous time; it is only due to our limitations that we discretize phenomena in some way (and subsequently distort it by reducing the quantity of information). Apart from the motivations given in the previous sections, a more remote incentive to study the continuous properties of economic phenomena dates back to Leibniz and his famous quote: "natura non facit saltus".[1] The same general idea has been adopted in time-series analysis with the development of continuous time econometrics and is providing significant contributions to many branches of economics (see Gandolfo 1990; Bergstrom 1990). The idea of continuous space modeling is not new in economic geography and spatial economics: it was present in Weber's studies of industrial location at the beginning of the twentieth century (Weber, 1909). More recently Beckmann (1970) and Beckmann and Puu (1985) analyzed equilibrium conditions of models defined in a continuous space. Griffith (1986) discusses a spatial demand curve based on a central place economic landscape defined on a continuous surface. Kaashoek and Paelinck (1994; 1996; 1998) derive the properties of a non-equilibrium

Firm demography and survival analysis 161

dynamic path of continuous space economic variables based on partial differential equation theory (John 1978; Toda 1989). However, these studies are all concerned with the theoretical properties of models, whereas we are interested in identifying models susceptible to statistical estimation and testing on the basis of existing data.

There are many reasons why such an approach has not been adopted thus far. The most obvious are lack of an appropriate statistical methodology, lack of accurate data (often not available for confidentiality reasons) and lack of appropriate computer technologies. However, the methods for analyzing spatial data on a continuous space now form a well-consolidated methodological body as it was extensively discussed in this book. The availability of statistical data at the individual agent level has also increased considerably in recent times, due to the diffusion of spatially referenced administrative records, new Big Data sources, as discussed at length in Chapter 1.3, and the development of methods to conceal confidential data without seriously distorting the statistical information (see Cox 1980; Duncan and Lambert 1986; De Waal and Willenborg 1998; Willenborg and De Waal 1996; Arbia et al., 2016; Chapter 3.5). As a consequence, there no longer appear to be any technical obstacles in a microeconomic approach to regional problems. We will formalize such an approach in the next section.

10.2 A spatial microeconometric model for firm demography

10.2.1 A spatial model for firm demography

10.2.1.1 Introduction

In this section we will introduce a class of testable models to help explain the concentration of firms in space. The formalism is taken from Arbia (2001) and derives from a model proposed by Rathbun and Cressie (1994) for the spatial diffusion of vegetation. Our modelling framework also shares a particular resemblance with the methodology employed by Van Wissen (2000) to simulate the dynamics of firm demography in space. However, even if the set-up of the model is similar, we must emphasize that in Van Wissen's approach (as in other recent works on firm demography, see Bade and Nerlinger 2000; Van Dijk and Pellenbarg 2000), the aim is to model firm behavior within regions. Our goal, however, is to explain why a firm locates (develops and dies) at a certain point in space. Indeed, the stochastic point processes theory presented in Part III is at the basis of possible firm demography models which account for the links of spatial interactions amongst individual economic agents. By treating the spatial distribution of the economic activities as the result of a dynamic process which occurs in space and time, the observed micro-geographical patterns can be modeled as realizations of a marked space–time survival point processes (see Chapter 6), where firms are created at some random location and at some point in time and then they operate, grow and attract (or repulse) other firms in their

162 *Looking ahead*

neighborhood. Following the reductionist approach already exploited by Arbia (2001), in this section we formalize three different model components:

i   a birth model,
ii a growth model and
iii a death/survival model.

Such an approach can prove very useful in that the model parameters can provide indications of how to validate the different paradigmatic economic-theoretical cases, such as the presence of spatial spillover effects, the effects of positive spatial externalities or hypotheses concerning the spatial inhibition processes among economic agents.

10.2.1.2 The birth model

The first element of the comprehensive spatial microeconometrics approach is constituted by an equation for the birth of new firms. In this methodological framework the observed spatial point pattern of new firms is assumed to be the realization of a point process conditional on the locations of existing firms in that moment.

In order to formalize our model, we rely on the spatial point process methodology (Diggle, 2003) introduced in Chapter 6. Within this framework, a spatial point process is considered as a stochastic mechanism that generates patterns of points on a planar map. The basic characteristic of a spatial point process is the intensity function, introduced in Equation 6.1 and denoted by the symbol $\lambda(x)$. Thus, by definition, the higher $\lambda(x)$, the higher the expected concentration of points around x (see Arbia et al., 2008).

Following the modeling framework originally proposed in a seminal paper by Rathbun and Cressie (1994) and imported by Arbia (2001) into the field of regional economics, the formation process of new firms can be modeled as an inhomogeneous Poisson process (see Diggle, 2003) with intensity function $\lambda(x)$ driven by the potential interaction effects of the existing firms. The values of $\lambda(x)$ constitute a realization of a random function parametrically specified by the following model:

$$\lambda(x) = exp\{\alpha + \beta_1 d(x) + \beta_2 W(x) + \beta_3 Z(x) + \Phi(x)\beta_k\} \qquad (10.1)$$

where α, β_1, β_2, β_3 are parameters to be estimated, $d(x)$ indicates the distance of point x from a conspicuous point (see Section 3.6) and $W(x)$ is a term measuring the sign and the intensity of the interaction between the firm located in point x and the other existing firms and incorporates the idea of non-constant spatial returns. A particular specification for the $W(x)$ function was suggested by Arbia (2001). Furthermore, in Equation 10.1, Z represents a vector of independent variables assumed to be spatially heterogeneous (such as demand or unitary transport costs and regional policy instruments such as local taxation, incentives) that can influence the birth of economic activities in the long-run. Finally $\Phi(x)$ is the error term of the model assumed to be spatially stationary, Gaussian and zero mean, but non-zero spatial correlations. Due to the nature of the error term, the estimation of Equation 10.1 presents some problems that will be discussed more thoroughly in Section 10.2.2 where we discuss a numerical application of the model. Notice that Equation 10.1 can be seen as a continuous space version of Krugman's concentration model that avoids the problems associated with arbitrary geographical partitions (see Krugman, 1991a). An example of the formalization of Equation 10.1 was already presented in Example 8.1.

10.2.1.3 The growth model

The second component of our model is the spatial growth dynamic of the firms. In this context, the growth of a single firm (proxied, for example, by the growth in the number of employees), is assumed to be a function of its stage of development at the beginning of the period and of the competitive (or cooperative) influences of the other firms located in the neighborhood.

Following the framework suggested by Rathbun and Cressie (1994) and Arbia (2001), the growth of the ith firm can be modeled as follows:

$$g_i = \varphi_0 + \varphi_1 D\ (x) + \varphi_2 W_i + \varepsilon_i \tag{10.2}$$

where g_i represents the growth of firm i in a certain period of time, $D\ (x)$ represents its dimension at the beginning of the period, and:

$$W_i = \sum_{j=1}^{n} \Phi_{ij} \tag{10.3}$$

represent measures of the level of spatial interaction between the firms, φ_1, φ_2 and φ_3 are parameters to be estimated and the ε_i's are independently and normally distributed errors with zero mean and a finite variance.

10.2.1.4 The survival model

The last component of the model is devoted to uncovering the death/survival process that together with the other two components brings the time dimension into the discussion and to fully describing the whole spatial demographic phenomenon. The death/survival process is fitted to the firms existing at a given moment of time which have survived or ceased to operate in a certain time interval. According to the methodological framework proposed by Rathbun and Cressie (1994) and Arbia (2001), a death/survival process can be developed as a survival conditional probability model which will be now described. Let x_i^t denote the spatial coordinates of firms, which survive at time t. Let also Z_i^t be a measure of firm dimension at time t (such as the number of employees). Finally let $M_i(t)$ denote a survivorship indicator variable such that $M_i(t) = 1$ if the ith

164   *Looking ahead*

firm survives at time t and $M_i(t) = 0$ if it ceases its activity at time t. The survival probability of the ith firm can then be defined as:

$$p_i(t;\theta) \equiv P\{M_i(t;\theta) = 1 \mid M_i(t-1;\theta) = 1\} \tag{10.4}$$

where θ is a set of unknown parameters. By assuming that the survival at time t is a function of the dimension of the firm at time $t-1$ and of the competitive or cooperative influences of the other neighboring firms also operating at time $t-1$, $p_i(t;\theta)$ is then modeled using the following space–time logistic regression (Rathbun and Cressie, 1994):

$$\ln\left[\frac{p_i(t,\theta)}{1 - p_i(t,\theta)}\right] = \theta_0 + \theta_1 D\ (x) + \theta_2 W_i \tag{10.5}$$

where again, as in Equation 10.2:

$$W_i = \sum_{j=1}^{n} \Phi_{ij}(Z_i, d = \left\| x_i^t - x_i^{t-1} \right\|) \tag{10.6}$$

represent measures of the level of spatial interaction of the ith firm, $\Phi_{ij}(Z,d)$ is a known function which can be specified by the same functional forms already proposed for the growth model's Equations 10.1 and 10.2, and θ_0, θ_1 and θ_2 are the parameters to be estimated.

Given a proper specification of $\Phi_{ij}(Z,d)$ and hence given Equation 10.6, θ for Equation 10.5 can be estimated using the standard maximum likelihood procedure.

This model aims to test the hypothesis that the presence of firms in one location can attract or inhibit the establishment of other firms in nearby locations.

10.2.2 A case study

10.2.2.1 Data description

In the past, most of the studies on firm demography were based on data on firm location aggregated at the level of geographical partitions such as regions, counties or countries mainly due to data limitations. The scenario, however, is rapidly changing and the accessibility of micro-geographical data related to single economic agents is becoming more and more common in many applied studies. In particular, when dealing with firm demography, many existing official databases are enriched with detailed information related to a single firm, including its geographical coordinates and a set of relevant variables, such as production, capital and labor inputs, level of technology and many others. A good example of such an informative database is the Statistical Register of Active Enterprises, managed and updated by the Italian Statistical Institute. At the firm level, this database currently contains information about firm code, tax code, business name, sector of activity (according to the NACE classification), number of employees, legal status (according to the current classification), class of sales, date of establishment and (if applicable) of termination. Drawn from such a rich database, the data employed in the case study analyzed in the present chapter refer to the geographical location and the number of employees of small retail food stores and big supermarkets[2] also selling food products operating in the town of Trento between 2004 and 2007. The model presented here draws heavily on work by Arbia et al. (2014a; 2017) and consists of the three basic components discussed in Section 10.2.1 We can conceive the three models as a way of describing different aspects of the phenomenon. Consequently (and consistently with Rathbun and Cressie, 1994), the three models are estimated separately and not simultaneously with no interaction effects, thus eliminating possible problems of simultaneity that could arise in the estimation methods and undermine their validity. More specifically, the case study refers to food stores in Trento, the birth component model will be fitted to the observed spatial distribution of 26 small retail food stores established after 2004 which were still active in 2007. Similarly, the growth component model will be fitted to the observed spatial pattern of the 72 small retail food stores established in 2004 or earlier, which were always active in the period from 2004 to 2007. Finally, the death/survival component process will be fitted to the 229 small retail food stores which were established in 2004 or earlier and that survived at least until 2007 or ceased to operate during the period 2004 to 2007. The three point patterns relative to birth, growth and survival, are represented in Figure 10.1.

In this methodological framework the observed spatial point pattern of the establishment of new small food stores is assumed to be the realization of a point process conditional on the locations of existing small food stores and big supermarkets in that moment. Our model aims to test the hypothesis that big

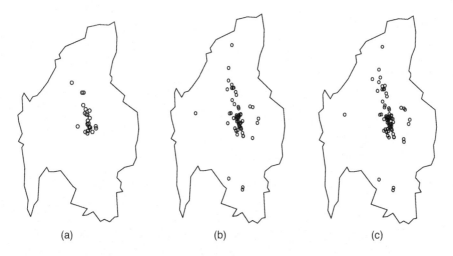

Figure 10.1 Spatial point patterns of small retail food stores used to estimate: (a) the firm establishment process, 2004–2007; (b) the firm growth process, 2004–2007; (c) the firm survival process, 2004–2007.

166 *Looking ahead*

supermarkets inhibit the establishment of small food stores in nearby locations, while, due to the presence of positive spatial externalities, the presence of small food stores attract other small food stores (see Igami, 2011; Borraz et al., 2014).

10.2.2.2 *The birth model*

Following the modelling framework described in Section 3.4.2 the new firm formation process of small food stores during the period 2004 to 2007 is modeled as an inhomogeneous Poisson process with intensity function $\lambda(x)$ driven by the potential interaction effects of the existing small food stores and big supermarkets. The values of $\lambda(x)$ can thus be conceived as a realization of a random function parametrically specified by the following model:

$$\lambda(x) = \exp\left\{\alpha + \beta_{ss} n_{ss}(x) + \beta_{bs} n_{bs}(x) + \beta_{nh} n_{nh}(x) + \beta_{af} n_{af}(x)\right\} \tag{10.7}$$

where $\beta_{ss}, \beta_{bs}, \beta_{nh}, \beta_{af}$ are the parameters to be estimated. The variables $n_{ss}(x)$ and $n_{bs}(x)$ measure the overall number of employees of the small food stores and, respectively, of big supermarkets, existing from before 2005 which are located around the arbitrary point x.

The two additional variables $n_{nh}(x)$ and $n_{af}(x)$ control for other factors that can affect the spatial intensity of the formation process of new small food stores. Locational choices of firms, and in particular of retail activities, can strongly depend on the potential market demand. As a proxy for the spatial distribution of potential customers in the city of Trento we use the number of households by census tract in 2004, which is at the finest level of spatial resolution. In order to properly include this data in the modeling framework of Equation 10.7 we can build up a marked point pattern (see Chapter 6) where the points are the centroids of the census tracts and the associated marks represent the number of household per census tract (see Figure 10.2). Then we could define the control variable $n_{nh}(x)$, which measures the number of households in 2004 that reside close to the arbitrary point x.

However, the decision to open a new firm in a particular location is also affected by the spatial characteristics of the territory (such as the urban structure, the presence of useful infrastructure or environmental and administrative limits). To control for these unidentified sources of spatial heterogeneity, we can include the variable $n_{af}(x)$, which is constructed as the overall number of employees of all firms of all industries, operating from before 2005, located around the generic point x. The use of this specific control variable is motivated by the assumption that the main unobserved exogenous spatial factors affecting the locational choices of firms are common for all the economic agents. The model is based on the working assumption that the locations of incumbent economic agents operating before 2005 are exogenously given. As already remarked by Arbia (2001), this hypothesis is consistent with Krugman's idea of "historical initial conditions" (Krugman, 1991a). The logarithmic transformation allows to fit the model maximizing the log pseudo-likelihood for $\lambda(x)$ (Besag, 1975) based on the points x constituting the observed point pattern.

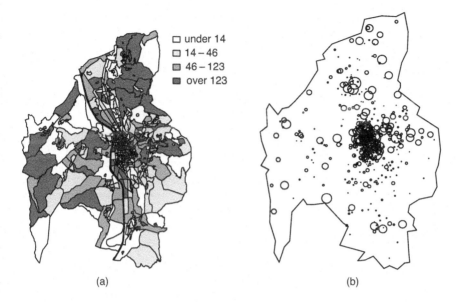

Figure 10.2 Number of households by census tract in 2004 in Trento: (a) as a census tracts map of the quartile distribution; (b) as a marked point pattern.

According to the current state-of-the-art in the spatial statistics literature, the most efficient and versatile method of maximizing the log pseudo-likelihood (thus obtaining unbiased estimates of the parameters) is the technique proposed by Berman and Turner (1992). (For a clear and detailed discussion of the method, see Baddeley and Turner, 2000.) As shown, for example, by Strauss and Ikeda (1990), maximum pseudo-likelihood is equivalent to maximum likelihood in the case of a Poisson stochastic process. Therefore, it is possible to test the significance of the estimated model parameters by using standard formal likelihood ratio criteria based on the χ^2 distribution.

The maximum pseudo-likelihood estimates of the parameters for the birth process model (Equation 10.7) are reported in Table 10.1. The significantly positive value of the estimate of β_{ss} indicates that establishment of small food stores is positively dependent on the locations and sizes of the existing small food stores, while the significantly negative value of the estimate of β_{bs} indicates that they are negatively dependent on the locations and sizes of the existing big supermarkets. Therefore, the probability of the establishment of new small food stores is higher in the locations characterized by the presence of other existing small food stores thus highlighting the presence of positive spatial externalities. On the other hand, such probability is lower in the locations characterized by the presence of existing big supermarkets, which indicates the presence of negative spatial externalities. The model also reveals the presence of a positive significant relationship between the spatial intensity and the two proxies of market potential and the urban structure (respectively the parameters β_{nh} and β_{af}).

168 Looking ahead

In the model considered, no measure is available to test the goodness-of-fit playing a role similar to that of R^2 in the OLS standard regression. To this aim, however, it is possible to rely on Monte Carlo simulations. The adequacy of the model to the observed data can indeed be visually assessed by looking at the behavior of the empirical inhomogeneous K-function (see Section 6.3.2.1) of the observed 26 new small retail food stores point pattern (see Figure 10.1a) plotted against the behavior of the inhomogeneous K-function, in terms of confidence bands, derived from 999 simulations of the estimated model.

Figure 10.3 shows the behavior of the empirical $\hat{K}_I(d) - \pi d^2$ calculated from the observed point pattern of the new small food stores against the upper and lower confidence bands calculated from 999 realizations of the estimated model. The benchmark value representative of a good fit is zero for each distance d. As it can be noted, the empirical function tends to be close to zero and lies entirely within the confidence bands thus indicating that the estimated model describes adequately the spatial birth phenomenon of small food stores.

Table 10.1 Estimates for the spatial establishment point process of new small food stores

Parameter	Estimate	Standard error	z-test
α	−18.900	0.8809	
β_{ss}	0.074	0.0234	**
β_{bs}	−0.028	0.0075	***
β_{nh}	0.004	0.0012	***
β_{af}	0.001	0.0003	***

Significant at 5%; * Significant at 1%.

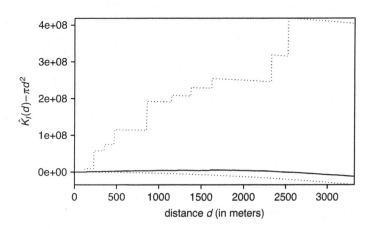

Figure 10.3 Behavior of the empirical $\hat{K}_I(d) - \pi d^2$ (continuous line) and the corresponding 99.9% confidence bands (dashed lines).

10.2.2.3 The growth model

The spatial growth dynamic of small food stores is modeled using the observed point pattern of small food stores that were established in 2004 or before and that survived for the whole period from 2005 to 2007 (see Figure 10.1b). As described in Equation 10.2, the growth of a single small food store is assumed to be a function of its stage of development at the beginning of the period and of the influences of the other food stores located in the neighborhood.

Let $\{x_{ss,i} : i = 1,\dots,n\}$ and $\{x_{bs,i} : i = 1,\dots,m\}$ denote, respectively, the spatial coordinates of small food stores and of big supermarkets existing from at least 2004 and that have survived until 2007. Let also $Z04_{ss,i}$ ($Z04_{bs,i}$) and $Z07_{ss,i}$ ($Z07_{bs,i}$) denote the number of employees of the ith small store (big supermarket) in 2004 and 2007, respectively, and let $g_i = Z07_{ss,i}/Z04_{ss,i}$ be a proxy for the growth of the ith small store.

Following the framework suggested by Rathbun and Cressie (1994), the growth of the ith small food store can be modeled as follows:

$$g_i = \alpha + \beta_Z Z04_{ss,i} + \beta_{ss} W_{ss,i} + \beta_{bs} W_{bs,i} + \varepsilon_i \tag{10.8}$$

where

$$W_{ss,i} \equiv \sum_{j=1}^{n} \Phi_{ij}\left(Z04_{ss,j}, d_{ij} = \|x_{ss,i} - x_{ss,j}\|\right) \tag{10.9}$$

and

$$W_{bs,i} \equiv \sum_{j=1}^{m} \Phi_{ij}\left(Z04_{bs,j}, d_{ij} = \|x_{ss,i} - x_{bs,j}\|\right) \tag{10.10}$$

measures the level of spatial interaction of the ith small food store with, respectively, other small food stores and big supermarkets, $\alpha, \beta_Z, \beta_{ss}, \beta_{bs}$ are the parameters to be estimated and the ε_i's are independently and normally distributed errors with zero mean and a finite variance. Relying on the idea that the level of spatial interaction of a neighboring economic activity should depend on the distance to that economic activity and on its size (here approximated by the number of employees), the two measures of spatial interaction reported in Equations 10.9 and 10.10 are derived by specifying the functional form of $\Phi_{ij}(Z, d)$. Rathbun and Cressie (1994) proposed choosing between the following functional forms: $\Phi_{ij}(Z, d) = 1/d$, $\Phi_{ij}(Z, d) = 1/d^2$, $\Phi_{ij}(Z, d) = Z/d$, $\Phi_{ij}(Z, d) = (Z/d)^2$ and $\Phi_{ij}(Z, d) = Z^2/d$. Having chosen a proper specification of $\Phi_{ij}(Z, d)$ and given Equations 10.9 and 10.10, the parameters of the growth model in Equation 10.7 can be estimated using OLS. The OLS estimates of the parameters for the growth process model fitted to the data of the small food stores are reported in Table 10.2. In our analysis we specified the spatial interaction term as

170   *Looking ahead*

Table 10.2 Estimates for the growth point process of new small food stores

Estimates	Full model	Restricted model
α	1.1600 ***	1.1190 ***
	(0.1145)	(0.0622)
β_Z	−0.0317	–
	(0.0364)	
β_{ss}	0.0446	–
	(0.0987)	
β_{bs}	0.0000 ***	0.0000 ***
	(0.0000)	(0.0000)
R^2	0.6811	0.6921

*** Significant at 1%.

$\Phi_{ij}(Z,d) = Z^2/d$, which is the one maximizing the fit in terms of the coefficient of determination R^2.

As can be seen, the parameters β_Z and β_{ss} are not significant, thus implying that in our specific case, the growth of small food stores is not affected by their size at the beginning of the period nor by the closeness to other economic activities of the same typology. On the other hand, the parameter β_{bs} is significant and positive (although very close to zero), thus indicating that spatial interactions with big supermarkets fosters firm growth. In other words, growth rates are higher for small food stores located in the proximity of big supermarkets than for those that are far from them. This evidence suggests the presence of some sort of cooperative behavior amongst competitive economic agents. Similar results have been found by Igami (2011) and Borraz et al. (2014).

10.2.2.4 The survival model

The death/survival process is fitted to the small food stores existing in 2004 and which have survived or ceased to operate during the period 2005 to 2007 (Figure 10.1c). Therefore, the data of interest consist of the spatial point patterns of small food stores observed at times $t = 2005, 2006, 2007$. According to the methodological framework described in Section 10.2.1.4, a death/survival process can be developed as a survival conditional probability model which will be now described. Let $\{x_{ss,i}(t): i=1,...,n\}$ and $\{x_{bs,i}(t): i=1,...,m\}$ denote the spatial coordinates of small food stores and big supermarkets, respectively, which survive at time t. Let also $Z_{ss,i,t}$ and $Z_{bs,i,t}$ represent the number of employees of the ith small store and of the ith big supermarket, respectively, at time t. Finally let $M_i(t)$ denote a survivorship indicator variable such that $M_i(t)=1$ if the ith small food store survives at time t and $M_i(t) = 0$ if the ith small food store ceases its activity at time t. The survival probability of the ith small food store can then be defined as described in Equation 10.4 by assuming that the survival at time t is a function of the dimension of the small food store at time $t-1$ and of the competitive or cooperative influences of the other neighboring small food stores and big supermarkets also operating at time $t-1$. $p_i(t;\theta)$ is then modeled using Equation 10.5, that now becomes:

$$\log \frac{p_i(t;\theta)}{1-p_i(t;\theta)} = \alpha + \beta_Z Z_{ss,i,t-1} + \beta_{ss} W_{ss,i,t-1} + \beta_{bs} W_{bs,i,t-1} \qquad (10.11)$$

where

$$W_{ss,i,t-1} \equiv \sum_{j=1}^{n} \Phi_{ij}\left(Z_{ss,j,t-1}, d_{ij} = \left\| x_{ss,i}(t-1) - x_{ss,j}(t-1) \right\| \right) \qquad (10.12)$$

and

$$W_{bs,i,t-1} \equiv \sum_{j=1}^{m} \Phi_{ij}\left(Z_{bs,j,t-1}, d_{ij} = \left\| x_{ss,i}(t-1) - x_{bs,j}(t-1) \right\| \right) \qquad (10.13)$$

represent measures of the level of spatial interaction of the ith small food store with, respectively, other small food stores and big supermarkets, $\Phi_{ij}(Z,d)$ is a known function which can be specified by the same functional forms already proposed for the growth model's (see Equations 10.9 and 10.10) and $\theta \equiv (\alpha, \beta_Z, \beta_{ss}, \beta_{bs})'$ is the vector parameter to be estimated. By choosing a proper specification of $\Phi_{ij}(Z,d)$ and given Equations 10.12 and 10.13, θ for Equation 10.11 can be estimated using the standard maximum likelihood procedure.

For estimation purposes, first of all let us specify the spatial interaction term again as $\Phi_{ij}(Z,d) = Z^2/d$, which is the specification that produces the best fit in terms of the value of the log likelihood. The ML estimates of the parameters for the death/survival model expressed in Equation 10.10 are shown in Table 10.3.

The results show that the parameters β_Z and β_{bs} are not significant, thus implying that the survivorship of small food stores is unaffected by their size and by the closeness of big supermarkets. Furthermore, since β_{ss} is significant and negative (although very close to zero), the estimated model indicates that spatial

Table 10.3 Estimates for the death/survival point process of new small food stores

Estimates	Full model	Restricted model
α	1.7220 ***	2.3076 ***
	(0.4842)	(0.2345)
β_Z	0.1811	–
	(0.1648)	
β_{ss}	−0.0003 ***	−0.0003 ***
	(0.0000)	(0.0000)
β_{bs}	2.6880	–
	(5.6140)	
Log likelihood	−70.7685	−72.4076

*** Significant at 1%.

172 *Looking ahead*

interactions with the other small food stores result in a relatively lower probability to survive. This evidence reinforces the conjecture of competitive behavior between small food stores.

10.2.3 Conclusions

In this section we discussed a model-based approach to the analysis of the dynamics of firm demography based on micro-geographical data. We presented a methodology to estimate a three-equations model dealing respectively with firms' birth, growth and survival. We argue that decomposing firm demography processes into these three sub-processes allows us to uncover the relative importance of competitive and cooperative spatial interactions in determining the spatial distribution of economic activities.

It is important to note that in the case study, the data allowed only the study of the spatial distribution of firm entries, exits and incumbent firms. Thus the conclusions are limited to the evidence of significant spatial interactions amongst economic agents. In order to uncover the entire locational process of economic agents, it would be necessary to access a larger information set of structural variables rather than just the mere geographical location of firms, such as, for instance, local demand, workforce skill and urban structure. However, this case study shows the potential of the proposed methodologies to study the spatial microeconomic behavior of firms. A possible extension of the techniques presented here could include more comprehensive studies which model the role of spatial proximity in the process of co-agglomeration and in the analysis of the joint locational behavior of the different economic sectors. In this way the global pattern of firm location, growth and survival observed at the level of the economy as a whole will be modeled as the outcome of the individual firm choices and their interaction in space and time.

10.3 A spatial microeconometric model for firm survival

10.3.1 Introduction

The presence of knowledge spillovers and shared human capital is at the heart of the Marshall–Arrow–Romer externalities (MAR) hypothesis (see Marshall, 1920; Arrow, 1962; Romer, 1986) which represented the fount of a flood of scientific contributions produced in the last decades in the field of firm formation, agglomeration, growth and survival. According to the MAR hypothesis, similar firms located nearby increase the chance of human interaction, labor mobility and knowledge exchange which in turn has an effect on firm creation, development and survival. Most of the earlier empirical contributions on knowledge externalities considered data aggregated at a regional level, mainly due to data limitation, leading to contrasting empirical results (Mansfield, 1995; Henderson, 2003; Rosenthal and Strange, 2003). In particular, the role of agglomeration economies has been considered to explain the establishment of firms at a

Firm demography and survival analysis 173

regional level and its effects on the growth of regional employment and regional production (Glaeser et al., 1992; Henderson, 2003). This is a further fruitful field for spatial microeconometric studies.

The present section tries to bridge the gap between the existing literature on point patterns presented in Part II with that on survival models. In particular our interest is in modeling the effects of spatial concentration and interaction on the probability of firm survival by incorporating spatial interaction effects amongst economic agents. We present a model for the probabilities of the failure of individual firms, which makes use of a survival regression model and which takes into account both the spatial interactions among firms and the potential effects deriving from agglomeration.

10.3.2 Basic survival analysis techniques

This chapter is devoted to introducing a spatial microeconometric version of the basic survival Cox model (Cox, 1972). Before presenting such a model, however, it is probably useful to introduce briefly the major concepts related to non-spatial survival analysis. Survival data analysis (or "failure time data") concentrates on the analysis of data corresponding to the time elapsed between a time origin and the time of occurrence of an event of interest (a "failure"). When the time elapsed represents the response variable of a model, standard statistical methods cannot be employed.

Perhaps the most striking feature of survival data is the presence of censoring: that is, the presence of incomplete observations, when the follow-up time is shorter than that necessary for an event to be observed. Censoring can arise due to time limits and other restrictions and makes it very hard to calculate even the simplest descriptive statistics, such as the mean or the median survival times. Furthermore, survival data often exhibit a positively skewed distribution with a high degree of asymmetry which makes the normal distribution assumption unreasonable.

Failure times can be considered empirical realizations of a positive random variable T related to time. In what follows we consider T as a continuous random variable characterized by a probability density function $f(t)$ and a (cumulative) distribution function $F(t) = \Pr[T \leq t] = \int_0^t f(x)\,dx$. The survival function $S(t)$ can therefore be defined as the complementary function of $F(t)$:

$$S(t) = 1 - F(t) = \Pr[T < t] \tag{10.14}$$

and represents the probability of surviving at t (Marubini and Valsecchi, 1995).

Apart from the three above mentioned functions $(f(t), F(t), S(t))$, two more functions are of interest when dealing with survival data. The first function,[3] say $\lambda(t)$, is called the "hazard function" and represents the instantaneous failure rate for an individual firm surviving to time t:

$$\lambda(t) = \lim_{\Delta t \to 0^+} \frac{\Pr\{t \leq T < t + \Delta t \mid T \geq t\}}{\Delta t}; \tag{10.15}$$

174 *Looking ahead*

In Equation 10.15, $\lambda(t)\,dt$ thus represents the probability that the event of interest occurs in the infinitesimal interval $(t, t + dt)$, given survival at time t (Marubini and Valsecchi, 1995).

The second function, say $\Lambda(t)$, is called the "cumulative hazard function" and represents the integral of the hazard function: $\Lambda(t) = \int_0^t \lambda(x)\,dx$. It is easy to show that $\lambda(t) = f(t)/S(t)$ and that, therefore, $\Lambda(t) = -\log S(t)$. From this relationship it can be immediately verified that $\Lambda(t)$ diverges so that $\lambda(t)$ is not a conditional density function.

Parametric survival models are commonly specified by defining a plausible functional form for $\lambda(t)$ from which $S(t)$ and $f(t)$ can be derived. The simplest distribution (which plays a central role in the analysis of survival and epidemiological data) is the exponential distribution (Marubini and Valsecchi, 1995) which assumes the hazard function to be constant through time ($\lambda(t) = \lambda$). The basic model can be then easily extended to include independent explanatory variables, which enable us to investigate the role of selected covariates taking into account the effect of confounding factors.

If Y is a continuous response, regression models are commonly used to model its expectation $E(Y)$. Since in the exponential distribution the expectation is $1/\lambda$, an alternative way (Glasser, 1967) is to model the hazard as:

$$\lambda(t, \mathbf{x}) = \lambda_0 \exp(\mathbf{b'x}) \tag{10.16}$$

In Equation 10.16, $\mathbf{x}$ is a vector of k covariates including a constant term and $\mathbf{b}$ is a vector of unknown regression parameters to be estimated. Since $\mathbf{b'x} = b_0 + b_1 x_1 + \ldots + b_k x_k$, the term $\lambda_0 \exp(b_0)$ represents the failure rate in the reference category (that is when $\mathbf{x} = 0$).

It is important to note that the model specified in Equation 10.16 relies on two basic assumptions: (i) the hazard function is independent of the values of the covariates and (ii) the covariates act in a multiplicative way on the baseline hazard. Therefore, if we consider two individuals characterized by covariate vectors $\mathbf{x}_1$ and $\mathbf{x}_2$, respectively, the hazard ratio:

$$\frac{\lambda(t, \mathbf{x}_2)}{\lambda(t, \mathbf{x}_1)} = \exp\left[\mathbf{b'}(\mathbf{x}_2 - \mathbf{x}_1)\right] \tag{10.17}$$

is independent on time. For this reason Equation 10.16 is called a "proportional hazard model".

In a seminal paper, Cox (1972) introduced a regression model which is currently the most widely used in the analysis of censored survival data. In the Cox model, the hazard function depends on both time and covariates, but through two separate factors:

$$\lambda(t, \mathbf{x}) = \lambda_0(t) \exp(\mathbf{b'x}) \tag{10.18}$$

In Equation 10.18, the baseline hazard $\lambda_0(t)$ is arbitrary defined (although it is assumed to be the same for all firms), while the covariates act in a multiplicative

Firm demography and survival analysis 175

way on the baseline hazard. In this sense, the Cox model is a semi-parametric model where the hazards are proportional, since the hazard ratio, given by

$$\frac{\lambda_0(t)\exp(\mathbf{b}'\mathbf{x}_2)}{\lambda_0(t)\exp(\mathbf{b}'\mathbf{x}_1)} = \exp\left[\mathbf{b}'(\mathbf{x}_2 - \mathbf{x}_1)\right] \qquad (10.19)$$

is independent of time. An important difference from the parametric model (Equation 10.16) is in the form of the linear predictor $\mathbf{b}'\mathbf{x} = b_1 x_1 + \ldots + b_k x_k$ which does not include an intercept term. In terms of the inferential strategy, the parameter estimators of a Cox model and the significance tests are usually based on the partial likelihood technique (Cox, 1975).

In the context of the exponential and Cox models, time is considered as measured on a continuous scale so that the exact survival and censoring times are recorded in relatively fine units without multiple survival times. However, data on the duration of firms are usually observed in discrete units of yearly length, so that we only know the time interval within which each event has occurred. In such cases, when many duration times are tied, the partial likelihood construction is not appropriate. Although some approximations of the exact marginal likelihood have been proposed, in particular those suggested by Breslow (1974) and Efron (1977), they are still inaccurate when the number of ties becomes high. In these cases a model for discrete times can be recommended.

In a discrete times model, each firm experiences a sequence of censorings at t_1, t_2, ... and either fails or is finally censored in its last interval. The likelihood function over all the firms is a product of a Bernoulli likelihood for each firm in each interval. A discrete time proportional hazard model can be fitted by treating the observations in each time interval as independent across intervals, including period-specific intercepts (as a set of dummy variables) and a complementary log-log link function (Rabe-Hesketh and Skrondal, 2008). The linear predictor includes the "baseline hazards" (without making any assumptions about their functional form) and the covariates whose effects are assumed to be linear and additive on the logit scale. According to this model, the difference in the log odds between firms with different covariates is constant over time. This model, known as "cloglog model", is the exact grouped-duration equivalent of the Cox model (for a formal derivation of the key link between the continuous-time Cox model and the discrete-time cloglog model, see the Appendix in Hess and Persson, 2012). Coefficient estimates obtained from these two model specifications should be identical, if the true underlying model were indeed a Cox model (Hess and Persson, 2012).

It is also possible to include in the cloglog model a random intercept for each region (Rabe-Hesketh and Skrondal, 2008) in order to accommodate dependence among the survival times of different firms located in the same small geographical area (regions of Italy), and to control for the presence of unobserved heterogeneity after conditioning on the covariates included in the regression model. The exponential of the random intercept is called "shared frailty" due to the fact that it represents a region-specific disposition or "frailty" that is shared among firms nested in a region.

176　*Looking ahead*

It is important to observe that survival regression models have been widely used in the empirical literature to model firm survival (see Audretsch and Mahmood, 1995; Dunne et al., 2005 among others); however, not many attempts have been made, thus far, to explain how spatial interactions among individual firms affect their survival probabilities and to model the effects on survival of spatial agglomeration. In this chapter, we show how it is possible to augment the explicative power of a survival regression model by explicitly taking into account spatial information while modeling the hazard function and survival probabilities by presenting the evidence of a case study.

10.3.3　*Case study: The survival of pharmaceutical and medical device manufacturing start-up firms in Italy*

10.3.3.1　*Data description*

In this section we illustrate the use of a survival regression model augmented with the inclusion of micro-founded spatial covariates in order to assess the effects of agglomeration externalities generated by incumbent firms on the survival of start-up firms. We will show how this framework allows us to overcome the methodological pitfalls met by the agglomeration measures typically used in the current literature while uncovering the problem of firm survival.

The case study involves the 3,217 firms in the pharmaceutical and medical-device manufacturing industry in Italy which started their activity between 2004 and 2008.[4] In order to assess the effects of agglomeration externalities on the survival of these firms, we can also use the data about the 10,572 incumbent firms of the same industry, established before 2004 and still surviving in 2009. This dataset is a subset of an internationally comparable database on Italian firm demography built up and managed by the Italian National Institute of Statistics, in accordance with the procedures suggested by OECD and EUROSTAT and based on the statistical information contained in the National Business Registers.

The business registers collect yearly a large set of information on the date of registration (firm entry) or deregistration (firm exit) for each business unit. However, this information does not purely represent firm demography, as registration and deregistration may also depend on non-demographic events such as changes of activity, mergers, break-ups, split-offs, take-overs and restructuring. Even if much of the literature on firm demography regularly makes use of data extracted from the business registers without any controls for the influence of non-demographic aspects, it should be noted that the mere observation of data from business registers does not allow a proper comparison at an international level due to a series of inconsistencies, such as different definitions, different units of observation, different national legal systems to name but a few. In this chapter, we specifically exploit data based on the true firm entries and exits with the explicit aim to remove some of these inconsistencies. For each firm, our database currently contains, for the period 2004 to 2009, information about firm code, sub-sector of activity (according to the NACE classification), number of employees, legal status (according to the current classification), date of establishment (if between 2004 and 2009), termination date (if the exit occurred before 2009) and the precise spatial location (in GMT longitude and latitude coordinates).

10.3.3.2 Definition of the spatial microeconometric covariates

In the empirical literature based on firm-level data (e.g. Staber 2001; Ferragina and Mazzotta, 2014 among others) agglomeration externalities effects on firm exit are typically assessed by regressing the probability (or hazard) of firm default on locational measures, such as industry specialization indices. Then the statistical significance, sign and magnitude of the associated estimated regression parameters are used to assess the empirical evidence indicating whether agglomeration externalities play a significant role in firm survival.

In this chapter, however, we argue that the locational measures commonly used by researchers (such as the locational quotient or the Ellison–Glaeser index (Ellison and Glaeser, 1997)) might not be adequate for at least three reasons.

First of all, these measures are calculated on regional aggregates built on arbitrarily defined geographical units (such as provinces, regions or municipalities). Hence, they introduce a statistical bias arising from the discretional definition of space (i.e. the modifiable areal unit problems bias. See Arbia, 1989). As evidence of this effect, Beaudry and Schiffauerova (2009) reviewed the relevant regional science literature and found that the emergence and intensity of agglomeration externalities are strictly dependent on the chosen level of spatial aggregation of data.

Secondly, the dependent variable (the hazard rate) is defined at the firm level while the locational measures are defined at the regional level. As a consequence the regression model will be necessarily based on the implicit assumption that the behavior of firms is homogeneous within each region, which is certainly too restrictive and unrealistic in many empirical situations.[5]

Thirdly, the sampling distribution of locational measures traditionally employed in the literature is unknown, and, therefore, we cannot establish in a conclusive way whether the phenomenon is characterized by significant spatial concentration.

In order to provide a solution to these problems, we develop a firm-level distance-based measure of spatial concentration to be included in the survival regression model thus taking into account the presence of spatial effects in firm survival analysis.

Furthermore, unlike the regional-level locational measures that can only detect the presence of externalities at the regional level, the firm-level measures proposed here allow us also to clearly identify which firms benefit from MAR externalities testing: for example, whether small firms benefit from this more than the big firms.

In order to build up a set of variables to capture MAR externalities, we rely on the well-established idea (see e.g. Glaeser et al., 1992) that the degree of

178   *Looking ahead*

specialization of an industry matters more than its size. The rationale behind this hypothesis is that the degree of specialization can be seen as a proxy for the intensity and density of interaction among firms (Beaudry and Schiffauerova, 2009). In what follows we build up a firm-level distance-based measure of spatial concentration which is able to capture the start-up firm's potential for Marshall externalities generated by incumbents. This measure can be seen as an application of the idea of LISA (see Chapter 2.3) to the standard Ripley's K-function (Chapter 7.1) introduced by Getis (1984). Basically a local K-function is a statistical measure allowing to assess spatial interactions among geo-referenced locations. Indeed, within the context of micro-geographical data identified by maps of point events in two-dimensional space (represented by their longitude/ latitude coordinates), Getis' local K-function can be seen as an explorative tool that summarizes the characteristics of a spatial distribution of point events relative to the location of a given point event. In our particular case the event of interest is represented by the presence of start-up firms in a particular location and our modeling framework aims at testing statistically if a given individual start-up firm is more likely to be localized in a clustering situation. For any given start-up firm i, located in a given geographical area, the local K-function can be defined as follows:

$$K_i(d) = E\left[\sum_{j \neq i} I\left(d_{ij} \leq d\right)\right]\Big/ \lambda \qquad (10.20)$$

where the term d_{ij} is the Euclidean distance between the ith start-up firm's and the jth incumbent firm's locations, $I\left(d_{ij} \leq d\right)$ represents the indicator function such that $I = 1$ if $d_{ij} \leq d$ and 0 otherwise, and λ represents the mean number of firms per unitary area (a parameter called "spatial intensity"). Therefore, $\lambda K_i(d)$ can be interpreted as the expected number of further incumbent firms located up to a distance d of the ith start-up firm. The local K-function quantifies the degree of spatial interaction between the ith start-up firm and all other incumbent firms at each possible distance d, and hence can be exploited to develop a micro-based measure of spatial concentration.

Turning now to the inferential aspects, following Getis (1984), a proper unbiased estimator of $K_i(s)$ for a study area with n firms is given by:

$$\hat{K}_i(s) = \frac{|A|}{n-1} \sum_{j \neq i}^{n-1} w_{ij} I\left(s_{ij} \leq s\right) \qquad (10.21)$$

where A is the study area and $|A|$ denotes its surface. Due to the presence of edge effects arising from the bounded nature of the study area, an adjustment factor, say w_{ij}, is introduced thus avoiding potential biases in the estimates close to the boundary.[6] The adjustment function w_{ij} represents the reciprocal of the proportion of the surface area of a circle centered on the ith start-up firm's location, passing through the jth incumbent firm's location, which lies within the area A (Boots and Getis, 1988).

Firm demography and survival analysis 179

As a final step, we use the function expressed in Equation 10.21 in order to obtain a measure of spatial concentration with a clear benchmark value allowing us to assess if the ith start-up firm is located in an agglomerated industrial area. The most popular strategy in the literature (see e.g. Beaudry and Schiffauerova, 2009) has been to refer to a relative benchmark, in which an industry in a region is considered as geographically concentrated (or dispersed) if it is over-represented (or under-represented) within the region with respect to the entire economy. A relative measure allows us to control for the presence of spatial heterogeneity in the study area and hence it is able to identify spatial concentration due to the genuine spatial interactions amongst economic agents (see e.g. Haaland et al., 1999; Espa et al., 2013). Following these considerations, a firm-level relative measure of spatial concentration for newly established economic activities in the health and pharmaceutical industry can be defined as:

$$RS_i(d) = \hat{K}_{i,sector}(d) / \hat{K}_{i,all}(d) \tag{10.22}$$

where $\hat{K}_{i,sector}(d)$ is the local K-function estimated on the incumbent firms belonging to the same health and pharmaceutical sub-sector of activity of the ith start-up firm and $\hat{K}_{i,all}(d)$ is the local K-function estimated on all incumbent firms of the entire health and pharmaceutical industry. If, at a given distance d, $RS_i(d)$ tends to be equal to 1 then the ith start-up firm is located in an area (a circle with radius d) where economic activities are randomly and independently located from each other, implying absence of spatial interactions. When, at a given distance d, the functional expressed in Equation 10.22 is significantly greater than 1, then the ith start-up firm is located in a cluster with a spatial extension of d where the incumbent firms of its sub-sector of activity are more concentrated then all incumbent firms of the dataset, implying the presence of spatial concentration. For example, a value of $RS_i(d) = 2$ indicates that, among the incumbent firms located within distance d from the ith firm, the expected number of incumbent firms belonging to the ith firm's sub-sector is two times the expected number of incumbent firms of the entire health and pharmaceutical industry. However, when at a given distance d, $RS_i(d)$ is significantly lower than 1, the ith start-up firm is located in a dispersed area, where the incumbent firms of its sub-sector of activity are less concentrated then all incumbent firms of the dataset, implying the presence of spatial dispersion. For example, $RS_i(d) = 0.5$ indicates that, among the incumbent firms located within distance d from the ith start-up firm, the expected number of incumbent firms belonging to the ith start-up firm's sub-sector is half the expected number of incumbent firms of the entire health and pharmaceutical industry.

The function expressed in Equation 10.22 represents a relative measure of spatial concentration with the benchmarking value (case of random localization) represented by the spatial distribution of all health and pharmaceutical firms. Hence a specific sub-sector exhibits over-concentration (or over-dispersion) if its spatial distribution is more concentrated (or dispersed) than the spatial distribution of health and pharmaceutical firms as a whole. In order to use this function

180 *Looking ahead*

as a proper measure of the level of spatial interactions among firms, however, it is necessary that the confounding exogenous factors of spatial heterogeneity (such as land regulation, topography lock in, proximity to raw materials and land use policies) affect all the considered sub-sectors in the same way. Since all firms belong to the same health and pharmaceutical industry, we can reasonably assume that their locational choices are affected by common unobserved exogenous spatial factors. Therefore, in this empirical case, Equation 10.22 can suitably represent a micro-geographical firm-level version of the location quotient that can be used to assess the presence of MAR externalities.

In order to evaluate the significance of the values of $RS_i(d)$ a proper inferential framework needs to be introduced. However, since the exact distribution of $RS_i(d)$ is unknown no exact statistical testing procedure can be adopted and we have to base our conclusions on Monte Carlo simulated confidence envelopes (Besag and Diggle, 1977). In practice, we generate n simulations in each of which the m incumbent firm locations are randomly labelled with the observed m sub-sector of activity "markers". Then, for each simulation, we calculate a different $RS_i(d)$ function. We are then able to obtain the approximate $n/(n+1) \times 100\%$ confidence envelopes from the highest and lowest values of the $RS_i(d)$ functions calculated from the n simulations under the null hypothesis. Finally, if the observed $RS_i(d)$ falls, at the given distance d, outside the envelopes – above or below – this will indicate a significant departure from the null hypothesis of absence of spatial interactions ($RS_i(d) = 1$).

10.3.3.3 Definition of the control variables

We considered three establishment-specific control variables: the number of employees in each firm, the legal status of the firm and the geographical area in which it was located. More specifically, the number of employees is measured as the annual mean number of employees classified into three categories: (i) small firms with only 1 employee (2,496 firms, representing 77.6% of all the firms in the database), (ii) medium-sized firms with between 2 and 5 employees (681 firms, representing 21.2% of the dataset) and (iii) large firms with more than 5 employees (40 firms, representing 1.2% of the dataset). In terms of legal status the 3,217 firms belonged to three main categories: sole trader (2,454 firms, representing 75.4% of the dataset), partnerships (365 firms, representing 11.3% of the dataset) and companies (412 firms, representing 12.8% of the dataset). Finally the variable defining the geographical area consisted of four categories: north-west (798 firms, representing 24.8% of the dataset), north-east (350 firms, representing 10.9% of the dataset), center (901 firms, representing 28.0% of the dataset) and south and islands (1,168 firms, 36.3% of the dataset).

According to the literature on spatial externalities (see e.g. Beaudry and Schiffauerova, 2009), other firm-level control covariates (such as proxies for the level of innovation and labor skills) should be taken into consideration but, because of data availability constraints, cannot be included in the model. However, since $RS_i(d)$ detects spatial interactions between firms belonging to the same narrow

Firm demography and survival analysis 181

sub-sectors of the health and pharmaceutical industry, with reasonably similar characteristics, these unobserved variables should not exert a relevant confounding effect. We also considered three region-specific control variables (defined at the second level of the European Nomenclature of Units for Territorial Statistics), namely the regional unemployment rate, the proportion of region population between 24 and 54 years old and rural land price, in order to control for regional heterogeneity.

10.3.3.4 Empirical results

Table 10.4 contains the Kaplan–Meier estimates of survival probability of the 3,217 start-up firms included in our database observed in the period 2004 to 2008. The table shows that after one year after being established, around 94% of firms still survived, while after four years around 1 firm out of 4 had failed. In the end, after five years of observation, the estimated survival probability is around 72%. A graphical representation is given in Figure 10.4 which shows that during the first five years of activity the propensity to failure tends to be constant over time.

Among the 3,217 start-up firms, 415 failed in the period 2004 to 2008. Since the sum of survival times of all start-up firms is 6,444 years, a rough estimate of the annual hazard of failure is given by the ratio of these two figures: 415/6,444 = 0.0644 firms/year. In epidemiology this is called the "raw (or crude) incidence rate". It means that if we observe 10,000 firms for one year, we expect that 644 will fail during that period. One of the most striking features of the data reported in Table 10.4 is that the incidence rate calculated within each year of follow-up (the age-specific incidence rate) is fairly constant so that the crude rate (0.0644) in this case could be considered a good synthesis of the data. When the incidence rate is constant we have the simplest and the best-known survival model: the exponential model. Such a model is not suitable, for example, in many medical studies, since for humans the incidence rate cannot be considered constant across years. However, it could be a suitable model in other contexts, such as engineering or physics. If the exponential model is the correct one, it is possible to estimate the mean survival time taking the reciprocal of the incidence

Table 10.4 Kaplan–Meier estimates of probability of survival of the 3,217 pharmaceutical and medical-device manufacturing start-up firms in Italy, 2004–2008

Time	Firms at risk	Firm exits	Survival probability	Lower 95% CI	Upper 95% CI	Incidence Rate
1	3,217	198	0.938	0.930	0.947	0.0615
2	1,595	109	0.874	0.860	0.888	0.0683
3	917	64	0.813	0.794	0.833	0.0698
4	496	32	0.761	0.736	0.787	0.0645
5	219	12	0.719	0.687	0.753	0.0548

182   *Looking ahead*

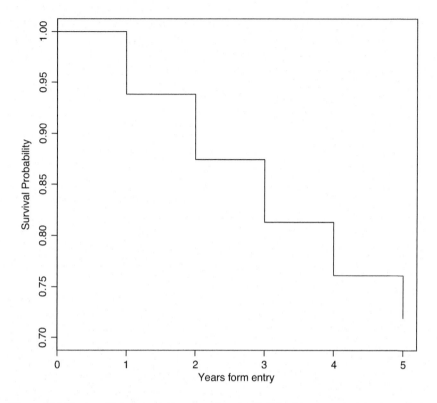

Figure 10.4 Kaplan–Meier survival curves for the 3,217 pharmaceutical and medical-device manufacturing start-up firms in Italy, 2004–2008.

rate; in our case we have about 15.5 years, a value that is fairly outside the follow-up time, so that it must be considered an extrapolation.

As explained in Section 10.4.2, in our empirical circumstances, due to the discrete characteristics of time observations, the best specification of the hazard of firm exit appears to be the complementary log-log model with frailty. However, in order to assess the robustness of our results to model specification, we also consider three alternative models: (i) the exponential model, (ii) the Cox proportional hazards model and (iii) the complementary log-log model without frailty. In all four models, we included the micro-founded spatial covariate of interest (the measure $RS_i(d)$) classified within three categories, namely "dispersion" (when $RS_i(d)$ is significantly lower than 1, the baseline category), "independence" (when $RS_i(d) = 1$) and "concentration" (when $RS_i(d)$ is significantly greater than 1). In order to avoid the imposition of a unique arbitrarily chosen spatial scale, and hence to control for the MAUP effects, the models have been estimated using a large set of different distances d, ranging from 5 to 100 kilometers, at which $RS_i(d)$ has been computed. Table 10.5 shows the estimates of the complementary log-log model with and without frailty for two relevant distances, 10 and 60 kilometers. Figure 10.5 summarizes the values of the estimated model coefficients of $RS_i(d)$ for all models and distances. Table 10.5 indicates that the coefficient associated to "$RS_i(d)$: independence" is positive and highly significant in all cases, while the coefficient associated to "$RS_i(d)$: concentration" is never significant.

According to how $RS_i(d)$ has been formalized, this implies that start-up firms located in a dispersed area (i.e. relatively far from the incumbent firms belonging to the same sub-sector) or in a cluster (i.e. relatively close to the incumbent firms belonging to the same sub-sector) will tend to have a lower exit hazard. In other words, geographical proximity to incumbent firms, on the one hand, and spatial differentiation, on the other hand, decrease the risk of failure, thus highlighting the presence of both negative and positive MAR externalities. This evidence suggests that in the industry of pharmaceutical and medical devices there are both competitive and cooperative behaviors amongst economic agents.

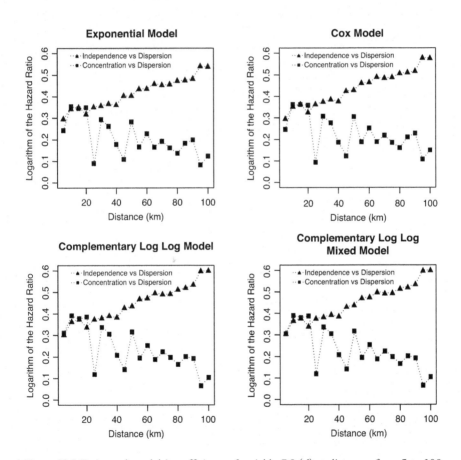

Figure 10.5 Estimated models' coefficients of variable $RS_i(d)$ at distances from 5 to 100 kilometers.

184 *Looking ahead*

Table 10.5 Complementary log-log model estimates (logarithm of hazard ratios) for the 3217 pharmaceutical and medical device manufacturing start-up firms in Italy, 2004–2008

	Cloglog model without frailty		*Cloglog model with frailty*	
	d = 10 km	*d = 60 km*	*d = 10 km*	*d = 60 km*
$RS_i(d)$: dispersion	Reference	Reference	Reference	Reference
$RS_i(d)$: independence	0.352***	0.464***	0.365***	0.474***
	(0.117)	(0.131)	(0.116)	(0.128)
$RS_i(d)$: concentration	0.363	0.253	0.390	0.254
	(0.316)	(0.190)	(0.315)	(0.190)
Employees: 1	Reference	Reference	Reference	Reference
Employees: 2–5	−0.137	−0.159	−0.147	−0.166
	(0.132)	(0.132)	(0.132)	(0.132)
Employees: >5	−1.160	−1.095	−1.178	−1.107
	(0.720)	(0.717)	(0.720)	(0.717)
Legal status: sole trader	Reference	Reference	Reference	Reference
Legal status: partnership	0.364**	0.38**	0.360**	0.380**
	(0.179)	(0.179)	(0.179)	(0.179)
Legal status: company	0.519***	0.487**	0.530***	0.500**
	(0.200)	(0.199)	(0.200)	(0.199)
Region: north-west	Reference	Reference	–	–
Region: center	0.061	0.152	–	–
	(0.318)	(0.319)		
Region: south	0.278	0.279	–	–
	(0.242)	(0.241)		
Region: north-east	0.363**	0.380**	–	–
	(0.177)	(0.177)		
Population aged 25–54	10.651**	10.476**	10.778**	10.395**
	(4.865)	(4.831)	(4.871)	(4.838)
Unemployment rate	0.301	0.165	0.128	0.071
	(0.309)	(0.313)	(0.150)	(0.152)
Rural land price	−0.181	−0.280	−0.447	−0.568
	(0.826)	(0.829)	(0.514)	(0.516)
Log incidence rate: first year	10.651***	10.476***	10.778***	10.395***
	(4.865)	(4.831)	(4.871)	(4.838)
Log incidence rate: second year	0.301***	0.165***	0.128***	0.071***
	(0.309)	(0.313)	(0.150)	(0.152)
Log incidence rate: third year	−0.181***	−0.280***	−0.447***	−0.568***
	(0.826)	(0.829)	(0.514)	(0.516)
Log incidence rate: fourth year	0.352***	0.464***	0.365***	0.474***
	(0.117)	(0.131)	(0.116)	(0.128)
Log incidence rate: fifth year	0.363***	0.253***	0.390***	0.254***
	(0.316)	(0.190)	(0.315)	(0.190)
ρ	–	–	0.004	0.004
Wald χ^2	2970.42***	2963.94***	2776.39***	2779.61***

*** Significant at 1% level; ** significant at 5%; * significant at 10%; standard errors are in parentheses.

Firm demography and survival analysis 185

All estimated coefficients associated with the control variables have the expected sign. In particular, they show that the risk of failure is negatively affected by legal status and that there is heterogeneity between geographical areas. Interestingly, the coefficients of the incidence rates at the various years from firm's entry have very similar values, indicating that in the first five years of activity the risk of failure of start-up firms is substantially constant over time. Finally, the parameter ρ, which accounts for the presence of a frailty effect, is not statistically significant. This means that spatial variability and heterogeneity of hazard rates is well captured by variable $RS_i(d)$.

Figure 10.5 displays the geographical dimension of MAR externalities by showing the way in which the coefficients associated to " $RS_i(d)$: independence" and " $RS_i(d)$: concentration" are affected by distance. The important evidence emerging from these results is that the way in which MAR externalities exert their effects on start-up firm survival in the first five years of activity strongly depends on the spatial dimension of the industrial site where they are located. Indeed, it can be seen that the two coefficients display a different magnitude depending on the value of the distance d. This implies that when we try to estimate the effect of MAR externalities on firm survival using region-level locational measures (thus referring to a fixed arbitrarily defined spatial scale), what we estimate is the combined result of different effects exerting their influence at different spatial scales. This result confirms the opportunity to use firm-level distance-based measures, such as the one proposed here, to better assess MAR externalities in their whole complexity. In particular, all the graphs in Figure 10.5 show that the relative advantage of dispersion over independence is positively related with the spatial scale since the coefficient for " $RS_i(d)$: independence" increases steadily over distance. In contrast, the relative advantage of dispersion over concentration is negatively related with the spatial dimension of the industrial site since the coefficient for " $RS_i(d)$: concentration" tends to decrease over distance. Therefore, Figure 10.5 unveils the action of Krugman's centrifugal and centripetal forces (Krugman, 1991a). Specifically, it shows that centrifugal factors dominate at large distances, making it advantageous to locate as far as possible from incumbent firms. On the other hand, centripetal forces are relevant at short distances, making it advantageous to locate close to incumbent firms. The opposite behaviors of the two lines of Figure 10.5 show that the choice of location to reduce the risk of failure and increase the probability of survival of a new medical-device manufacturing firm in Italy, should take into consideration the distance from incumbent firms. The economic agent should choose the optimal distance from incumbents that avoids their competition but, at the same time, does not limit the opportunity to exploit MAR externalities that cannot occur at large distances.

Figure 10.5 also shows that the four different models considered produce substantially the same results. There is therefore strong evidence that (at least in the first five years), the underlying model explaining the survival of start-up firms

186   *Looking ahead*

can be considered to belong to the exponential family. This evidence is further corroborated by Grambsch and Therneau's proportional hazards test (1994). Indeed, at all distances, the global chi-square test leads to the non-rejection of the proportional hazards assumption of a Cox regression. It is thus possible to conclude that, at least until 5 years of activity, experience does not help start-up firms to survive in the pharmaceutical and medical devices market.

10.4 Conclusion

In this chapter we have discussed some pioneering models that try to capture simultaneously both the aspect of individual agents location and their spatial behavior. In this sense we tried to summarize the message of the whole book by showing how the spatial econometric methods presented in Part II can be integrated with the point pattern analysis literature of Part III to form a unique body of theory. The literature in this area is still relatively scarce and scattered, but it is easy to forecast that it will grow quickly in the near future under the rapidly increasing availability of reliable micro-data and the impulse of an increasing demand for more realistic testable behavioral models which involve space and spatial relationships. The methods and the applications presented here are only a small example of the vast possibilities offered to the analysis of the microeconomic behavior of individual economic agents.

Notes

1 G.W. Leibniz, *Neuveaux essaies sur l'entendement humain* (1703), bk 4, ch. 16.
2 The identification of these two kinds of economic activities has been made referring to the OECD/Eurostat classification scheme (NACE Rev 2).
3 Notice that in this section symbols are used with a different meaning with respect to those used elsewhere in the book.
4 This section draws heavily on Arbia et al., 2015b.
5 For a comprehensive discussion of the weaknesses of the regional-level location measures, see Duranton and Overman, 2005; Combes et al., 2008.
6 Firms located near the boundary of the study area may be close to unobserved firms located outside the study area. Therefore, for these firms, it may not be possible to count the actual number of further incumbent firms located up to a distance d. An estimator of the local K-function that does not account for this circumstance would tend to underestimate the actual degree of spatial interaction and hence would lead to biased estimates. For further details about the estimation biases generated by the presence of boundary limits, see Diggle, 2003.

Appendices

Appendix 1: Some publicly available spatial datasets

The package spdep contains some datasets that are useful for additional practice.
In particular, to download the dataset Baltimore, type:

```
data(baltimore)
```

To visualize the content type the command:

```
> str(baltimore)
```

which shows the following variables:

```
'data.frame': 211 obs. of 17 variables:
$ STATION: int 1 2 3 4 5 6 7 8 9 10 …
$ PRICE: num 47 113 165 104.3 62.5 …
$ NROOM: num 4 7 7 7 7 6 6 8 6 7 …
$ DWELL: num 0 1 1 1 1 1 1 1 1 1 …
$ NBATH: num 1 2.5 2.5 2.5 1.5 2.5 2.5 1.5 1 2.5 …
$ PATIO: num 0 1 1 1 1 1 1 1 1 1 …
$ FIREPL: num 0 1 1 1 1 1 1 0 1 1 …
$ AC: num 0 1 0 1 0 0 1 0 1 1 …
$ BMENT: num 2 2 3 2 2 3 3 0 3 3 …
$ NSTOR: num 3 2 2 2 2 3 1 3 2 2 …
$ GAR: num 0 2 2 2 0 1 2 0 0 2 …
$ AGE: num 148 9 23 5 19 20 20 22 22 4 …
$ CITCOU: num 0 1 1 1 1 1 1 1 1 1 …
$ LOTSZ: num 5.7 279.5 70.6 174.6 107.8 …
$ SQFT: num 11.2 28.9 30.6 26.1 22 …
$ X: num 907 922 920 923 918 900 918 907 918 897 …
$ Y: num 534 574 581 578 574 577 576 576 562 576 …
```

The last two variables are the spatial coordinates.
To download the dataset Boston, type:

```
data(boston)
```

188 *Appendices*

which downloads three objects:

```
(i) boston.c
(ii) boston.soi
(iii) boston.utm.
```

In particular, the object (boston.c) contains 506 observations of the following 20 variables:

```
$ TOWN: Factor w/ 92 levels "Arlington","Ashland", … : 54 77
77 46 46 46 69 69 69 69 …
$ TOWNNO: int 0 1 1 2 2 2 3 3 3 3 …
$ TRACT: int 2011 2021 2022 2031 2032 2033 2041 2042 2043
2044 …
$ LON: num -71-71-70.9-70.9-70.9 …
$ LAT: num 42.3 42.3 42.3 42.3 42.3 …
$ MEDV: num 24 21.6 34.7 33.4 36.2 28.7 22.9 27.1 16.5 18.9
…
$ CMEDV: num 24 21.6 34.7 33.4 36.2 28.7 22.9 22.1 16.5 18.9
…
$ CRIM: num 0.00632 0.02731 0.02729 0.03237 0.06905 …
$ ZN: num 18 0 0 0 0 0 12.5 12.5 12.5 12.5 …
$ INDUS: num 2.31 7.07 7.07 2.18 2.18 2.18 7.87 7.87 7.87
7.87 …
$ CHAS: Factor w/ 2 levels "0","1": 1 1 1 1 1 1 1 1 1 1 …
$ NOX: num 0.538 0.469 0.469 0.458 0.458 0.458 0.524 0.524
0.524 0.524 …
$ RM: num 6.58 6.42 7.18 7 7.15 …
$ AGE: num 65.2 78.9 61.1 45.8 54.2 58.7 66.6 96.1 100 85.9
…
$ DIS: num 4.09 4.97 4.97 6.06 6.06 …
$ RAD: int 1 2 2 3 3 3 5 5 5 5 …
$ TAX: int 296 242 242 222 222 222 311 311 311 311 …
$ PTRATIO: num 15.3 17.8 17.8 18.7 18.7 18.7 15.2 15.2 15.2
15.2 …
$ B: num 397 397 393 395 397 …
$ LSTAT: num 4.98 9.14 4.03 2.94 5.33 …
```

including longitude (LONG) and latitude (LAT) of the point data that can be used to create the W matrix. Furthermore, the object boston.utm contains the universal transverse Mercator (UTM) coordinates of the points that can also be used to build up the weight matrix.

Appendix 2: Creation of a W matrix and preliminary computations

Most of the R procedures that will be presented, are contained in the package (spdep). When needed we will present other libraries. To install the package, type the command:

Appendices 189

```
> install.packages("spdep")
```

for the first time and then at the beginning of each new session, call it back by typing:

```
> library(spdep)
```

In order to create a W matrix the starting point is always a system of point coordinates. If we have, say, the s1 and s2 coordinates of a map of n points, first of all we need to combine them together into an n-by-2 matrix with the command:

```
> coordinates <-cbind(s1,s2)
```

Before creating a weight matrix, we need to identify a list of neighbors. Different procedures are necessary for different neighbors definition.

First of all, in order to generate a list of neighbors based on a minimum threshold distance we use the command:

```
> nbnear <- dnearneigh(coordinates, 0, t, longlat=F)
```

where t is a threshold distance. If longlat = TRUE, the distance is measured in great circle kilometers (that is the distance along a path on a sphere). Conversely, longlat = FALSE do not require a sphere correction and it is the right choice for small areas. In practical cases the threshold distance t has to be identified as the smallest possible distance (so as to keep the matrix as sparse as possible) which ensures that each point has at least one neighbor.

As an alternative, to calculate a list of neighbors based on a k nearest neighbor criterion, first of all we have to use the following command:

```
> knn <- knearneigh(coordinates, k)
```

where k is the number of neighbors assigned to each spatial unit. Then, we proceed to the storage of the neighbors with the command:

```
> nbk <- knn2nb(knn)
```

which has to be interpreted as a transformation from the object knb to (2) the object nb. This a general feature to all the R transformation commands.

The objects nb or knb created with the previous procedures are only lists of neighbors. Once these object are created, we have to transform it into an actual matrix, say W, through the command:

```
> W <- nb2mat(nb)
```

The command indicates that we want to change our data from a list of neighbors (nb) to (2) a weight matrix (mat).

In many R procedures it is not necessary to create and store an actual matrix, but only an object called listw which contains only the relevant information. In this case we type:

```
> W <- nb2listw(nb)
```

We can swap from a matrix to a listw object with the command:

```
> listw2mat(nb)
```

190 *Appendices*

or, vice versa, as:

```
> mat2listw(nb)
```

To calculate an inverse distance weight matrix, we proceed in a different way. First of all, we have to generate a matrix of distances through the command:

```
> D <- as.matrix(dist(coordinates))
```

Default is euclidean, but we can use several alternatives such as: ("euclidean", "maximum", "manhattan", "canberra", "binary" or "minkowski").

Then we create a W matrix where each element is the algeabric inverse of each entry of the matrix D:

```
> W <-1/D
```

but taking care of setting to zero the main diagonal:

```
> for(i in 1:dim(W)[1]) {W[i,i] = 0}
```

To calculate an inverse distance with threshold, we proceed as before to generate the inverse distance W matrix and then we set:

```
W <- ifelse(W < invthreshold, 0, W)
```

where "invthreshold" is the inverse of the maximum threshold distance that we can to arbitrarily fix.

As said already, if we need a listw instead, we can use the inverse transformationa already reported (mat2listw).

Once the weight matrix W is created with any of the previous criteria, a spatially lagged variable of a variable X (say WX) can be easily obtained through the command:

```
> WX <- lag.listw(W,X)
```

If we wish to row-standardize the weights we will have to add the extra option:

```
> W <- nb2listw(contnb, glist=NULL, style ="W")
```

In order to compute Moran's I on the residuals of a model previously estimated with OLS (command lm) (say model1), we use the command:

```
> lm.morantest(model1, W)
```

which uses a W matrix contained in the object W. By default, the randomization option and the one-sided test are considered for the hypothesis testing. To change the default, introduce the option:

```
> lm.morantest(model1, W, randomization=FALSE), alternative
"two-sided")
```

which considers the hypothesis of normality and a two-sided alternative hypothesis of positive or negative spatial autocorrelation.

Appendices 191

Appendix 3: Spatial linear models

All the R commands related to the procedures described in this chapter are contained in the libraries (spdep) and spatialreg. We assume that we want to estimate the model $y = \beta_0 + \beta_1 x + \beta_2 z + \varepsilon$ (possibly with the addition of a spatial lag or a spatial error or both) using a weight matrix contained in object *W*. We also assume that the observations of the variables y, *x* and *z* are stored in a file called filename. If the data are stored in the active R session, all the options including this specification can be omitted.

To start, if we want to estimate the parameters of a purely autoregressive model, the command is:

```
> model0 <- spautolm(X~1, data=filename, listw=W)
```

and provides the ML solution to the estimation problem.

If we want to estimate a spatial error model using maximum likelihood, we use the command:

```
> model1 <- errorsarlm(formula= y~x + z, data=filename,
listw=W)
```

Instead, if we want to use the feasible generalized least squares procedure we use the command:

```
> model2 <- GMerrorsar (formula= y~x + z, data=filename,
listw=W)
```

When dealing with a spatial lag model, if we wish to employ the ML method, we use the command:

```
> model3 <- lagsarlm(formula= y~x+z, data=filename, listw=W)
```

whereas, if we want to use the two-stage least squares estimator, we use the command:

```
> model4 <- stsls (formula= y~x+z, data=filename, listw=W)
```

For the spatial Durbin model the command for ML is:

```
> model5 <- lagsarlm(formula= y~x+z, data=filename, listw=W,
type="mixed")
```

which is basically a spatial lag model with the additional spatial lag of all independent variables.

In order to estimate the parameters of a complete SARAR model, using ML we have command:

```
> model6 <- sacsarlm(formula= y~x+z, data=filename, listw=W)
```

and using the generalized spatial two-stage least squares, we use the command:

```
> model7 <- gstsls(Y~X+Z, listw = w)
```

192 *Appendices*

For the calculation of the autocorrelation test for residuals of a regression, but with a clearly specified alternative hypothesis, we use the command:

```
> lm.LMtests(Model1, listw=W, test="all")
```

which produces the LM test with the spatial error or the spatial lag model as alternatives (LM_{SEM} and LM_{LAG}) and, in addition, the robust test RLM_{SEM} and RLM_{LAG} discussed in the text.

For the calculation of the impact measures, the spdep and the spatialreg libraries contain a command for impacts in a spatial lag model. If we call such a model, say, model3, we can obtain the three impact measures (direct, indirect and total) by typing the command:

```
> impact <- impacts(model3, listw = W)
```

Appendix 4: Non-linear spatial models

The R commands related to the various procedures to estimate the spatial version of the probit and logit models are contained in the library (McSpatial). In all cases we assume that we want to estimate a probit/logit model where the latent variable is expressed as: $y^{\bullet} = \beta_0 + \beta_1 X + \beta_2 Z + \lambda W y^{\bullet} + \varepsilon$ and we also assume that the observations of the variables y, X and Z are stored in the active R session. As for the weight matrix W we have to use the mat specification and not the listw as in the linear models.

Let us now consider the various estimators of a spatial probit model. To start with, if we want to estimate the parameters of a spatial probit model using the ML technique, type the command:

```
> model8 <- spprobitml(y~x+z,wmat=W,stdprobit=F)
```

If we want estimate the same model using a generalized method of moments approach, we need to initialize the parameter ρ before starting the iterative search of a solution. So, before starting the procedure we have to type:

```
> rho=rho0
```

rho0 being any value such that |rho0 | < 1. The robustness of the results with respect to different initial values should be tested in any practical circumstances. Having done so, now type:

```
> model9 <-gmmprobit(y~x+z,wmat=W,startrho=rho)
```

and similarly gmmlogit for the logit version.

Finally, if we wish to estimate the same model using the linearized generalized method of moments approach, type instead:

```
> model10<-spprobit(y~x+z,wmat=W)
```

And, again, splogit for the logit version.

For the spatial tobit, instead, we use the following command contained in the library {spatialprobit}:

```
> model11<-sartobit(y~x+z,listw=W)
```

Appendix 5: Space–time models

The procedures for estimating spatial panels are contained in the R package called (splm) (Millo and Piras, 2012). With this command we also automatically load the (plm) package (Croissant and Millo, 2008) for the estimation of non-spatial models.

Both packages have very few formal requirements. The dataset can be stored in a regular dataset object, provided it contains the pair of indices related to individual locations and time so as to be unambiguously identified. The packages assume that the individual index are stored in the first column of the dataset and the time index the second column. If data are arranged in a different way, this must be stated explicitly.

The two main functions to be used are spml (spatial panel maximum likelihood) for ML estimation and spgm (spatial panel generalized method of moments) for GMM estimation.

If we ignore space, we use the plm function included in the (plm) package.

The a-spatial fixed effects model, then can be simply estimated typing:

```
> model0 <- plm(y~x+z)
```

If we add the option model="pooling" we can estimate a model with OLS model by pooling together all data (spatial and temporal):

```
> model0 <- plm(y ~ x+z, model="pooling", data=datafile)
```

For the spatial models estimated with ML the command is spml. This function makes use of three arguments:

- "Model", which could assume the value of "random" or "fixed"
- "Spatial.error", which may include the error component or not. This could assume the values n for no component, kkp for the Kapor–Kalejian–Prucha specification or b for Baltagi specification
- "Lag", which may include the dependent variable lag component or not specified assuming the values TRUE or FALSE

In case of a random effect, we distinguish 4 cases.

i No spatial component, when both spatial.error and lag are both set to null. In this case the ML estimation can be performed using the command spml with the following specifications:

```
> model1 <- spml(y~x+z, listw=W, model="random", spa-
tial.error="n", lag=FALSE)
```

194   *Appendices*

where W is the usual weight matrix.

ii   Spatial lag. In this case we must set the lag argument to TRUE:

```
> model2 <- spml(y~x+z, listw=W, model="random", spa-
tial.error="n", lag=TRUE)
```

iii Spatial error using the Baltagi specification discussed in Section 5.3. In this case we set the lag argument to FALSE and the spatial.error argument to "b":

```
> model3 <- spml(y~x+z, listw=W, model="random", spa-
tial.error="b", lag=FALSE)
```

iv   Spatial error using the Kapor–Kelejian–Prucha specification expressed in Section 5.3. In this case we set the lag argument to FALSE and the spatial.error argument to "kkp":

```
> model4 <- spml(y~x+z, listw=W, model="random", spa-
tial.error="kkp", lag=FALSE)
```

If, alternatively, we wish to use the generalized method of moments instead of the maximum likelihood we use the command spgm with similar arguments:

```
> model5 <- spgm(y~x+z, listw=W, model="random", spatial.
error="kkp", lag=FALSE)
```

For fixed effects models estimated with maximum likelihood the command is always spml and the logic is similar. We only need to exclude the argument model="random" which by default considers the fixed effect.

If we wish to add a spatial lag to the specification, we can estimate it with the additional argument lag=TRUE:

```
> model7 <- spml(y~x+z, listw=W, spatial.error="none",
lag=TRUE)
```

If, conversely we want to specify a spatial error component, we add the argument spatial.error="b":

```
> model8 <- spml(y~x+z, listw=W, spatial.error="b",
lag=FALSE)
```

Appendix 6: Preliminary definitions and concepts in point pattern analysis

Appendix 6.1: Point pattern datasets

Many R packages are available for analyzing point pattern data. The most up-to-date and comprehensive is certainly (spatstat) (Baddeley et al., 2015). The functions contained in this library to analyze a point pattern require it to be in the form of an object of class ppp, which states for planar point pattern. A ppp object is made up of at least the spatial coordinates of the points and the data identifying the study area of the pattern. Such an object can be created using the function ppp, whose essential inputs that the user has to provide are the x and y vectors of spatial coordinates of the points and the argument that specifies the study area. If the study area is a square or a rectangle, it can be specified using the arguments xrange and yrange that indicate the ranges of the horizontal and vertical sides of the study area, respectively. If the study area has a more complex polygonal shape, the proper argument is poly, which has to be provided as a list with elements x and y representing the spatial coordinates of the polygon's vertices.

As an example, let us see how to create a ppp object representing a point pattern with 30 observations in a rectangular study area from spatial coordinates data. First of all, let us generate the hypothetical arbitrary x and y coordinates of the points with ranges [0, 20] and [0,10] respectively:

```
> xcoord <- runif(30, min=0, max=20)
> ycoord <- runif(30, min=0, max=10)
```

Then, let us create the desired object and visualize it using the plot method for ppp class:

```
> library(spatstat)
> ptsdata <- ppp(x=xcoord, y=ycoord, xrange=c(0,20),
+ yrange=c(0,10))
> plot(ptsdata)
```

As a second example, let us consider the case of a polygonal study area, specified using the argument poly:

```
> ptsdata2 <- ppp(x=xcoord, y=ycoord,
+ poly=list(x=c(20,20,15,8,0,0), y=c(0,10,12,10,15,0)))
> plot(ptsdata2)
```

The ppp function allows us also to deal with other types of data for the study area, such as pixel images. Type?ppp to get further details.

Appendix 6.2: Simulating point patterns

The spatstat package contains functions to simulate the main point processes, such as the homogeneous and inhomogeneous Poisson processes, Cox processes, Poisson cluster processes, Matern processes, simple sequential inhibition processes and Strauss processes.

Appendix 6.2.1: Homogeneous Poisson processes

A homogeneous Poisson process with given constant first-order intensity in a given study area can be simulated using the function rpoisp, which requires at least the arguments lambda, that is the value of the first-order intensity, and win, that is the study area that can be specified as in the ppp function. The result is a ppp object. For example, a realization of a homogeneous Poisson process with intensity 50 in a unit square can be obtained with:

196   *Appendices*

```
> csrpattern <- rpoispp(lambda=50, win=owin(c(0,1),c(0,1)))
> plot(csrpattern)
```

Appendix 6.2.2: Inhomogeneous Poisson processes

The function rpoispp can be used also to simulate inhomogeneous Poisson processes by making the argument lambda equal to a function or a pixel image, instead of a constant value, that provide the differing values of the first-order intensity. For example, if we type:

```
> lambdaFun <- function(x,y) {x^2+y^2}
> inhompat <- rpoispp(lambda=lambdaFun,
win=owin(c(0,4),c(0,4)))
> plot(inhompat)
```

we obtain a partial realization of an inhomogeneous Poisson process on a square of side of 4 units with spatially varying intensity function $\lambda(x_1,x_2) = x_1^2 + x_2^2$.

Appendix 6.2.3: Cox processes

The spatstat function rLGCP allows us to simulate the log-Gaussian Cox process. It makes use of at least three arguments: mu, var and model, which are the mean, variance and covariance function, respectively, of the underlying Gaussian process for the intensity. In order to specify the exponential covariance function, model has to be set equal to "exp"; otherwise, for instance, model="matern" gives the Whittle–Matérn specification. To see the complete list of the available functional forms for the covariance function type?rLGCP. Depending on the choice of the covariance function, it is also possible to use the argument scale. For example, the following code allows to obtain a partial realization of a log-Gaussian Cox process on a unit square with mean $\mu = 4$, variance $\sigma^2 = 0.25$ and correlation function $\rho(d) = \exp\{-d/0.2\}$:

```
> LGCPpattern <- rLGCP(model="exp", mu=4, var=0.25,
scale=0.2,+ win=owin(c(0,1),c(0,1)))
> plot(LGCPpattern)
```

Appendix 6.2.4: Poisson cluster processes

To simulate a Poisson cluster process with radially symmetric normal dispersion of followers, that is a Thomas model, the spatstat package provides us with the function rThomas, whose main arguments, kappa, scale and mu indicate, respectively, the process parameters ρ, σ and μ.

Therefore, for example, to obtain a realization of a Thomas process in unit square with $\rho = 25$, $\sigma = 0.025$ and $\mu = 4$, we can type:

```
> ThomasPattern <- rThomas(kappa=25, scale=0.025, mu=4,+
win=owin(c(0,1),c(0,1)))
> plot(ThomPattern)
```

In a very similar way, to simulate a Poisson cluster process with uniform dispersion of followers, that is a Matérn cluster process, we can use the function rMatClust. To obtain a realization of a Matérn cluster process in a unit square with $\rho = 25$, $R = 0.025$ and $\mu = 4$, we can type:

```
> MatClustPattern <- rMatClust(kappa=25, scale=0.025, mu=4,+
win=owin(c(0,1),c(0,1)))
> plot(MatClustPattern)
```

Appendix 6.2.5: Regular processes

Spatstat allows us to simulate the main regular point processes. First of all, the spatstat functions rMaternI and rMaternII generate random point patterns according to the Matérn model I and Matérn model II inhibition processes, respectively. They both require, at least, the values for the intensity and inhibition distance parameters, represented by the arguments kappa and r, respectively. For example, to simulate regular point processes with intensity 50 and inhibition distance 0.08:

```
> MatPatternI <- rMaternI(kappa=50, r=0.08,
+ win=owin(c(0,1),c(0,1)))
> plot(MatPatternI)
> MatPatternII <- rMaternII(kappa=50, r=0.08,
+ win=owin(c(0,1),c(0,1)))
> plot(MatPatternII)
```

Secondly, the function rSSI generates realizations of the simple sequential inhibition process. In order to implement it, it is necessary to specify the value for the inhibition distance, that is the argument r. It is also possible to set n, the (maximum) number of points allowed. By way of illustration, the following syntax returns a ppp object as a realization of a simple sequential inhibition process in a unit square with 50 points and inhibition distance equal to 0.08:

```
> SSIpattern <- rSSI(r=0.08, n=50, win=owin(c(0,1),c(0,1)))
> plot(SSIpattern)
```

Finally, the function rStrauss provides realizations of the Strauss process. Its use is characterized by the essential arguments beta, gamma and R, which refer to the β, γ and δ parameters, respectively. For example, to obtain a realization of this process with $\beta = 50$, $\delta = 0.08$ and $\gamma = 0.1$, we can type:

```
> StrPattern <- rStrauss(beta=50, gamma=0.1, R=0.08)
> plot(StrPattern)
```

Appendix 6.3: Quadrat-based analysis

The fundamental spatstat function to perform quadrat count analysis of a spatial point pattern is the function quadratcount, which subdivides the study area of

198 *Appendices*

a point pattern into quadrats and provides the count for each quadrat. Its essential inputs are the point pattern of interest X, which has to be in the form of an object of class ppp, and the pair of scalars nx and ny that define the nx by ny grid of quadrats. The output of the function is an object of class quadratcount, which essentially consists of a nx by ny contingency table whose elements are the quadrat counts.

For example, to get the 4-by-4 grid of quadrat counts for the simulated point pattern data simdat, type:

```
> QC <- quadratcount(X=simdat, nx=4, ny=4)
> QC
           x
y  [0,2.5)  [2.5,5)  [5,7.5)  [7.5,10]
  [7.5,10]  15 15 15 8
  [5,7.5)   8 19 17 10
  [2.5,5)   8 11 12 8
  [0,2.5)   8 15 17 11
```

Various functions dedicated to the class quadratcount are available. Among others, plot provides a graphical representation of quadrat counts, intensity computes the quadrat-based intensity and quadrat.test performs the quadrat-based chi-squared CSR test,

```
> plot(QC)
> intensity(QC)
> quadrat.test(QC)
```

Appendix 6.4: Clark–Evans test

The CSR test based on the Clark–Evans index can be performed with the function clarkevans.test, which simply requires the user to indicate the point pattern under study, X, as a ppp object. Among other options, the function also allows us, through the argument alternative, to choose the type of test: "two.sided", for the two-tailed test; "greater", for the upper-tailed test; and "less", for the lower-tailed test. For example, to perform the two-tailed Clark–Evans test for the simdat point pattern, type:

```
> clarkevans.test(X=simdat, alternative="two.sided")
Clark-Evans test
No edge correction
Z-test
data: simdat
R = 1.1175, p-value = 0.001603
alternative hypothesis: two-sided
```

Appendix 7: Models of the spatial location of individuals

Appendix 7.1: K-function-based CSR test

To perform a CSR test based on the *K*-function we can use the R function envelope from the (spatstat) package. This is a general command to compute simulated confidence envelopes of a summary function according to a given generating point process. By default, if the user does not specify which summary function should be considered and which point process should be simulated, envelope uses the *K*-function and the homogeneous Poisson process.

As an example, let us see how to conduct the CSR test for a simulated point pattern dataset. First of all, we generate the point pattern ptsdata within a unit square study area and according to an homogeneous Poisson process with $\lambda = 100$:

```
> library(spatstat)
> set.seed(1234)
> ptsdata <- rpoispp(lambda=100)
> plot(ptsdata)
```

Secondly, we create the object CSRbands which, among other elements, contains the vectors of the empirical *K*-function computed on ptsdata and the upper and lower confidence envelopes for 999 realizations of a homogeneous Poisson process conditional on the same number of points of ptsdata:

```
> CSRbands <- envelope(ptsdata, nsim=999)
```

where the option nsim refers to the desired number of simulated point patterns to be generated.

Finally, the graphical comparison between the empirical *K*-function and the corresponding upper and lower confidence envelopes can be made through the function plot.envelope, that is:

```
> plot(CSRbands, fmla=sqrt(./pi) ~ r)
```

where the option fmla allows to specify which transformation of the function has to be plotted. The string sqrt(./pi) ~ r indicates the Besag's *L* transformation.

Appendix 7.2: Point process parameters estimation by the method of minimum contrast

The spatstat functions thomas.estK, matclust.estK and lgcp.estK apply the method of minimum contrast using the *K*-function to estimate the parameters of the Thomas process, the Matérn cluster process and the log-Gaussian Cox process, respectively. Their usage is similar and, in its simpler form, only requires to indicate the dataset, as a ppp class object, to be fitted. For example, to fit the three processes to the simulated point pattern data simdat, type:

200 *Appendices*

```
> library(spatstat)
> plot(simdat)
> fitThomas <- thomas.estK(simdat)
> fitMatern <- matclust.estK(simdat)
> fitLgcp <- lgcp.estK(simdat)
> fitThomas
> fitMatern
> fitLgcp
```

The resulting objects contain the estimated parameters, the observed values of the empirical K-function and the values of the theoretical K-function computed from the fitted model parameters. In particular, fitThomas contains the parameters kappa and scale which represent the intensity of the leader points, ρ, and the standard deviation σ of the followers' spatial dispersion; fitMatern contains the parameters kappa and scale which represent the intensity of the leader points, ρ, and the radius R centered on each leader point; fitLgcp contains the parameters var and scale which represent the variance of the underlying Gaussian random field and the scale of the spatial autocorrelation.

In all three cases, the user can specify the value of the constants, q and p, for the contrast criterion. By default, q = 1/4 and p = 2. It is also possible to indicate the interval, rmin and rmax, of the distance values for the contrast criterion. All the three functions have a sensible default.

Appendix 8: Points in a heterogeneous space

Appendix 8.1: D-function-based test of spatial interactions

The (spatstat) function envelope that we introduced in Appendix 7 does not allow direct computation of the random labelling simulated confidence envelopes for Diggle and Chetwynd's D-function. Therefore, we need to write our own R code. Let us start by loading demopat, a useful example dataset contained in the spatstat library:

```
> library(spatstat)
> data(demopat)
```

The demopat dataset is an artificial multitype point pattern, in the form of a ppp object characterized by two different types of points, labelled A and B. Let us suppose that we are interested in performing a D-function-based test of spatial interactions in which the points of type A are treated as cases and the points of type B are treated as controls. The empirical K-function for the cases and controls, $\hat{K}_{cases}(d)$ and $\hat{K}_{controls}(d)$, can be obtained using the function Kest, which at least requires a ppp object as an input, and hence typing

```
> KdemopatCases <- Kest(subset(demopat, marks=="A"),
+ correction="isotropic")
> KdemopatControls <- Kest(subset(demopat, marks=="B"),
+ correction="isotropic")
```

Appendices   201

where subset(demopat,marks=="A") and subset(demopat,marks=="B") provide, respectively, the ppp objects for the point pattern of type A (the cases) and the point pattern of type B (the controls). The option correction allows us to specify the method to correct for edge effects. The choice isotropic indicates, in particular, to use the Ripley (1976) method.

The output of Kest contains the vector iso of the values of the empirical K-function and the vector r of the corresponding distance values d. Therefore, we can obtain $\hat{D}(d) = \hat{K}_{cases}(d) - \hat{K}_{controls}(d)$ and the corresponding vector of d with:

```
> Demp  <- KdemopatCases$iso-KdemopatControls$iso
> d  <- KdemopatCases$r
```

In order to compute the confidence envelopes under the null hypothesis of random labelling, we need to generate nsim randomly labelled versions of demopat in which the cases and controls labels are randomly permuted amongst the observed locations. If we run rlabel(demopat) we obtain a point pattern where the labels A and B are randomly permuted among the points of demopat. Therefore, for example, to obtain a list of 29 randomly labelled patterns of A and B points, we can type:

```
> nsim  <-29
> RLsim
```

For each of the 29 simulated patterns we need to compute the D-function. To avoid the use of loops, we can again rely on the function lapply, which applies a given function to all the elements of a list. It is then convenient to first build a function to compute the D-function for a two types point pattern:

```
> DenvFunct <- function(pattern, idcases, idcontrols) {
+ Kcases <- Kest(subset(pattern, marks==idcases))
+ Kcontrols <- Kest(subset(pattern, marks==idcontrols))
+ D <- Kcases - Kcontrols
+ D$iso
+ }
```

and next apply it to the list of the nsim simulated randomly labelled patterns with the aim of obtaining a matrix of the resulting D-function, that is:

```
> Denv <- lapply(RLsim, FUN=DenvFunct, idcases="A",
+ idcontrols="B")
> Denv <- matrix(unlist(Denv), ncol=nsim)
```

Each column of the matrix Denv contains the D-function values for each randomly labelled pattern. As a consequence, the maximum and minimum values across the rows of Denv provide, respectively, the values of the upper and lower confidence envelopes. These can be obtained with

```
> EnvUpper <- apply(Denv, 1, max)
> EnvLower <- apply(Denv, 1, min)
```

202 *Appendices*

Finally, the graphical comparison between the empirical D-function and the corresponding upper and lower confidence envelopes under random labelling can then be made by typing:

```
> plot(d, Demp, type="n",
ylim=c(min(EnvLower),max(EnvUpper)),
+ xlab="d", ylab=expression(hat(D)))
> bandx <- c(d, rev(d))
> bandy <- c(EnvLower, rev(EnvUpper))
> polygon(bandx, bandy, border="grey", col="grey")
> lines(d, Demp)
```

Appendix 8.2: K_{inhom}*-function-based test of spatial interactions*

To perform a test of spatial interactions based on the K_{inhom}-function we can use the R function envelope from the spatstat package introduced in Appendix 7. By way of illustration, let us see how to conduct the test for the artificial point pattern dataset simdat. If we opt to estimate the first-order intensity non-parametrically using Gaussian kernel smoothing, we can use the function density.ppp, which simply requires, among other possible options, to specify the ppp object of interest and, sigma, that is the bandwidth for the Gaussian kernel:

```
> library(spatstat)
> lambda <- density.ppp(simdat, sigma=1.5)
> plot(lambda)
> plot(simdat, add=T)
```

Then, we have to create the object KinhomBands which, among other elements, contains the vectors of the empirical K_{inhom}-function computed on simdat and the upper and lower confidence envelopes for 39 realizations of an inhomogeneous Poisson process conditional on the same number of points of simdat and first-order intensity values provided by lambda:

```
> KinhomBands <- envelope(simdat, fun=Kinhom, nsim=39,
+ simulate=expression(rpoint(n=simdat$n, f=lambda)),
sigma=1.5)
```

With the option fun=Kinhom we have specified that we want to compute the simulated confidence envelopes using the K_{inhom}-function as a summary function; the option nsim indicates, as usual, the number of simulations to perform; and simulate allows us to choose the kind of simulation we need. The function rpoint generates a random point pattern containing n independent, identically distributed random points according to a given first-order intensity. With the syntax expression(rpoint(n=simdat$n, f=lambda)) we can simulate inhomogeneous Poisson patterns with a fixed number of points equal to the size of simdat and first-order intensity values provided by lambda.

Finally, the graphical comparison between the empirical L_{inhom}-function with the corresponding upper and lower confidence envelopes can be made through the function plot.envelope, that is:

```
> plot(KinhomBands, fmla=sqrt(./pi) ~ r)
```

Alternatively, in order to perform the K_{inhom}-function-based test with the first-order intensity function estimated by a parametric regression model, the function ppm can be used. For example, to estimate $\lambda(x)$ with a model that assumes that the intensity depends on a quadratic trend in the spatial coordinates, we may run:

```
> fit <- ppm(simdat, ~ polynom(x,y,2), Poisson())
> lambda <- predict(fit)
```

Appendix 8.3: Duranton–Overman K-density and Marcon–Puech M-function

To implement the Duranton–Overman K-density and Marcon–Puech M-function measures of spatial concentration of economic activities in R, the library (dbmss) (Marcon et al., 2015) provides, respectively, the functions KdEnvelope and MEnvelope. Let us see how to use them while assuming that we are interested in assessing the level of relative spatial concentration of points of type A in the spatstat example dataset demopat. Both the functions require that the point pattern under study is in the form of a on R-object of class "wmppp". We can create a wmppp object using the function wmppp that takes as inputs a dataframe – containing the point coordinates and the potential associated typologies and weights – and the polygon defining the study area. Therefore, to convert demopat into a wmpp object we can type:

```
> demopat2 <- wmppp(data.frame(X=demopat$x, Y=demopat$y,
+ PointType=demopat$marks), window=demopat$win)
```

and then, to perform the analysis based on the K-density and M-function we can run, respectively:

```
> Kd <- KdEnvelope(demopat2, NumberOfSimulations=39, Alpha =
0.01,
+ ReferenceType="A")
> plot(Kd)
```

and

```
> M <- MEnvelope(demopat2, NumberOfSimulations=39, Alpha =
0.01,
+ ReferenceType="A")
> plot(M)
```

204   *Appendices*

where, quite intuitively, the options NumberOfSimulations, Alpha and ReferenceType refer, respectively, to the number of simulations for the confidence envelopes, the level of significance and typology of points for which we want to analyze the relative spatial concentration.

Appendix 9: Space–time models

Appendix 9.1: Space–time K-function

To estimate the Diggle, Chetwynd, Häggkvist and Morris space–time K-function and perform the associated test of space–time interactions, it is possible to use functions contained in the library (splancs) (Rowlingson and Diggle, 2015). To illustrate their use, we refer to an artificial, simulated, spatio-temporal point pattern dataset. First of all, we generate the spatial coordinates of the dataset according to a homogeneous Poisson process using the spatstat function rpoispp:

```
> library(spatstat)
> points <- rpoispp(lambda=100, win=owin(c(0,1),c(0,1)))
> plot(points)
```

Secondly, we simulate the associated time labels according to a Poisson distribution with mean equal to 10 using the function rpois:

```
> times <- rpois(n=points$n, lambda=10)
> hist(times)
```

The space–time K-function can be estimated using the splancs function stkhat, which requires the following inputs:

- pts, the spatial coordinates of the points in the form of a matrix where the rows identify the observations and the columns represent the horizontal and vertical coordinates, respectively;
- times, the vector of time labels associated to the points;
- poly, the study area of the point pattern as a matrix containing the spatial coordinates of its vertices;
- tlimits, the vector specifying the range of the time interval to be considered;
- s, the vector of spatial distances to be used for the estimation;
- tm, the vector of temporal distances to be used for the estimation.

If we consider a unit square as the study area, we can estimate the space–time K-function for the points point pattern with the times time labels by running the following code:

```
> library(splancs)
> ptsData <- as.points(points$x, points$y)
> area <- matrix(c(0,1,1,0,0,0,1,1), nrow=4, ncol=2)
```

```
> s <- seq(0,0.25,0.25/99)
> tm <-0:15
> STK <- stkhat(pts=ptsData, times=times, poly=area,
+ tlimits=c(0,max(times)), s=s, tm=tm)
```

where as.points is a convenient function to easily organize the spatial coordinates of the points in a matrix.

The resulting STK object is made of STK$kst, the values of the estimated space–time K-function; STK$ks, the values of the estimated Ripley's K-function; and STK$kt, the values of the temporal K-function. Therefore, it is possible to easily obtain also $\hat{D}(d,t)$ and $\hat{D}_0(d,t)$:

```
> oprod <- outer(STK$ks, STK$kt)
> st.D <- STK$kst - oprod
> st.D0 <- STK$kst / oprod
```

which can be graphically represented using some 3D plotting utilities, such as the function persp. For example:

```
> persp(STK$s, STK$t, st.D, xlab="d", ylab = "t",
+ zlab = "D", expand = 0.5, ticktype = "detailed",
+ theta = -30, shade = 0.4, cex = 0.7)
```

The associated Monte Carlo test of space–time clustering can be performed using the function stmctest, which, in addition to the same arguments of stkhat, allows us to specify the number of simulations to do by setting the option nsim. The output of stmctest is given by the value of the test statistic, tp, and the vector of the resulting Monte Carlo distribution, t. To perform the test for the points dataset we can then type:

```
> STtest <- stmctest(pts=ptsData, times=times, poly=area,
+ tlimits=c(0,max(times)), s=s, tt=tm, nsim=999)
> plot(density(STtest$t), xlim=range(c(STtest$t0,
STtest$t)))
> abline(v=STtest$t0)
```

Appendix 9.2: Gabriel and Diggle's **STIK-***function*

Gabriel and Diggle's *STIK*-function can be estimated using the function STIKhat contained in the library (stpp). This function is characterized by essentially the same inputs as function stkhat, but it additionally requires the user to provide lambda, a vector of values of the estimated first-order intensity function evaluated at the points of the pattern. For the purpose of illustration, let us refer, as in the previous paragraph, to a simulated example dataset:

```
> points <- rpoispp(lambda=100, win=owin(c(0,1),c(0,1)))
> times <- rpois(n=points$n, lambda=10)
```

206 *Appendices*

In order to apply STIKhat to these data we then first need to estimate the first-order intensity function: that is, we need to obtain the separated spatial and temporal intensities $\hat{m}(s)$ and $\hat{\mu}(t)$. Let us estimate the former using the spatial kernel estimator and hence by means of the spatstat function density.ppp:

```
> mhat <- density.ppp(x=points, at="points")
```

where the option at="points" implies that the computations are made at observed points. To estimate the temporal intensity, we can rely on standard kernel density smoothing and hence on the function density:

```
M <- density(x=times, n=1000)
mut <- M$y[findInterval(times, M$x)]*points$n
```

Moreover, before implementing STIKhat, it is necessary to convert the data into an object of class "stpp", that is a 3 vectors matrix made of the spatial coordinates and time labels, which can be done using the function as.3dpoints:

```
> stppData <- as.3dpoints(points$x, points$y, times)
> area <- matrix(c(0,1,1,0,0,0,1,1), nrow=4, ncol=2)
> s <- seq(0,0.25,0.25/99)
> tm <-0:15
> stikPoints <- STIKhat(xyt=stppData, s.region=area,
+ t.region=c(0,max(times)), lambda=mhat*mut/points$n,
+ dist=s, times=tm, infectious=T)
```

The created output stikPoints is a list containing, among other elements: Khat, the matrix of the estimated values of $K_{ST}(u,v)$; and Ktheo, the matrix of the values of $\pi u^2 v$.

To graphical represent the estimated *STIK*-function, the function plotK is available, which is mainly characterized by argument L, that implies the plot of $\hat{K}_{ST}(u,v)$ if it is set to FALSE and the plot of $\hat{K}_{ST}(u,v) - \pi u^2 v$ if it is set to TRUE, and argument type that allows us to choose between a 3D surface plot, persp; a contour plot, contour; or a grid of colored rectangles, image. For example:

```
> plotK(K=stikPoints,type="image", L=T)
> plotK(K=stikPoints,type="contour", L=T)
> plotK(K=stikPoints,type="persp", L=T)
```

For further details, see?plotK.

Bibliography

Amemiya, T. (1985) *Advanced Econometrics*. Oxford: Basil Blackwell.

Anselin, L. (1988) *Spatial Econometric: Methods and Models*. Dordrecht: Kluwer Academic.

Anselin, L. (1995) Local indicators of spatial association. *Geographical Analysis*, 27: 93–115.

Anselin, L., Bera, A., Florax, R.J.G.M. and Yoon, M. (1996) Simple diagnostic tests for spatial dependence. *Regional Science and Urban Economics*, 26: 77–104.

Anselin, L., Le Gallo, J. and Jayet, H. (2008) Spatial panel econometrics. In Matyas, L. and Silvestre, P. (eds.), *The Econometrics of Panel Data: Fundamentals and Recent Developments in Theory and Practice*, 3rd edn., 625–660. Berlin: Springer.

Arbia, G. (1989) *Spatial Data Configuration in the Statistical Analysis of Regional Economics and Related Problems*. Dordrecht: Kluwer Academic.

Arbia, G. (1990) On second order non-stationarity in two-dimensional lattice processes. *Computational Statistics and Data Analysis*, 9: 147–160.

Arbia, G. (2001) Modelling the geography of economic activities on a continuous space. *Papers in Regional Sciences*, 80: 411–424.

Arbia, G. (2006) *Spatial Econometrics: Statistical Foundations and Applications to Regional Economic Growth*. Heidelberg: Springer.

Arbia, G. (2012) Pairwise likelihood inference for spatial regressions estimated on very large datasets. Paper presented at the 6th Annual World Conference of the Spatial Econometrics Association, Salvador, Brazil, 11–13 July 2012.

Arbia, G. (2014a) Pairwise likelihood inference for spatial regressions estimated on very large datasets. *Spatial Statistics*, 7: 21–39.

Arbia, G. (2014b) *A Primer for Spatial Econometrics: With Applications in R*. Basingstoke: Palgrave Macmillan.

Arbia, G. (2016) Spatial econometrics: A broad view. *Foundations and Trends in Econometrics*, 8: 3–4.

Arbia G. (forthcoming) *Statistics, New Empiricism and Society in the Era of Big Data*. Heidelberg: Springer.

Arbia, G. and Espa, G. (1996) *Statistica economica territoriale*. Padua: Cedam.

Arbia, G. and Nardelli, V. (2020) On spatial lag models estimated using crowdsourcing, web-scraping or other unconventionally collected Big Data. arXiv:2010.05287.

Arbia, G. and Petrarca, F. (2011) Effects of MAUP on spatial econometrics models. *Letters in Spatial and Resource Sciences*, 4: 173–185.

Arbia, G., Espa, G. and Quah, D. (2008) A class of spatial econometric methods in the empirical analysis of clusters of firms in the space. *Empirical Economics*, 34: 81–103.

208 Bibliography

Arbia, G., Espa G., Giuliani, D. and Mazzitelli, A. (2010) Detecting the existence of space–time clustering of firms. *Regional Science and Urban Economics*, 40: 311–323.

Arbia, G., Bee, M. and Espa, G. (2013) Testing isotropy in spatial econometric models. *Spatial Economic Analysis*, 8: 228–240.

Arbia, G., Espa, G., Giuliani, D. and Dickson, M. (2014a) Spatio-temporal clustering of pharmaceutical and medical device manufacturing industry: A geographical micro-level analysis. *Regional Science and Urban Economics*, 49: 298–304.

Arbia, G., Espa, G. and Giuliani, D. (2014b) Weighting Ripley's K-function to account for the firm dimension in the analysis of spatial concentration. *International Regional Science Review*, 3: 247–268.

Arbia, G., Espa, G. and Giuliani, D. (2015a) Measurement errors arising when using distances in spatial microeconometric modelling and the individuals' position is geomasked for confidentiality. *Econometrics*, 3: 709–718.

Arbia, G., Cella, P., Espa, G. and Giuliani, D. (2015b) A micro spatial analysis of firm demography: The case of food stores in the area of Trento (Italy). *Empirical Economics*, 48: 923–937.

Arbia, G., Espa, G. and Giuliani, D. (2016) Dirty spatial econometrics. *Annals of Regional Science*, 56: 177–189.

Arbia, G., Espa, G., Giuliani, D. and Micciolo, R. (2017) Spatial analysis of start-up health and pharmaceutical firm survival. *Journal of Applied Statistics*, 44: 9.

Arbia, G., Berta, P. and Dolan, C.B. (2019a) Measurement error induced by locational uncertainty when estimating discrete choice models with a distance as a regressor. arXiv:1904.01849.

Arbia, G., Ghiringhelli, C. and Mira, A. (2019b) Estimation of spatial econometric linear models with large datasets: How big can spatial Big Data be?, *Regional Science and Urban Economics*, 76: 67–73.

Arbia G., Solano-Hermosilla, G., Genovese, G. Nardelli, V. and Micale, F. (2020) Post-sampling crowdsourced data to allow reliable statistical inference: The case of food price indices in Nigeria. arXiv:2003.12542.

Arbia, G., Billè, A.G. and Leorato, S. (forthcoming) Feasible ML estimator for dynamic spatial panel data probit models with fixed effects and large datasets.

Arrow, K. (1962) The economic implications of learning by doing. *Review of Economic Studies*, 29: 155–172.

Aten, B. (1996) Evidence of spatial autocorrelation in international prices. *Review of Income and Wealth*, 42: 149–163.

Aten, B. (1997) Does space matter? International comparison of the prices of tradables and nontradables. *International Regional Science Review*, 20: 35–52.

Audretsch, D.B. and Mahmood, T. (1995) New firm survival: New results using a hazard function. *Review of Economics and Statistics*, 77: 97–103.

Autant-Bernard, C. and LeSage, J. (2011) Quantifying knowledge spillovers using spatial econometric models. *Journal of Regional Science*, 51: 471–496

Baddeley, A.J. and Turner, R. (2000) Practical maximum pseudolikelihood for spatial point patterns. *Australian and New Zealand Journal of Statistics*, 42: 283–322.

Baddeley, A.J. and Turner, R. (2005) Spatstat: An R package for analyzing spatial point patterns, *Journal of Statistical Software*, 12: 1–42.

Baddeley, A.J., Møller, J., and Waagepetersen, R. (2000) Non- and semi-parametric estimation of interaction in inhomogeneous point patterns. *Statistica Neerlandica*, 54: 329–350.

Baddeley, A., Rubak, E. and Turner, R. (2015) *Spatial Point Patterns: Methodology and Applications with R*. London: Chapman & Hall/CRC.

Bibliography 209

Bade, F.J. and Nerlinger, E.A. (2000) The spatial distribution of new technology-based firms: Empirical results from West Germany. *Papers in Regional Science*, 79: 155–176

Bai, J. and Li, K. (2018) Theory and methods of panel data models with interactive effects. *Annals of Statistics*, 42: 142–170.

Baltagi, B.H. (2008) *Econometric Analysis of Panel Data*, 4th edn. Hoboken, NJ: Wiley.

Baltagi, B.H. and Pesaran, H. (2007) Heterogeneity and cross-section dependence in spatial panel data models: Theory and application: Introduction. *Journal of Applied Econometrics*, 22: 229–232.

Baltagi, B., Song, S.H. and Koh, W. (2003) Testing panel data regression models with spatial error correlation. *Journal of Econometrics*, 117: 123–150.

Baltagi, B.H, Egger, P. and Pfaffermayr, M. (2013) A generalized spatial panel data model with random effects. *Econometric Reviews*, 32: 650–685.

Banerjee, S. and Gelfand, A.E. (2002) Prediction, interpolation and regression for spatially misaligned data. *Sankhyā: The Indian Journal of Statistics*, 64: 227–245.

Barff, R.A. (1987) Industrial clustering and the organization of production: A point pattern analysis of manufacturing in Cincinnati, Ohio. *Annals of the Association of American Geographers*, 77: 89–103.

Barker, T. and Pesaran, M.H. (eds.) (1989) *Disaggregation in Econometric Modeling*. London: Routledge.

Bartlett, M.S. (1964) The spectral analysis of two-dimensional point processes. *Biometrika*, 51: 299–311.

Beaudry, C. and Schiffauerova, A. (2009) Who's right, Marshall or Jacobs? The localization versus urbanization debate. *Research Policy*, 38(2): 318–337.

Beckmann, M.J. (1970) The analysis of spatial diffusion processes. *Papers of Regional Science Association*, 25: 109–117.

Beckmann, M.J. and Puu, T, (1985) *Spatial Economics: Density, Potential and Flow*. Amsterdam: North-Holland.

Behrens, K. and Bougna, T. (2015) An anatomy of the geographical concentration of Canadian manufacturing industries. *Regional Science and Urban Economics*, 51: 47–69.

Bennett, R.J., Haining, R.P. and Griffith, D.A. (1984) The problem of missing data on spatial surfaces. *Annals of the Association of American Geographers*, 74: 138–156.

Beręsewicz, M. (2015) On the representativeness of internet data sources for the real estate market in Poland. *Austrian Journal of Statistics*, 44(2): 45–57.

Bergstrom, A.R. (1990) *Continuous Time Econometric Modelling*. Oxford: Oxford University Press.

Berman, M. and Diggle, P.J. (1989). Estimating weighted integrals of the second-order intensity of a spatial point process. *Journal of the Royal Statistical Society: Series B*, 51: 81–92.

Berman, M. and Turner, T.R. (1992) Approximating point process likelihoods with GLIM. *Applied Statistics*, 41: 31–38.

Beron, K.J. and Vijverberg, W.P. (2004) Probit in a spatial context: A Monte Carlo approach. In Anselin, L., Florax, R.J.G.M. and Rey, S. (eds.), *Advances in Spatial Econometrics: Methodology, Tools and Applications*, 169–195. Heidelberg: Springer.

Besag, J. (1975) Statistical analysis of non-lattice data. *The Statistician*, 24: 179–195.

Besag, J. (1977) Contribution to the discussion of Dr. Ripley's paper. *Journal of the Royal Statistical Society: Series B*, 39: 193–195.

Besag, J. and Diggle, P.J. (1977) Simple Monte Carlo tests for spatial pattern. *Applied Statistics*, 26: 327–333.

210 *Bibliography*

Boeing, G. and Waddell, P. (2017) New insights into rental housing markets across the United States: Web scraping and analyzing Craigslist rental listings. *Journal of Planning Education and Research*, 37: 457–476.

Boots, B.N. and Getis, A. (1988) *Point Pattern Analysis*, Sage Scientific Geography Series, 8. London: Sage.

Borraz, F., Dubra, J., Ferrés, D. and Zipitría, L. (2014) Supermarket entry and the survival of small stores. *Review of Industrial Organization*, 44: 73–93.

Breslow, N. (1974) Covariance analysis of censored survival data. *Biometrics*, 30: 89–99.

Burridge, P. (1980) On the Cliff–Ord test for spatial correlation. *Journal of the Royal Statistical Society: Series B*, 42: 107–108.

Cameron, A.C. and Trivedi, P.K. (2005) *Microeconometrics: Methods and Applications.* Cambridge: Cambridge University Press.

Case, A. (1992) Neighborhood influence and technological change. *Regional Science and Urban Economics* 22: 491–508.

Case, A., Rosen, H. and Hines, J.R. (1993) Budget spillovers and fiscal policy interdependence: Evidence from the States. *Journal of Public Economy*, 52: 285–307.

Cavallo, A. and Rigobon, R. (2016) The Billion Prices Project: Using online data for measurement and research. *Journal of Economic Perspectives*, 31(2): 151–178.

Christaller, W. (1933) *Die zentralen Orte in Süddeutschland.* Jena: Fischer.

Clark, P.J. and Evans, F.C. (1954) Distance to nearest neighbor as a measure of spatial relationships in populations. *Ecology*, 35: 445–453.

Cliff, A.D. and Ord, J.K. (1972) *Spatial Autocorrelation.* London: Pion,

Cliff, A.D. and Ord, J.K. (1981) *Spatial Processes.* London: Pion.

Collins, B. (2011) *Boundary Respecting Point Displacement.* Arlington, Va.: Blue Raster.

Combes, P.-P., Mayer, T. and Thisse, J.F. (2008) *Economic Geography: The Integration of Regions and Nations.* Princeton, NJ: Princeton University Press.

Conley, T.G. and Topa, G. (2002) Socio-economic distance and spatial patterns in unemployment. *Journal of Applied Econometrics*, 17: 303–327.

Conrow, L., Aldstadt, J. and Mendoza, N.S. (2015) A spatio-temporal analysis of on-premises alcohol outlets and violent crime events in Buffalo, NY. *Applied Geography*, 58: 198–205.

Corrado, L. and Fingleton, B. (2012) Where is the economics in spatial econometrics? *Journal of Regional Science*, 52: 210–239.

Cox, D. (1972). Regression models and life-tables. *Journal of the Royal Statistical Society: Series B*, 34: 187–220.

Cox, D.R. (1955) Some statistical models related with series of events. *Journal of the Royal Statistical Society: Series B*, 17: 129–164.

Cox, L.H. (1980) Suppression methodology and statistical disclosure control. *Journal of the American Statistical Association*, 75: 377–385

Cozzi, M. and Filipponi, D. (2012) The new geospatial Business Register of Local Units: potentiality and application areas. Paper presented at the 3rd Meeting of the Wiesbaden Group on Business Registers-International Roundtable on Business Survey Frames, Washington, DC, 17–20 September 2012.

Cramer, J.S. (1964) Efficient grouping, regression and correlation in Engel curve analysis. *Journal of the American Statistical Association*, 59: 233–250.

Crequit, P.P., Mansouri, G., Benchoufi, M., Vivot, A. and Ravaud, P. (2018) Mapping of crowdsourcing in health: Systematic review. *Journal of Medical Internet Research*, 20. doi: 10.2196/jmir.9330.

Cressie, N. (1993) *Statistics for Spatial Data.* New York: Wiley.

Cressie, N. and Wikle, C.K. (2011) *Statistics for Spatio-Temporal Data*. Hoboken, NJ: Wiley.

Croissant, Y. and Millo, G. (2008) Panel data econometrics in R: The plm package. *Journal of Statistical Software*, 27: 1–43.

Cuzick, J. and Edwards, R. (1990) Spatial clustering for inhomogeneous populations (with Discussion). *Journal of the Royal Statistical Society: Series B*, 52: 73–104.

Dagenais, M.G. (1994) Parameter estimation in regression models with errors in the variables and autocorrelated disturbances. *Journal of Econometrics*, 64: 145–163.

Daley, D.J. and Vere-Jones, D. (2003) *An Introduction to the Theory of Point Processes*, Volume 1: *Elementary Theory and Methods*, 2nd edn. New York: Springer.

De Waal, A.G. and Willenborg, L.C.R.J. (1998) Optimal local suppression in microdata, *Journal of Official Statistics*, 14: 421–435.

Dempster, A.P., Laird, N.M. and Rubin, D.B. (1977) Maximum likelihood from incomplete data via the EM algorithm. *Journal of the Royal Statistical Society: Series B*, 39: 1–38.

Diggle, P.J. (2003) *Statistical Analysis of Spatial Point Patterns*, 2nd edn. London: Edward Arnold.

Diggle, P.J. (2007) Spatio-temporal point processes: Methods and applications. In Finkenstadt, B., Held, L. and Isham V. (eds), *Statistical Methods for Spatio-Temporal Systems*, 1–45. Boca Raton, Fla.: Chapman & Hall/CRC.

Diggle, P.J. and Chetwynd, A.G. (1991) Second-order analysis of spatial clustering for inhomogeneous populations. *Biometrics*, 47: 1155–1163.

Diggle, P.J. and Gratton, R.J. (1984) Monte Carlo methods of inference for implicit statistical models. *Journal of the Royal Statistical Society: Series B*, 46: 193–212.

Diggle, P.J., Chetwynd, A.G., Haggkvist, R. and Morris, S. (1995) Second-order analysis of space–time clustering. *Statistical Methods in Medical Research*, 4: 124–136.

Diggle, P.J., Gomez-Rubio, V., Brown, P.E., Chetwynd, A.G., and Gooding, S. (2007) Second-order analysis of inhomogeneous spatial point processes using case-control data, *Biometrics*. 63: 550–557.

Dixon, P. (2002) Ripley's K-function. In El-Shaarawi, A.H. and Piergorsch, W.W. (eds.), *The Encyclopedia of Environmetrics*, 1976–1803. New York: Wiley.

Donfouet, H.P.P., Jeanty, P.W. and Malin, É. (2012) Accounting for spatial interactions in the demand for community-based health insurance: A Bayesian spatial tobit analysis. Paper presented at the 11th International Workshop Spatial Econometrics and Statistics, Avignon, 15–16 November 2012.

Donnelly, K. (1978) Simulations to determine the variance and edge-effect of total nearest neighbor distance. In Hodder, I. (ed.), *Simulation Studies in Archaeology*, 91–95. Cambridge: Cambridge University Press.

Doreian, P. (1980) Linear models with spatially distributed data, spatial disturbance or spatial effects? *Sociological Methods and Research*, 9: 29–60.

Dubé, J. and Legros, D. (2014) *Spatial Econometrics Using Microdata*. Hoboken, NJ: Wiley.

Dubin, R.A. (1992) Spatial autocorrelation and neighborhood quality. *Regional Science and Urban Economics*, 22: 433–452.

Duncan, G.T. and Lambert, D. (1986) Disclosure-limited data dissemination (with discussion). *Journal of Official Statistics*, 81: 10–28.

Dunne, T., Klimek, S.D. and Roberts, M.J. (2005) Exit from regional manufacturing markets: The role of entrant experience. *International Journal of Industrial Organization*, 23: 399–421.

Duranton, G. and Overman, H.G. (2005) Testing for localization using micro-geographic data. *Review of Economic Studies*, 72: 1077–1106.

212   *Bibliography*

Duranton, G. and Overman, H.G. (2008) Exploring the detailed location patterns of UK manufacturing industries using microgeographic data. *Journal of Regional Science,* 48: 213–243.

Durbin, J., and Watson, G.S. (1951) Testing for serial correlation in least squares regression, I. *Biometrika,* 37: 409–428.

Durlauf, S.N. (1989) *Locally Interacting Systems, Coordination Failure and the Long Run Behaviour of Aggregate Activity.* Working paper, Department of Economics, Stanford University.

Durlauf, S.N. (1999) How can statistical mechanics contribute to the study of social science? *Proceedings of the National Academy of Sciences,* 96: 10582–10584.

Efron, B. (1977) The efficiency of Cox's likelihood function for censored data. *Journal of the American Statistical Association,* 72: 557–565.

Elhorst, J.P. (2003) Specification and estimation of spatial panel data models. *International Regional Sciences Review,* 26: 244–268.

Elhorst, J.P. (2009) Spatial panel data models. In Fischer, M.M. and Getis, A. (eds.), *Handbook of Applied Spatial Analysis: Software Tools, Methods and Applications,* 377–408. Berlin: Springer.

Elhorst, J.P. (2010) Applied spatial econometrics: Raising the bar, *Spatial Economic Analysis,* 5: 9–28.

Elhorst, J.P. (2014) *Spatial Econometrics: From Cross-Sectional Data to Spatial Panels.* Berlin: Springer.

Ellison, G. and Glaeser, E.L. (1997) Geographic concentration in U.S. manufacturing industries: A dartboard approach. *Journal of Political Economy,* 105: 889–927.

Espa, G., Arbia, G. and Giuliani, D. (2013) Conditional vs unconditional industrial agglomeration: Disentangling spatial dependence and spatial heterogeneity in the analysis of ICT firms' distribution in Milan. *Journal of Geographical Systems,* 15: 31–50.

Ferragina, A.M. and Mazzotta, F. (2014) Local agglomeration economies: What impact on multinational and national Italian firms' survival? *Procedia: Social and Behavioral Sciences,* 110: 8–19.

Feser, E.J. and Sweeney, S.H. (2000) A test for the coincident economic and spatial clustering of business enterprises. *Journal of Geographical Systems,* 2: 349–373.

Fleming, M.M. (2004) Techniques for estimating spatially dependent discrete choice models. In Anselin, L., Florax, R.J.G.M. and Rey, S. (eds.), *Advances in Spatial Econometrics: Methodology, Tools and Applications,* 145–168. Heidelberg: Springer.

Flores-Lagunes, A. and Schnier, K. (2012) Estimation of sample selection models with spatial dependence. *Journal of Applied Econometrics,* 27: 173–204.

Forni, M. and Lippi, M. (1997) *Aggregation and the Microfoundations of Dynamic Macroeconomics.* Oxford: Oxford University Press.

Gabriel, E. and Diggle, P.J. (2009) Second-order analysis of inhomogeneous spatio-temporal point process data. *Statistica Neerlandica,* 63: 43–51.

Gandolfo, G. (1990) *Continuous Time Econometrics.* London: Chapman & Hall.

Geary, R.C. (1954) The contiguity ratio and statistical mapping. *Incorporated Statistician,* 5: 115–127, 129–146.

Gehlke, C.E. and Biehl, K. (1934) Certain effects of grouping upon the size of the correlation coefficient in census tract material. *Journal of the American Statistical Association,* 29: 169–170.

Getis, A. (1984) Interaction modelling using second-order analysis. *Environment and Planning A,* 16: 173–183.

Getis, A. and Boots, B. (1978) *Models of Spatial Processes.* Cambridge: Cambridge University Press.

Bibliography 213

Getis, A. and Ord, J.K. (1995) Local spatial autocorrelation statistics: Distributional issues and an application, *Geographical Analysis*, 27: 286–306.

Gilley, O.W. and Pace, R.K. (1996) On the Harrison and Rubinfeld data. *Journal of Environmental Economics and Management*, 31: 403–405.

Glaeser, E.L. and Kerr, W.R. (2009) Local industrial conditions and entrepreneurship: How much of the spatial distribution can we explain? *Journal of Economics and Management Strategy*, 18: 623–663.

Glaeser, E.L., Kallal, H.K., Scheinkman, J.A. and Shleifer, A. (1992) Growth in cities. *Journal of Political Economy*, 100: 1126–1152.

Goldberger, A.S. (1964) *Econometric Theory*. New York: Wiley.

Goodchild, M. (2007) Citizens as sensors: The world of volunteered geography. *GeoJournal*, 69: 211–221.

Goreaud, F. and Pélissier, R. (1999) On explicit formulas of edge-effect correction for Ripley's *K*-function. *Journal of Vegetation Science*, 10: 433–438.

Grambsch, P. and Therneau, T. (1994) Proportional hazard tests and diagnostics based on weighted residuals. *Biometrika*, 81: 515–526.

Grandell, J. (1976) *Doubly Stochastic Poisson Processes*. Berlin: Springer.

Green, H.A.J. (1964) *Aggregation and Disaggregation in Economics Analysis*. Princeton, NJ: Princeton University Press.

Greene, W. (2018) *Econometric Analysis*, 8th edn. Upper Saddle River, NJ: Pearson Educational.

Greig-Smith, P. (1952) The use of random and contiguous quadrats in the study of the structure of plant communities. *Annals of Botany*, 16: 293–316.

Grether, D. and Maddala, G.S. (1973) Errors in variables and serially correlated disturbances in distributed lag models. *Econometrica*, 41: 255–262.

Griffith, D.A. (1986) Central place structures using constant elasticity of consumption demand cones, Part I: The infinite plane. *Economic Geography*, 62: 74–84.

Griffith, D.A., Bennett, R.J. and Haining, R.P. (1989) Statistical analysis of spatial data in the presence of missing observations: A methodological guide and an application to urban census data. *Environment and Planning A*, 21: 1511–1523.

Griffith, D.A., Wong, D.W.S. and Whitfied, T. (2003) Exploring relationships between the global and regional measures of spatial autocorrelation. *Journal of Regional Science*, 43: 683–710.

Haaland, J.I., Kind, H.J., Midelfart-Knarvik, K.H. and Torstensson, J. (1999) *What Determines the Economic Geography of Europe?* Centre for Economic Policy Research, discussion paper.

Haitovsky, J. (1973) *Regression Estimation from Grouped Observations*, Griffin's Statistical Courses and Monographs, 33. London: Griffin.

Hall, A.R. (2005) *Generalized Method of Moments*. Oxford: Oxford University Press.

Hannan, E.J. (1970) *Aggregation and Disaggregation in Sociology*. Lexington, Mass.: Lexington Books.

Hansen, M.H., Hurwitz, W.N. and Madow, W.G. (1953) *Sample Survey Methods and Theory*. New York: Wiley.

Harrison, D. and Rubinfeld, D.L. (1978) Hedonic housing prices and the demand for clean air. *Journal of Environmental Economics and Management*, 5: 81–102.

Hausman, J. (1978) Specification tests in econometrics. *Econometrica*, 46: 1251–1271.

Henderson, J.V. (2003) Marshall's scale economies. *Journal of Urban Economics*, 53: 1–28.

Hess, W. and Persson, M. (2012) The duration of trade revisited: Continuous-time versus discrete-time hazards. *Empirical Economics*, 43: 1083–1107.

214 Bibliography

Hopenhayn, H. (1992) Entry, exit and firm dynamics in long run equilibrium. *Econometrica*, 60: 1127–1150.

Igami, M. (2011) Does big drive out small? Entry, exit, and differentiation in the supermarket industry. *Review of Industrial Organization*, 38: 1–21.

Illian, J., Penttinen, A., Stoyan, H. and Stoyan, D. (2008) *Statistical Analysis and Modelling of Spatial Point Pattern*. Chichester: Wiley.

Isard, W. (1956) *Location and Space Economy*. Cambridge, Mass.: MIT Press.

Jensen, P. and Michel, J. (2011) Measuring spatial dispersion: Exact results on the variance of random spatial distributions. *Annals of Regional Science*, 47: 81–110.

John, F. (1978) *Partial Differential Equations*. Berlin: Springer.

Kaashoek, J.F. and Paelinck, J.H.P. (1994) On potentialized partial differential equations in theoretical spatial economics. *Chaos, Solitons and Fractals*, 4: 585–594

Kaashoek, J.F. and Paelinck, J.H.P. (1996) Studying the dynamics of pre-geographical space by means of space and time-potential partial differential equations. *Geographical Systems*, 3: 259–277.

Kaashoek, J.F. and Paelinck, J.H.P. (1998) Potentialized partial differential equations in economic geography and spatial economics: Multiple dimension and control. *Acta Applicandae Mathematicae*, 51: 1–23.

Kang, H. (2010) Detecting agglomeration processes using space–time clustering analyses. *Annals of Regional Science*, 45: 291–311.

Kapoor, M., Kelejian, H. and Prucha, I. (2007) Panel data model with spatially correlated error components. *Journal of Econometrics*, 140: 97–130.

Kelejian, H. and Prucha, I. (1998) A generalized spatial two-stage least squares procedure for estimating a spatial autoregressive model with autoregressive disturbances. *Journal of Real Estate Finance and Economics*, 17: 99–121 .

Kelejian, H. and Prucha, I. (1999) A generalized moments estimator for the autoregressive parameter in a spatial model. *International Economic Review*, 40: 509–533.

Kelejian, H.H., Tavlas, G.S. and Hondronyiannis, G. (2006) A spatial modeling approach to contagion among emerging economies. *Open Economies Review*, 17: 423–442.

Kelly, F.P. and Ripley, B.D. (1976) On Strauss's model for clustering. *Biometrika*, 63: 357–360.

Kerr, W.R. and Kominers, S.D. (2015) Agglomerative forces and cluster shapes. *Review of Economics and Statistics*, 97: 877–899.

Kirman, A.P. (1992) Whom or what does the representative individual represent? *Journal of Economic Perspectives*, 6(2): 117–136.

Klein, L.R. (1946) Remarks on the theory of aggregation. *Econometrics*, 14: 303–312.

Klier, T. and McMillen, D.P. (2008a) Clustering of auto supplier plants in the United States: Generalized method of moments spatial logit for large samples. *Journal of Business and Economic Statistics*, 26: 460–471.

Klier, T. and McMillen, D.P. (2008b) Evolving agglomeration in the U.S. auto supplier industry. *Journal of Regional Science*, 48: 245–267.

Koh, H.J. and Riedel, N. (2014) Assessing the localization pattern of German manufacturing and service industries: A distance-based approach. *Regional Studies*, 48: 823–843.

Kosfeld, R., Eckey, H.-F. and Lauridsen, J. (2011) Spatial point pattern analysis and industry concentration. *Annals of Regional Science*, 47: 311–328.

Krueger, N.F., Jr. (2003) The cognitive psychology of entrepreneurship. In Acs, Z. and Audrestsch, D.B. (eds.), *Handbook of Entrepreneurial Research*, 105–140. London: Kluwer Law International.

Bibliography 215

Krugman, P. (1991a) *Geography and Trade*. Cambridge, Mass.: MIT Press.

Krugman, P. (1991b) Increasing returns and economic geography. *Journal of Political Economy*, 99: 183–199.

Lazear, E.P. (2005) Entrepreneurship. *Journal of Labor Economics*, 23: 649–680.

Lang, G. and Marcon, E. (2013) Testing randomness of spatial point patterns with the Ripley statistic. *ESAIM: Probability and Statistics*, 17: 767–788.

Le Gallo, J. and Fingleton, B. (2012) Measurement error in a spatial context. *Regional Science and Urban Economics*, 42: 114–125.

Lee, L.-F. (2003) Best spatial two-stages least squares estimators for a spatial autoregressive model with autoregressive disturbances. *Econometric Reviews*, 22: 307–335.

Lee, L.-F. (2004) Asymptotic distribution of maximum likelihood estimators for spatial autoregressive models. *Econometrica*, 72: 1899–1925.

Lee, L.-F. and Yu, J. (2010a) Estimation of spatial autoregressive panel data models with fixed effects. *Journal of Econometrics*, 154: 165–185.

Lee, L.-F. and Yu, J. (2010b) Some recent developments in spatial panel data models. *Regional Science and Urban Economics*, 40: 255–271.

Lee, L.-F. and Yu, J. (2011) Estimation of spatial panels. *Foundation and Trends in Econometrics*, 4: 1–164.

Lee, L.-F. and Yu, J. (2012) Spatial panels: Random components versus fixed effects. *International Economic Review*, 53: 1369–1412.

LeSage, J. (2000) Bayesian estimation of limited dependent variable spatial autoregressive models. *Geographical Analysis*, 32: 19–35.

LeSage, J. and Pace, R.K. (2009) *Introduction to Spatial Econometrics*. Boca Raton, Fla.: Chapman & Hall/CRC.

LeSage, J., Pace, R.K., Lam, N., Campanella, R. and Liu, X. (2011) New Orleans business recovery in the aftermath of Hurricane Katrina. *Journal of the Royal Statistical Society: Series B*, 174: 1007–1027.

Lewis, P.A.W. and Shedler, G.S. (1979) Simulation of non-homogeneous Poisson processes by thinning. *Naval Research Logistics Quarterly*, 26: 403–413.

Li, H., Calder, C.A. and Cressie, N. (2007) Beyond Moran's I: Testing for spatial dependence based on the spatial autoregressive model. *Geographical Analysis*, 39: 357–375.

Li, L., Hong, X. and Peng, K. (2019) A spatial panel analysis of carbon emissions, economic growth and high-technology industry in China. *Structural Change and Economic Dynamics*, 49: 83–92

Little, R.J.A. (1988) Missing-data adjustments in large surveys. *Journal of Business and Economic Statistics*, 6: 287–296.

Little, R.J.A. and Rubin, D.B. (2002) *Statistical Analysis with Missing Data*, 2nd edn. New York: Wiley.

Lösch, A. (1954) *The Economics of Location*. New Haven, Conn.: Yale University Press.

McMillen, D.P. (1992) Probit with spatial autocorrelation. *Journal of Regional Science*, 32: 335–348.

Madsen, L., Ruppert, D. and Altman, N.S. (2008) Regression with spatially misaligned data. *Environmetrics*, 19: 453–467.

Mansfield, E. (1995) Academic research underlying industrial innovations: Sources, characteristics, and financing. *Review of Economics and Statistics*, 77: 55–65.

Marcon, E. and Puech, F. (2003) Evaluating the geographic concentration of industries using distance-based methods. *Journal of Economic Geography*, 3: 409–428.

Marcon, E. and Puech, F. (2009) *Generalizing Ripley's K Function to Inhomogeneous Populations*. <https://halshs.archives-ouvertes.fr/halshs-00372631>.

216 Bibliography

Marcon, E. and Puech, F. (2010) Measures of the geographic concentration of industries: Improving distance-based methods. *Journal of Economic Geography*, 10: 745–762.

Marcon, E. and Puech, F. (2017) A typology of distance-based measures of spatial concentration. *Regional Science and Urban Economics*, 62: 56–67.

Marcon, E., Traissac, S. and Lang, G. (2013) A statistical test for Ripley's K function rejection of Poisson null hypothesis. *ISRN Ecology*, art. 753475.

Marcon, E., Traissac, S., Puech, F. and Lang, G. (2015) Tools to characterize point patterns: dbmss for R. *Journal of Statistical Software*, 67: 1–15.

Marshall, A. (1920) *Principles of Economics*, revd edn. London: Macmillan.

Marubini, E. and Valsecchi, M.G. (1995) *Analysing Survival Data from Clinical Trials and Observational Studies*. Chichester, Wiley.

Matérn, B. (1960) *Spatial Variation*, Meddelanden fran statens skogsforsningsinstitut, 49/5. Stockholm: Statens Skogsforsningsinstitut.

Matérn, B. (1986) *Spatial Variation*, Lecture Notes in Statistics, 36. Berlin: Springer.

Millo, G. and Pasini, G. (2010) Does social capital reduce moral hazard? A network model for non-life insurance demand. *Fiscal Studies*, 31: 341–372.

Millo, G. and Piras, G. (2012) Splm: Spatial panel data models in R. *Journal of Statistical Software*, 47: 1–43.

Modigliani, F. and Brunberg, R. (1955) Utility analysis and consumption function an interpretation of cross-section data. In Kurihara, K.K. (ed.), *Post-Keneysian Economics*, 388–436. London: Allen & Unwin.

Møller, J. and Waagepetersen, R. (2003) *Statistical Inference and Simulation for Spatial Point Processes*. Boca Raton, Fla.: Chapman & Hall/CRC.

Møller, J. and Waagepetersen, R. (2007) Modern statistics for spatial point processes (with discussion). *Scandinavian Journal of Statistics*, 34: 643–711.

Møller, J., Syversveen, A. and Waagepetersen, R. (1998) Log Gaussian Cox processes. *Scandinavian Journal of Statistics*, 25: 451–482.

Moran, P.A.P. (1950) Notes on continuous stochastic phenomena. *Biometrika*, 37: 17–23.

Moreno-Monroy, A.I. and García, G.A. (2016) Intra-metropolitan agglomeration of formal and informal manufacturing activity: Evidence from Cali, Colombia. *Tijdschrift Voor Economische en Sociale Geografie*, 107: 389–406.

Mugglin, A.S., Carlin, B.P. and Gelfand, A.E. (2000) Fully model-based approaches for spatially misaligned data. *Journal of the American Statistical Association*, 95: 877–887.

Murdoch, J.C., Sandler, T. and Sargent, K. (1997) A tale of two collectives: Sulphur versus nitrogen oxide emission reduction in Europe. *Public Finance Quarterly*, 21: 334–350.

Mutl, J. and Pfaffermayr, M. (2011) The Hausman test in a Cliff and Ord panel model. *Econometrics Journal*, 14: 48–76.

Newey, W. and West, K. (1987) A simple positive semi-definite heteroscedasticity and autocorrelation consistent covariance matrix. *Econometrica*, 55: 703–708.

Neyman, J. and Scott, E.L. (1958) Statistical approach to problems of cosmology (with discussion). *Journal of the Royal Statistical Society: Series B*, 20: 1–43.

Oberhofer, W. and Kmenta, J. (1974) A general procedure for obtaining maximum likelihood estimates in generalized regression models. *Econometrica*, 42: 579–590.

Okabe, A. and Tagashira, N. (1996) Spatial aggregation bias in a regression model containing a distance variable. *Journal of Geographical Systems*, 2: 83–202.

Openshaw, S. and Taylor, P.J. (1979) A million or so of correlated coefficients: Three experiments on the modifiable areal unit problem. In Wrigley, N. and Bennet, R.J. (eds.), *Statistical Applications in the Spatial Sciences*, 127–144. London: Pion.

Bibliography 217

Orcutt, G.H., Watts, H.W. and Edward, J.B. (1968) Data aggregation and information loss. *American Economic Review*, 58: 773–787.

Ord, J.K. (1975) Estimation methods for spatial interaction. *Journal of the American Statistical Association*, 70: 120–126.

Ord, J.K. and Getis, A. (1992) The analysis of spatial association by use of distance statistics. *Geographical Analysis*, 24: 189–206.

Orwat-Acedańska, A. (2019) Dynamic spatial panel data models in identifying socio-economic factors affecting the level of health in selected European countries. *European Spatial Research and Policy*, 26: 195–211.

Pesaran, M.H., Pierse, R.G. and Kumar, M.S. (1987) On the problem of aggregation in econometrics. Discussion paper on structural analysis of economic systems, Department of Applied Economics, Cambridge University.

Pinkse, J. and Slade, M.E. (1998) Contacting in space: An application of spatial statistics to discrete-choice models. *Journal of Econometrics*, 85: 125–154.

Pinkse, J. and Slade, M.E. (2010) The future of spatial econometrics. *Journal of Regional Science*, 50: 103–117.

Prais, S. and Aitchinson, J. (1954) The grouping of observations in regression analysis. *Revue de l'Institut International de Statistique*, 1: 1–22.

Qu, X. and Lee, L.-F. (2012) LM tests for spatial correlation in spatial models with limited dependent variables. *Regional Science and Urban Economics*, 42: 430–445.

Qu, X. and Lee, L.-F. (2013) Locally most powerful tests for spatial interactions in the simultaneous SAR tobit model. *Regional Science and Urban Economics*, 43: 307–321.

Quah, D. (1993) Galton's fallacy and the convergence hypothesis. *Scandinavian Journal of Economics*, 95: 427–443.

Rabe-Hesketh, S. and Skrondal, A. (2008) *Multilevel and Longitudinal Modeling using Stata*. College Station, Tex.: Stata Press.

Rathbun, S.L. and Cressie, N. (1994) A space time survival point process for a longleaf pine forest in Southern Georgia. *Journal of the American Statistical Association*, 89: 1164–1174.

Ripley, B.D. (1976) The second-order analysis of stationary point processes. *Journal of Applied Probability*, 13: 255–266.

Ripley, B.D. (1977) Modelling spatial patterns (with discussion). *Journal of the Royal Statistical Society: Series B*, 39: 172–212.

Robinson, W.S. (1950) Technological correlations and the behavior of individuals. *American Sociologic Review*, 15: 351–357.

Roderick, J.L. and Rubin, D.B. (2007) *Statistical Analysis with Missing Data*. Hoboken, NJ: Wiley.

Romer, P. (1986) Increasing returns and long-run growth. *Journal of Political Economy*, 94: 1002–1037.

Rosenthal, S.S. and Strange, W.C. (2003) Geography, industrial organization and agglomeration. *Review of Economic Studies*, 85: 377–393

Rowlingson, B. and Diggle, P.J. (2015) *Splancs: Spatial and Space-Time Point Pattern Analysis*. R package version 2.01–38. <https://CRAN.R-project.org/package=splancs>.

Rubin, D.B. (1976) Inference and missing data. *Biometrika*, 63: 581–592.

Rubin, D.B. (1987) *Multiple Imputation for Nonresponse in Surveys*. New York: Wiley.

Silverman, B.W. (1986) *Density Estimation for Statistics and Data Analysis*. London: Chapman & Hall.

Smirnov, O. (2010) Modelling spatial discrete choice. *Regional Science and Urban Economics*, 40: 292–298.

218   *Bibliography*

Staber, U. (2001) Spatial proximity and firm survival in a declining industrial district: The case of knitwear firms in Baden-Wurttemberg. *Regional Studies*, 35: 329–341.

Stocker, T.M. (1982) The use of cross-section data to characterize macro functions. *Journal of the American Statistical Association*, 77: 369–380.

Strauss, D.J. (1975) A model for clustering. *Biometrika*, 62: 467–475.

Strauss, D. and Ikeda, M. (1990) Pseudolikelihood estimation for social networks. *Journal of the American Statistical Association*, 85: 204–212.

Sweeney, S.H. and Feser, E.J. (1998) Plant size and clustering of manufacturing activity. *Geographical Analysis*, 30: 45–64.

Tagashira, N. and Okabe, A. (2012) The modifiable areal unit problem in a regression model whose independent variable is a distance from a predetermined point. *Geographical Analysis*, 34: 1–20.

Theil, H. (1954) *Linear Aggregation in Economic Relations*. Amsterdam: North-Holland.

Thomas, M. (1949) A generalisation of Poisson's binomial limit for use in ecology. *Biometrika*, 36: 18–25.

Tobin, J. (1958) Estimation of relationships for limited dependent variables. *Econometrica*, 26: 24–36.

Tobler, W. (1970) A computer movie simulating urban growth in the Detroit region. *Economic Geography*, 46: 234–240.

Toda, M. (1989) *Nonlinear Waves and Solitons*. Dordrecht: Kluwer Academic.

USAID (2013) *Geographical Displacement Procedure and Georeferenced Data Release Policy for the Demographic and Health Surveys*, DHS Spatial Analysis Report, 7 Calverton, Md.: ICF International.

Van Dijk, J. and Pellenbarg, P.H. (2000) Firm relocation decisions in the Netherlands: An ordered logit approach. *Papers in Regional Science*, 79: 191–219

Van Wissen, L. (2000) A micro-simulation model of firms: Application of concepts of the demography of the firm. *Papers in Regional Science*, 79: 111–134

Waagepetersen, R. (2007) An estimating function approach to inference for inhomogeneous Neyman–Scott processes. *Biometrics*, 63: 252–258.

Wang, H., Iglesias, E.M. and Wooldridge, J.M. (2013) Partial maximum likelihood estimation of spatial probit models. *Journal of Econometrics*, 172: 77–89.

Wang, X. and Kockelman, K.M. (2009) Bayesian inference for ordered response data with a dynamic spatial ordered probit model. *Journal of Regional Science*, 49: 877–913.

Weber, A. (1909) *Über den Standort der Industrien*. Tubingen: Mohr.

Whittle, P. (1954) On stationary processes in the plane. *Biometrika*, 41: 434–449.

Willenborg, L.C.R.J. and De Waal, T. (1996) *Statistical Disclosure Control in Practice*. Berlin: Springer.

Wooldridge, J. (2002) *Econometric Analysis of Cross-Section and Panel Data*. Cambridge, Mass.: MIT Press.

Xu, X. and Lee, L.-F. (2015) Maximum likelihood estimation of a spatial autoregressive tobit model. *Journal of Econometrics*, 188: 264–280.

Yule, U. and Kendall, M.S. (1950) *An Introduction to the Theory of Statistics*. London: Charles Griffin.

Zellner, A. (1962) An efficient method of estimating seemingly unrelated regression equations and tests for aggregation bias. *Journal of the American Statistical Association*, 57: 348–368.

Index

Note: **Bold** page numbers refer to tables; *italic* page numbers refer to figures and page numbers followed by "n" denote endnotes.

a-spatial fixed effects model 193
a-spatial probit model 64–65
ADI (average direct impact) 47
agglomeration economies 172–173
agglomeration externalities 176, 177
aggregate shocks 5
aggregated point pattern 111
aggregated point processes 98
aggregation 5, 98; problem 6
AII (average indirect impact) 47
analysis advantages, of spatial
    macroeconometrics 5–7
Anselin, L. 28–29; *et al.* 45, 83
Arbia, G. 7, 161, 162, 163, 166; and Espa,
    G. 101–102; *et al.* 54–55, 73, 130, 148,
    165; and Petrarca, F. 7
ASIA 31, 34
asymptotic theory xv
ATI (average total impact) 47
ATIF (average total impact from) and
    observation 47
ATIT (average total impact to) and
    observation 47
attenuation effect 50–51, 53, 54–55
autocorrelation 7, 22, 192; *see also* spatial
    autocorrelation
autoregressive model, spatial 50, 51–52

Baddeley, A.J. 154; *et al.* 132–134, 152,
    154; and Turner, T.R. 135
Baltagi, B.H., *et al.* 87, **87**
Baltimore house prices and characteristics
    62–63, *62*, **62**, **63**, 67, **67**, 69, **69**,
    71, **71**
Bartlett, M.S. 113
Beaudry, C., and Schiffauerova, A. 177

Beckmann, M.J. 160; and Puu, T. 160
behavior: competitive 172, 183;
    cooperative 170, 183; firm xvi–xvii, 6,
    93, 159–160, 161, 172, 177
benchmark 93, 117, 132, 144, 152;
    hypothesis for spatial point pattern 95,
    98; model 96, 98; value 139, 140, 146,
    168, 179
Berman, M.: and Diggle, P.J. 134; and
    Turner, R. 167
Berman–Turner approximation 135
Bernoulli likelihood 175
Bernoulli variables 58–59
Beron, K.J., and Vijverberg, W.P. 73
Besag, J. 117; and Diggle, P.J. 118
BFGS2SLS (best feasible generalized
    spatial two-stage least squares) 43
bias, statistical 177
Big Data 7
Billion Prices Project 8
birth model 162–163, 165, 166–168
bivariate normal distribution 102
bivariate uniform distribution 102
Boots, B.N., and Getis, A. 143
Boston: dataset 24–25, 187–188; house
    price locations 24, *24*
Boston house price determinants: local
    Moran I example 27, *27*; Moran's I
    example 24–25, **25**, 27, *28*; residual
    correlation tests **45**; SARAR model
    example 43–44, *43*, **44**; SDM example
    40–41; SDM regression residuals **41**;
    SLM example 37–39; SLM marginal
    impacts 47–48, **48**; SLM regression
    residuals 38, **38**, *39*
boundaries 160

220 *Index*

Breslow, N. 175
business units 107, *108*; point pattern 109–110, *110*

Cameron, A.C., and Trivedi, P.K. 6
cell phone data 8
censoring 173, 175
census tract, Trento (2004) 166, *167*
central place model 104
centrifugal and centripetal forces 185
centroids, Italian provinces *86*
chi-squared test 107–109
Christaller, W. 104
Clark, P.J., and Evans, F.C. 111
Clark–Evans index 111, 112, 198
Clark–Evans test 112, 198
classical spatial microeconometrics xix
Cliff, A.D., and Ord, J.K. 22, 23
cloglog model 175
closeness concept 11
clustering, space–time 145–148, *149*, *150*
clusters: of ICT firms in Rome 155; space–time 151, 155; spatio-temporal 155; *see also* Matérn cluster process; Poisson cluster point processes; Poisson cluster process
Cochrane–Orcutt transformation 83, 85
cold spots 26
competing stores 105, 106
competition of supermarkets (Trento, Italy) 136–138, *136*, *137*
competitive behavior 172, 183
complementary log-log mixed model *183*
complementary log-log model 182–183, *183*; estimates 183, **184**; with or without frailty 182–183
composite error u_{it} 77
confidence envelopes: Monte Carlo-simulated 135, 139, 180; random labelling simulated 200, 201
connectivity matrix *see* W matrix (weights matrix)
Conrow, L., *et al.* 148
consumption 6
contagion xvi, 98, 100, 127
continuous space modelling 160–161
continuous time econometrics 160
control variables 180–181, 185
convenience sampling 10
cooperative behavior 170, 183
correlation, spatial 15, 26
correlation coefficient 7
covariates 174, 175; micro-founded spatial 176, 177–180, 182

Cox, D. 174
Cox processes 100–101, *100*, 196; *see also* log-Gaussian Cox process
Cox proportional hazards model 182, *183*
Cox (regression) model 173, 174–175
Cressie, N., and Rathbun, S.L. 161, 162, 163–165, 169
cross-sectional models xv, 78, 84; spatial linear 30–56
crowd-sourced data 8
crowdsourcing 6, 10
CSR (complete spatial randomness): hypothesis xvi, 96–97, 107–110, 117; test 116–120, *119–120*, *123*
cumulative hazard function 174
Cuzick, J., and Edwards, R. 128

D-function xvi, 127–132, 200–202; firms' exit from Sicily hospitality market example 130–132, *130*, *131*; tests of spatial interactions 128–130, *129*, 200–202
data: acquisition 8; alternative sources 6–7; cell phones 8; crowd-sourced 8; description of firm demography case study 164–166; extraction from web 8; failure time 173; geo-coded 7, 9; insurance 86–88; micro- 8–10, 48–53, 159; micro-geographical 164–172, 178; missing 9–10, 50–51, 53; panel 76; regional 6, 8–9, 86, 159; simulated 55–56, *55*; for survival of pharmaceutical and medical device manufacturing firms in Italy case study 176–177; uncertainty 49, 50; *see also* panel data models
data analysis, survival 173
data modelling, spatial panel 85–89
data-generating point process 133, *134*
databases xix; enrichment for firm demography 164; geographical 4
datasets: Baltimore 187; Baltimore house prices and characteristics 62–63, 67, **67**; Boston 24–25, 187–188; demopat 200; local units in Macerata industrial sectors 31–32, *32*, **32**, 34–35, **34**, **35**; long-run spatial dynamics of Rome ICT firms 153–154; micro- 141; Veneto pharmaceutical and medical device manufacturing firms 122; point pattern 194–195
death/survival process xvii, 163, 165, 170–172
demopat dataset 200

Diggle and Chetwynd's D-function
see D-function
Diggle, P.J. 96, 99, 100, 102, 114–116, 121, 134; and Berman, M. 134; and Besag, J. 118; *et al.* 143–144, 145–147, 148–149; and Gabriel, E. 148–155; and Gratton, J.R. 121
discrete choice modeling 55, 57, 58, 73
discrete outcomes xiv, 57
discrete time proportional hazard model 175
discrete times model 175
dispersion index 109–110, *110*
distance 115; inhibition 104; nearest-neighbor 17, *19*, 21, 38, 111; optimal 185; pair-wise 52, 54; regressions on 53–56; threshold 17, *18*, *19*, 21, 25
distance-based approaches 110–112
distribution: bivariate normal 102; bivariate uniform 102; ICT firms in Rome 154, *154*
Donnelly, K. 111–112
doubly stochastic processes 100
Duranton, G., and Overman, H.G. 138, 139
Duranton and Overman's K-density 138, 139–140, 141–142, *142*
duration times 175
Durbin model, spatial (SDM) 39–41, 191
Durbin term xiv
Durbin–Watson statistic 22
Durlauf, S.N. 4
dynamic spatial panel data models 85

$\hat{E}$ *(d)* function 115
ecological fallacy 11n1
econometric analysis 94
econometric modelling 6, 7, 10, 72
econometrics, continuous time 160
economic activities, space–time clusters of 151
economic agents 93–94, 127, 135, 166, 172, 185
economic dynamics 159
economic events, detecting space–time clustering of 145–148
economy 4–5; agglomeration 172–173; lattice 4; spatial random 7
Edwards, R., and Cuzick, J. 128
efficiency loss 7
Efron, B. 175
Elhorst, J.P. 80, 82, 85
Ellison–Glaeser index 138

EM (expectation-maximization) algorithm 66
employee numbers 180
endogeneity problem 41–42
error: composite error u_{it} 77; idiosyncratic 81; locational 49, 52–53; measurement 48, 49, 50–53; positional 9–10; pseudo- (generalized-) 67; term 77, 163; *see also* SEM (spatial error model); spatial error
Espa, G., and Arbia, G. 101–102
estimation 80–85; complementary log-log model 183, *184*; of generalized logit model 70; iterative 82–83; of K-function 114–116; of K_{inhom}-function 133–135; of non-linear spatial models 73; nonparametric 134, 153; problems of spatial lag probit model equation 64; of space–time K-function 145; of spatial lag logit model 69–71; of spatial tobit model 72–73; of $STIK$-function 152–153; *see also* parameters estimation
estimators, OLS 22, *25*, 37, *38*, 47, 84–85, 169, *170*
Evans, F.C., and Clark, P.J. 111
exponential model 175, 181–182, *183*
externalities: agglomeration 176, 177; knowledge 172; MAR 177–178, 183, *183*, 185; Marshall 178; spatial 180–181

failure 181; hazard of 181; risk for start-up firms 185; time 173
family budgets 6
Feser, E.J., and Sweeney, S.H. 130
FGLS (feasible GLS) 33–34, 35, 191
firm demography: models 159; spatial microeconometric model for 161–172; and survival literature 159
firm demography case study 164–172; birth model 166–168; data description 164–166; growth model 169–170; survival model 170–172
firm survival spatial microeconometric model 172–186
firms: behaviors xvi–xvii, 6, 93, 159–160, 161, 172, 177; exit from hospitality in Sicily 130–132, *130*, *131*; exit hazard 182, 183; ICT in Rome 153–155, *154*; incumbent 76, 176, 178, 183, 185; legal status 180; model components xvi–xvii; spatial interactions between individual 176, 180; spatial point pattern of Sicily tourism and hospitality start-up 93–94, *94*; start-up 176, 178,

222 *Index*

181, 185, 186; survival model 172–186; *see also* pharmaceutical and medical device manufacturing firms in Veneto
first-order intensity function 95–96, 102
Fisher information matrix 59
fixed effect spatial model 79–80
fixed effects (or within) model 77, 82–83, 85, 88, 193, 194
food stores in Trento (Italy): case study 165–172; spatial establishment point process 167, **168**
frailty 175, 182–183

Gabriel, E., and Diggle, P.J. 148–155
Gaussian geo-masking 55–56, *56*
Gaussian kernel smoother 140
Geary's index 25–26
general spatial model *see* SARAR model
geo-coded data 7, 9
geo-masking: Gaussian 55–56, *56*; uniform 51, 54–55, 55–56, *56*
geographical area variable 180
geographical databases 4
geographical proximity, to incumbent firms 183
Getis, A. 178; and Boots, B.N. 143; and Ord, J.K. 27–28
Getis–Ord G* 28
Getis–Ord index 28
Gibbs sampler algorithm 73
GLS (generalized least squares) procedure 33–34; feasible (FGLS) 33–34, 35, 191
GMM (generalized method of moments) xiv, xv, 6, 34, 67, 68, **69**, **71**, 194; for fixed effects models 84–85, 88, **88**; linearized 192; for random effects models 84–85, 88, **88**; for spatial panel models 83–85
goodness-of-fit *125*, 126, 135, 168
Google Maps 8
Goreaud, F., and Pélissier, R. 115
Grambsch, P., and Therneau, T. 186
Gratton, J.R., and Diggle, P.J. 121
Grieg-Smith, P. 109, 110
Griffith, D.A. 160
growth model 163, 165, 169–170, **170**
GS2SLS (generalized spatial two-stage least squares) 42–43, 44, **44**

Hausman test xv, 80
hazard: baseline 174–175; cumulative function 174; of failure 181; of firm exit 182, 183; function 173–174; rate 177
hazard model, proportional 174
hazard test, proportional 186
health economics 53

Hessian matrix 59–60
heterogeneity: spatial 134, 166, 180; spatio-temporal 150–151, 153; unobserved 76–77
heterogeneous space, points in 200–204
heteroscedastic measurement error 50
heteroscedasticity 64, 65; locational error 53
HH (high–high) points 26
historical initial conditions 166
HL (high–low) points 27
homogeneous Poisson point process 96–98, *97*, 99, 106, 107, 111, 112, *112*, 117, 132; Monte Carlo simulations of 118; simulating 195–196
hospitality (Sicily): firms' exit 130–132, *130*, *131*; and tourism start-up firms 93–94, *94*
hot spots 26
house prices *see* Baltimore house prices and characteristics; Boston house price determinants

ICT firms in Rome, long-run spatial dynamics 153–155, *154*
idiosyncratic component 77
idiosyncratic error 81
Igami, M. 160
Ikeda, M., and Strauss, D. 135, 167
imperfections, spatial 48–53
incidence rate 181, **181**
income 6
incumbent firms 176, 178, 183, 185
independence 95
industries, spatial concentration of 138–142
inference: for K_{inhom}-function 135; of *STIK*-function 152–153
information 8
inhibition xvi, 104; distance 104; spatial xvi–xvii, 162
inhibition processes: hard-core 105–106; Matérn 104–105, *105*, 112, *112*; simple sequential (SSI) 105, *105*, 197; soft-core 106
inhomogeneous *K*-function 168, *168*
inhomogeneous Poisson point process 98–100, *99*, 132–133, 135, 155, 162, 166; simulating 196; spatio-temporal 152
insurance: data 86–88; Italian provinces consumption 86–89, *86*
intensity function xvi, 162; first order 95–96, 102; of ICT firms in Rome 154, *154*; second order 95–96, 132–133, 151, 152

interaction: space–time 146, 148–149; spatio-temporal 144, 153, 155, *155*; *see also* spatial interactions
internet of things 8
isotropic spatio-temporal point process 152
ISTAT (Italian National Statistical Institute) 31, 122, 131, 141, 176
Italy: dataset of local units in Macerata industrial sectors 31–32, *32*, **32**, 34–35, **34**, **35**; provinces insurance consumption 86–89, *86*; Veneto pharmaceutical and medical device manufacturing firms 122–124, *122*, *123*, 125–126, *125*; *see also* ICT firms in Rome (Italy); Sicily (Italy); Trento (Italy)
iterative estimation 82–83

$K(d)$, linear transformation 117
K-density 138, 139–140; spatial pattern of Trento single-plant metallurgy manufacturing example 141–142, *142*
K-function xvi, 113–114, 121–122, 124–126, 127–128, 138, 143; CSR test based on 116–120, *119–120*; estimation 114–116; inhomogeneous 168, *168*; local 178, 179, 186n6; for Matérn cluster process 124–125; space–time 143–148, *148*; space–time inhomogeneous (*STIK*-function) 148–155; spatio-temporal xvi, 143–148, 148–155; for Thomas cluster process 121
K-nearest neighbor contiguity criterion 16, *16*
Kaashoek, J.F., and Paelinck, J.H.P. 160–161
Kang, H. 148
Kaplan–Meier probability estimates 181–182, **181**, *182*
Kapoor, M., *et al.* 79, 84, 85, 88
Kelejian, H., and Prucha, I. 34, 37, 41
kernel estimator 134, 154
kernel smoother, Gaussian 140
kernel smoothing technique 134
Kest function 200–201
K_{inhom}-function xvi, 132–138; competition of Trento supermarkets example 136–138, *136*, *137*; estimation of 133–135; inference for 135
K_{inhom}-function-based test of spatial interactions 202–203
Kirman, A. xix, 4–5
Klier, T., and McMillan, D.P. 69–71
Kmenta, J., and Oberhofer, W. 81–82

knowledge externalities 172
Kosfeld, R., *et al.* 130
Krugman, P. 160, 163, 166, 185; historical initial conditions 166

lag *see* SLM (spatial lag model); spatial lag
Lagrange multiplier test 44–45
Lang, G., and Marcon, E. 118
latent SAR tobit model 72
latent spatial lag tobit model 72; log likelihood function of 72–73
lattice economy 4
leader–follower framework 101–102
Lee, L.-F. 33–34, 43; and Qu, X. 72–73; and Yu, J. 83, 85
legal status, of firms 180
Leibniz, G.W. 160
LeSage, J.: *et al.* 74–75; and Pace, R.K. 40, 46, 47, 73, 75
Lewis, P.A.W., and Shedler, G.S. 99
LH (low–high) points 27
likelihood: procedures for random effects models 80–82; *see also* ML (maximum likelihood)
linear models xiv; cross-sectional spatial 30–56; quantifying marginal effects 46–48; spatial 190–192
linear spatial regression model 74
linear transformation 133; of $K(d)$ 117
linearized GMM 192
LISA (local indicators of spatial association) 26, 178
LL (low–low) points 26
local K-function 178, 179, 186n6
local Moran's I 26, 27, **27**
location of individuals models, spatial 198–200
location patterns *see* spatial location patterns
location quotient 138
locational choices 180, 185
locational error 49, 53; heteroscedasticity 53; intentional 52–53
locational measures 177
locational uncertainty 51–53
locations: Baltimore house prices and characteristics *62*; Boston house prices 24–25, *24*; of economic agents 127; known 9; missing 9–10; Sicily hospitality market firms *130*, 131, 132; Trento metallurgy manufacturing 141, *141*; Trento supermarkets 136–137, *136*
log likelihood function 66
log-Gaussian Cox process 100–101, 198; parameter estimation 126, 199–200; simulation 196

224 *Index*

log-log mixed model, complementary *183*
log-log model, complementary 182–183, *183*, **184**
logit models 58–60; example 63, **63**; generalized 70; spatial 63–72

M-function 138, 140–142; spatial pattern of Trento single-plant metallurgy manufacturing example 141–142, *142*
Macerata (Italy), dataset of local units in industrial sectors 31–32, *32*, **32**, 34–35, **34, 35**
McMillen, D.P. 66–67; and Klier, T. 69–71
macroeconomic modelling 4
macroeconomics, modern 5
macroeconomy 4
McSpatial 192
mapped point pattern 10
MAR (Marshall–Arrow–Romer): externalities 177–178, 183, *183*, 185; hypothesis 172, 177
Marcon, E.: *et al.* 118; and Lang, G. 118; and Puech, F. 130, 138, 139
Marcon and Puech's *M*-function 138, 140–142, *142*
marginal impacts: on spatial linear models 46–48; on spatial non-linear models 74–75
Marshall externalities 178
Matérn, B. 104–105
Matérn cluster process 102, 198; example 125–126, *125*; *K*-function for 124–125; parameter estimation 124–126, 199–200; simulating 197
Matérn inhibition process 112, *112*
Matérn model 1 104–105, *105*, 197
Matérn model II 105, *105*, 197
MAUP (modifiable areal unit problem) 6, 7, 117, 159, 182
maximum likelihood *see* ML (maximum likelihood)
maximum pseudo-likelihood 167
MCMC (Markov chain Monte Carlo) sampler 73
measurement error 48; due to locational uncertainty 51–53; heteroscedastic 50; in SEMs 49; in SLMs 50–53
measures, location 177
measuring spatial concentration of industries 138–142
meso-level approach 160
metallurgy manufacturing in Trento, spatial pattern 141–142, *141, 142*

method of minimum contrast 121, 123, 198
micro-data: effects of spatial imperfections 48–53; sources 7–8; systematic analysis 159; uncertainty sources 8–10
micro-founded spatial covariates 176, 177–180, 182
micro-geographical data 164–172, 178
micro-geographical patterns 161
micro-level approach 3–5, 160
microeconomic panels 76
microsimulation study 7
Millo, G., and Pasini, G. 83
missing data 9–10, 50–51, 53
missing location 9–10
mixed model, complementary log-log *183*
ML (maximum likelihood) xiv, xv, 33–34, 35, 36, 38, **39**, 87–88; for death/survival model of small food stores 171–172, **171**; for logit and probit models 58–59; solution for SARAR model 42, 43–44, **43**; spatial error model using 191; for spatial lag and spatial error panels 80–83; for tobit models 73
modifiable areal unit problem *see* MAUP
Møller, J., and Waagepetersen, R. 121, 124–125, 126
Monte Carlo procedures xvi, 73, 128, *129*; global test for space–time interaction 146, 148–149; simulations 118, 139, 140, 146, 168
Monte Carlo-simulated confidence envelopes 135, 139, 180
Monte Carlo-simulated tolerance envelopes 153, 155
Moran scatterplot 28–29, *28*
Moran's I xiv, 22–26, **25**, 29, **38**; example 24–26, 27–29; local 26, 27, *27*
Mutl, J., and Pfaffermayr, M. 85

n-dimension integral 73
Nash equilibrium 72
National Business Registers 176
nearest-neighbor, *K* 16, *16*
nearest-neighbor distance W matrix 17, **19**, 21, 38, 111
neighborhood: effects 160; and W matrix 15–22
Newey, W., and West, K. 68
Neyman, J., and Scott, E.L. 101
non-linear spatial models 57–75, 192–193; standard 58–63
non-linear spatial regressions 57

Index 225

non-spatial panel data models 76
nonparametric estimation 134, 153
normal distribution, bivariate 102

Oberhofer, W., and Kmenta, J. 81–82
OLS (ordinary least squares) estimators 22, **25**, 37, **38**, 47, 84–85, 169, **170**
omitted variables 40
Orcutt, G.H., *et al.* 7
Ord, J.K. 34; and Cliff, A.D. 22, 23; and Getis, A. 27–28
Ord's decomposition 34
outcomes: discrete xiv, 57; limited xiv, xv, 57
Overman, H.G., and Duranton, G. 138, 139–140

Pace, R.K., and LeSage, J. 40, 46, 47, 73, 75
Paelinck, J.H.P., and Kaashoek, J.F. 160–161
pair-wise distances 52, 53
panel data 76
panel data modelling, spatial 85–89
panel data models xv, 76–77; non-spatial 76; spatial dynamic 85; static 85; without spatial effects 86, **87**; *see also* random effects panel data models
panel models, spatial 80–85
panel regression models 77
panel time model, short xv
panels: microeconomic 76; spatial 76
parameters estimation: log-Gaussian Cox process 126, 199–200; Matérn cluster process 124–126, 199–200; spatial lag probit model 65–67; Thomas cluster process 121–126, *124*, 199–200
parameters interpretation: for logit and probit models 60; *see also* linear models
parametric regression model 134–135, 153, 174, 175
parametric survival models 174
Pasini, G., and Millo, G. 83
Pearson's chi-squared test 107–109
Pearson's correlation coefficient 7
Pélissier, R., and Goreaud, F. 115
Petrarca, F., and Arbia, G. 7
Pfaffermayr, M., and Mutl, J. 85
pharmaceutical and medical device manufacturing firms in Veneto 122–124, *123*, 125–126, *125*; locations *122*
Pinkse, J., and Slade, M.E. 3, 67, 68
plm package 193

point pattern analysis 93–112; definitions and concepts 194–198
point patterns 169; aggregated 111; business units 109–110, *110*; datasets 194–195; mapped 10; regular 111; sample 10; simulating 195–197; spatio-temporal 147; *see also* spatial point patterns
point processes 95; data-generating 133, 134; isotropic spatio-temporal 152; Poisson xvi; regular 104–106, 197; spatial xvi, 95–106, 114, 162; survival 161; for Trento food stores 167, **168**; *see also* homogeneous Poisson point process; inhomogeneous Poisson point process
points in a heterogeneous space 200–204
Poisson cluster point processes 101–104
Poisson cluster process xvi, 102, *102*, *103*, *104*, 112, *112*; simulating 196–197; *see also* Matérn cluster process; Thomas cluster process
Poisson point process xvi; *see also* homogeneous Poisson point process; inhomogeneous Poisson point process
Poisson random variable 107, 109, 121, 124
Poisson stochastic processes xvi, 167
pooled model 86, **87**
pooling model 77
positional error, intentional/unintentional 9–10
ppp object 194–195, *195*
probit models 58–60, 65; a-spatial 64–65; example 62, **62**; SAR xiv–xv
proportional hazard model 174
proportional hazard test 186
Prucha, I., and Kelejian, H. 34, 37, 41
pseudo- (generalized) error 67
pseudo-likelihood 135, 167
Puech, F., and Marcon, E. 130, 138, 139
Puu, T., and Beckmann, M.J. 160

Qu, and Lee, L.-F. x, 72–73
quadrat-based analysis 197–198
quadrat-based methods 107–110, *108*
quadratcount function 197–198
quadrats 107–110
Quah, D. 5

R packages 193, 194–195
random direction, random distance method 51
random effects 77

226 *Index*

random effects models: GMM for 84–85, 88, **88**; likelihood procedures for 80–82; spatial error 87, **87**, 88, **88**, **89**; spatial lag 87, **87**, 88, **88**

random effects panel data models 77–78; spatial error version 78, 80–82; spatial lag version 79, 81–82; standard cross-sectional models 78

random effects spatial models 77–79

random labelling hypothesis 128

random labelling simulated confidence envelopes 200, 201

randomness: spatial 94–95, 144; spatio-temporal 144, 145–146, 147, *148; see also* CSR (complete spatial randomness)

Rathbun, S.L., and Cressie, N. 161, 162, 163–165, 169

raw (or crude) incidence rate 181, **181**

region-specific control variables 181

regional data 6, 8–9, 86, 159

regional econometric modelling 6

regional economics 160

regression models xiv, 46, 174, 177; linear spatial 74; panel 77; parametric 134–135, 153, 174, 175; survival 176, 177

regression residuals 25, **25**, 29; of Boston house prices 38, **38**, **39**, **41**

regressions: non-linear spatial 57; on a spatial distance 53–56

regular point pattern 111

regular point processes 104–106; simulating 197

regular processes 98

regularity 104

relative benchmark 179

residual correlation tests **45**

residual spatial autocorrelation, test with explicit alternative hypotheses 44–46

residuals *see* regression residuals

Ripley, B.D. 113–114, 115–116, 117

Ripley's *K*-function *see K*-function

Rome (Italy), long-run spatial dynamics of ICT firms 153–155

row standardization 16

SAC (spatial autocorrelated) model *see* SARAR model

sample point pattern 10

sampling, convenience 10

SAR (spatial autoregression) model xiii, xiv, 30–32; example 31–32; probit xiv–xv; tobit 72

SARAR model 41–44, 47, 83, 191; example 43–44, **43**, **44**

Schiffauerova, A., and Beaudry, C. 177

Scott, E.L., and Neyman, J. 101

SDM (spatial Durbin model) 39–41

second-order intensity function 96, 151

second-order intensity-reweighted stationary 132–133, 152

SEM (spatial error model) 32–35, 39–40, 45, 46–47, 65, 83; example 34–35; measurement error in 49; using maximum likelihood 191

semi-parametric model 175

shared frailty 175

Shedler, G.S., and Lewis, P.A.W. 99

short panel time model xv

Sicily (Italy): firms' exit from hospitality market 130–132, *130*, *131*; spatial point pattern of tourism and hospitality start-up firms 93–94, *94*

simple sequential inhibition (SSI) process 105, *105*, 197

simulated data 55–56, *55*

simulation: log-Gaussian Cox process 196; Matérn cluster process 197; Monte Carlo procedures 118, 139, 140, 146, 168; Monte Carlo-simulated confidence envelopes 135, 139, 180; Monte Carlo-simulated tolerance envelopes 153, 155; point patterns 195–197; regular point processes 197

simultaneous spatial lag tobit model 72

Slade, M.E., and Pinkse, J. 3, 67, 68

SLM (spatial lag model) 35–39, 45, **45**, 191; adaptation 63–64; example 37–39, **38**; measurement error in 50–53

smart phones, data 8

space, heterogeneous 200–204

space modelling, continuous 160–161

space–time clustering 145–148, *149*; inhibition 147, *150*

space–time clusters 151, 155

space–time interaction 148–149; Monte Carlo test 146, 148–149

space–time *K*-function 143–148, *148*; detecting space–time clustering of economic events 145–148; estimation of 145

space–time models 76–89, 143–155, 193–194

space–time survival point process 161

spatial autocorrelation 15, 22, 25, 29, 44–46, 65, 126; negative 32; residual 43–44, 44–46

spatial autoregressive model 50, 51–52

spatial concentration 177–178, 179

spatial concentration of industries 138–142

spatial correlation 15, 26
spatial dependence 134
spatial differentiation 183
spatial dynamics, of ICT firms in Rome 153–155
spatial error 78–79, 194; random effects 80–82; random effects model 87, **87**, **88**, **88**, **89**; version of random effects panel data models 78, 80–82
spatial error probit model 67–68
spatial externalities 180–181
spatial heterogeneity 134, 166, 180
spatial imperfections, effects on micro-data 48–53
spatial inhibition xvi–xvii, 162
spatial intensity 100
spatial interactions: D-function-based test of 200–202; between economic agents 172; between individual firms 176, 180; K_{inhom}-function-based test of 202–203; null hypothesis of 139
spatial lag 23, 194; random effects model 87, **87**, **88**, **88**; version of random effects panel data models 79, 81–82
spatial lag logit model 69; estimation 69–71; example 71, **71**
spatial lag model *see* SLM (spatial lag model)
spatial lag probit model 64; estimation of parameters 65–67, 73; examples 67, **67**, 69, **69**, 71, **71**
spatial lag tobit model 72; latent 72–73; simultaneous 72
spatial linear models 190–192
spatial location of individuals models 198–200
spatial location patterns 113; firms' exit from Sicily hospitality market example 130–132, *130*, *131*; identification 116–126; Veneto pharmaceutical and medical device manufacturing example 122–124, 125–126, *125*
spatial logit model 63–72
spatial microeconometric approach xix, 4
spatial microeconometric model 159, 162
spatial microeconometric model for firm survival 172–186; basic survival analysis techniques 173–176
spatial non-linear models, marginal impacts 74–75
spatial panel data modelling 85–89
spatial panel data models, dynamic 85
spatial panel models: estimation 80–85; GMM for 83–85
spatial panels 76

spatial pattern of Trento single-plant metallurgy manufacturing example 141–142, *141*, *142*
spatial point patterns 93, 112, *112*; classic exploratory tools and summary statistics 107–112; of economic agents 93–94; paradigmatic examples 94, *95*; reasons for analysis 93; of small food store 165, *165*, 170; of tourism and hospitality start-up firms in Sicily 93–94, *94*
spatial point process xvi, 95–106, 114, 162
spatial probit model 63–72, 74, 192
spatial processes framework 143
spatial random economy 7
spatial randomness 94–95, 144
spatial tobit model 72–73, 193
spatial units xiii–xiv
spatio-temporal clusters, of ICT firms in Rome 155
spatio-temporal heterogeneity 150–151, 153
spatio-temporal interactions 144, 153, 155, *155*
spatio-temporal K-function xvi, 143–148, 148–155
spatio-temporal point patterns 147
spatio-temporal point process, isotropic 152
spatio-temporal randomness 144, 145–146, 147, *148*
spatstat 193, 196, 197
spatstat function envelope 199, 200
spdep package 187
specialization 178
splm package 193
start-up firms 176, 178, 181, 185, 186
static models xv
static panel data models 85
stationarity 95; lack of 98
Statistica economica territoriale (Arbia and Espa) xix–xx
statistical bias 177
statistical mechanics 4
Statistical Register of Active Enterprises 164–165
STIK-function 148–155; estimation and inference of 152–153; long-run spatial dynamics of Rome ICT firms example 153–155
stochastic processes 95; doubly 100; Poisson xvi, 167; *see also* spatial point process
stores: competing 105, 106; Trento food stores case study 165–172; *see also* supermarkets
Strauss, D., and Ikeda, M. 135, 167

228 *Index*

Strauss process 106, *106*; regular 197
supermarkets 167, 169, 170–171;
   competition of 136–138, *136, 137*; new
   establishment 160
survival: data analysis 173; firm 172–186,
   181, *182*
survival analysis techniques, basic 173–176
survival conditional probability model
   163–164, 170–171
survival model 163–164; parametric 174
survival of pharmaceutical and medical
   device manufacturing firms in Italy case
   study: control variables definition
   180–181; data 176–177; empirical
   results 181–186; Kaplan–Meier
   probability estimates 181–182, **181**,
   182; spatial microeconometric covariates
   definition 177–180
survival point process, space–time 161
survival regression models 176, 177
Sweeney, S.H., and Feser, E.J. 130

ten points map 16, *18*, 21
Therneau, T., and Grambsch, P. 186
thinning 99
Thomas cluster process 102, 196, 198;
   example 122–124, *123, 124*; *K*-function
   for 121; parameter estimation 121–126,
   124, 199–200
time 175; continuous time econometrics
   160; elapsed 173; lag 85; series xiii
time-demeaning 79–80, 83
time-invariant unobservables xv
tobit model 60–63, **63**; spatial 72–73, 193
tobit SAR model xiv–xv; latent 72
tolerance envelopes, Monte
   Carlo-simulated 153, 155
tourism and hospitality start-up firms in
   Sicily, spatial point patterns 93–94, *94*
Trento (Italy): census tract (2004) 166,
   167; competition of supermarkets
   136–138, *136, 137*; food stores case
   study 165–172; spatial pattern of
   single-plant metallurgy manufacturing
   141–142, *141, 142*
Trivedi, P.K., and Cameron, A.C. 6
Turner, T.R.: and Baddeley, A.J. 135; and
   Berman, M. 167
2SLS (two-stage least squares) 36, 37,
   39, 191; generalized spatial (GS2SLS)
   42–43, 44, **44**

uncertainty: data 49, 50; locational 51–53;
   sources in micro-data 8–10
uniform geo-masking 51, 54–55,
   55–56, *56*
unobservables xv
unobserved effects model 77
unobserved heterogeneity 76–77
US (United States): Census Bureau,
   Longitudinal Business Database 4;
   Department of Homeland Security
   (DHS) 51; *see also* Baltimore house
   prices and characteristics; Boston;
   Boston house price determinants
UTM (Universal Transverse Mercator)
   system 24

Van Wissen, L. 161
variables: Bernoulli 58–59; control
   180–181, 185; omitted 40; Poisson
   random 107, 109, 121, 124
variance–covariance matrix 64–66, 68,
   69, 79
Veneto (Italy), pharmaceutical and medical
   device manufacturing firms 122–124,
   122, 123, 125–126, *125*
VGI (volunteered geographic
   information) 8
Vijverberg, W.P., and Beron,
   K.J. 73

W matrix (weights matrix) 15–22, 29,
   31; binary threshold distance 17, **18**,
   19, 21, 25; creation and preliminary
   computations 188–190; density 17;
   examples 17–22; inverse distance
   38; inversion 73; nearest neighbor
   distance 17, **19**, 21, 38; pair-wise
   distance matrix 17, **19**; spatially lagged
   variable 21, **22**; squared inverse distance
   17, **20**, 21, **21**; ten points map 16, *18*,
   21; threshold distance-based 31, 35,
   35, 38
Waagepetersen, R., and Møller, J. 121,
   124–125, 126
Wang, H., *et al.* 73
web, data extraction 8
web scraping 76
Weber, A. 160
West, K., and Newey, W. 68

Yu, J., and Lee, L.-F. 83, 85